THIRTY YEARS AFTER

THIRTY YEARS AFTER

·

An Artist's Memoir of the Civil War

·

Text and Illustrations by

EDWIN FORBES

Introduction by William J. Cooper, Jr.

LOUISIANA STATE UNIVERSITY PRESS

Baton Rouge and London

Introduction copyright © 1993 by Louisiana State University Press
All rights reserved
Manufactured in the United States of America
First printing
02 01 00 99 98 97 96 95 94 93   5 4 3 2 1

Library of Congress Cataloging-in-Publication Data

Forbes, Edwin, 1839–1895.
    Thirty years after : an artist's memoir of the Civil War / text
and illustrations by Edwin Forbes ; introduction by William J.
Cooper, Jr.
        p.   cm.
    Originally published: New York : Fords, Howard & Hulbert, [c1890].
    ISBN 0-8071-1877-X (cloth)
    1. United States—History—Civil War, 1861–1865—Pictorial works.
2. United States—History—Civil War, 1861–1865—Portraits.
I. Title.
E468.7.F69   1993   93-11083
973.7—dc20   CIP

The paper in this book meets the guidelines for permanence and durability of the Committee on
Production Guidelines for Book Longevity of the Council on Library Resources. ⊗

CONTENTS

INTRODUCTION

EDWIN FORBES AND THE CIVIL WAR
William J. Cooper, Jr.

EDWIN FORBES went to war in 1862, just as tens of thousands of other young northerners and southerners did early in the Civil War. He did not, however, shoulder a rifle or wear a sword, or even carry a pistol. Instead he was armed with a pencil and a sketch pad. The twenty-three-year-old Forbes marched to war under the banner of *Frank Leslie's Illustrated Newspaper.*

When young Edwin Forbes started south, he was a member of the Bohemian Brigade, the name given collectively to the multitude of reporters who followed the northern armies into the South and into battle. That name derived from the appellation *Bohemian* given around 1860 to reporters centered in New York City. At that time the profession of reporting was basically new; American newspapers had been chiefly editorial. Reporters were generally considered on the margin of both the newspaper business and respectability. Many of them thought of themselves as vagabonds and free spirits.[1]

Forbes was a new recruit for the Bohemians. Although information about his early life is quite scarce, no evidence indicates that before 1860 he had anything to do with newspapers, much less with reporting. He was born in New York County, New York, in 1839 and given the name John Edwin Forbes, but early on he dropped "John." Traditional sources indicate that he began to study art in 1857. Trained in classical fashion, Forbes painted animals, landscapes, and genre. In 1860, while living in Hoboken, New Jersey, a suburb of New York City and in the 1850s and 1860s a popular art colony, Forbes had a painting accepted at the National Academy of Design.

The outbreak of war in 1861 turned Forbes's artistic career in a completely different direction. In 1862 Frank Leslie, the owner of *Frank Leslie's Illustrated Newspaper,* hired Forbes to join the corps of artists he was sending south to provide illustrations for his paper. These pictorial reporters were known as "special correspondents" or "special artists." Forbes immediately left for the front in Virginia, where he would remain until the autumn of 1864.

The youthful Forbes headed to the South for what would become the pivotal experience of his life. In the two-and-a-half years Forbes covered the war, he spent most of his time with the Army of the Potomac, though his initial campaign experience occurred in the Shenandoah Valley in the spring of 1862. From then until the fall of 1864 he observed most of the major battles in the eastern theater of the war, including Cedar Mountain, Second Manassas, Antietam, Chancellorsville, Gettysburg, the Wilderness, and Petersburg.

Forbes had a straightforward mission—to sketch scenes of the war that would end up as illustrations in *Frank Leslie's Illustrated Newspaper.* He had to learn his craft quickly, for he had not previously done any commercial artwork. His artistic ability along with his energy and determination enabled him to become proficient rapidly. Like so many other new soldiers, Forbes discovered that battles were not exactly what he had imagined. He remarked that he had expected to accompany troops into battle and "seat myself complacently on a convenient hillside and sketch exciting incidents at my leisure."[2] Forbes found that strategy to be impossible, however. At his first battle, Cross Keys, in the Shenandoah Valley on June 8, 1862, he heard musket fire and wanted to watch the infantry charge. But he quickly learned that Confederate artillery raked the ridge which offered the best view of the fighting. In addition, Forbes admitted that the sight of wounded soldiers being moved toward the rear did not serve to drive him forward. He did know about combat, however. At Second Manassas he found himself in the midst of

---

1. Louis M. Starr, *Bohemian Brigade: Civil War Newsmen in Action* (New York, 1954), 3–11.
2. Page 257 herein. Subsequent citations are given parenthetically in the text.

"Going into Winter Quarters," pencil sketches made on the spot. *Reproduced, with permission, from Print Collection, Miriam and Ira D. Wallach Division of Art, Prints, and Photographs, The New York Public Library, Astor, Lenox, and Tilden Foundations.*

heavy fire, and he spent the final day at Gettysburg just on the rear side of Cemetery Hill from the point assaulted by Confederate Major General George Pickett.

Forbes did not make many sketches of actual fighting. The etching in *Thirty Years After* entitled *The Distant Fighting* gives a good sense of the perspective from which he felt safe (p. 259). Although he did not usually chronicle the fighting from up close, he did sketch from personal observation such combat scenes as a battle line forming, an artillery section going into action, and a cavalry charge. Forbes concentrated, however, on scenes he could witness close at hand. The bulk of his sketches deal with the everyday life of the soldiers, and their variety makes clear that he could do almost as he pleased in observing the army and following its movements. His employer liked the action coverage best, and because of that preference fewer than half of Forbes's wartime sketches ended up being reproduced in *Frank Leslie's Illustrated Newspaper*.[3]

Forbes departed the army and returned to New York City in the autumn of 1864. Precisely why he left his position and the war at that time is not at all clear. In a real sense, however, he never left; the war and his experiences in it remained central to him for the rest of his life.

Details about Forbes's postwar life and career remain almost as murky as those of his youth, except for his artistic endeavors that focused on the war. The story of his first marriage is a mystery. By 1875 he was a resident of Brooklyn, where he lived until his death. Sometime in the early 1880s he married for a second time. His second wife, Ida Batty, a schoolteacher, survived him. There were children, probably a son and a daughter, the former most likely with Ida Forbes, and the latter most likely with his first wife. Almost immediately upon his resettling in New York City, Forbes reclaimed his original sketches from his employer and began work on a project that would become his greatest artistic achievement. Between 1865 and 1868 he completed drawings of forty scenes based on his wartime sketches, which were then transferred to ground copper plates. In 1876 he exhibited the resulting etchings as *Life Studies of the Great Army* at the Philadelphia Centennial Exhibition.

Life Studies received considerable critical acclaim. For it Forbes won an award from the Centennial Exhibition. A contemporary critic called *Life Studies* "the first notable example of etchings as yet produced in this country." Forbes sent a portfolio of the etchings to the London Etching Club, which named him an honorary member, and he also belonged to the French Etching Club. Without question, *Life Studies* was a major achievement that represented a notable step forward in establishing etching as a fine art in the United States. Twentieth-century historians of etching consider Edwin Forbes a founder of etching as art in this country.[4]

Forbes was eager for *Life Studies* to become a commercial success as well as an artistic triumph. To sell it he published a catalog that also contained favorable comments from leading war figures, including President Ulysses S. Grant, to whom he had sent editions of the portfolio. William T. Sherman, commanding general of the United States Army, bought the original portfolio to decorate his office. The outcome of Forbes's promotional campaign is not known, but in 1884 a bill was introduced in Congress to purchase Forbes's collection of sketches and drawings for $100,000. It failed. The collection survives today because in 1901 Forbes's widow sold it for $25,000 to J. P. Morgan, who donated it to the Library of Congress in 1919.[5]

While trying to market *Life Studies*, Forbes busied himself with other artistic enterprises. In the 1870s and 1880s he produced a number of oil paintings, including war scenes. Most have disappeared, though the Library of Congress possesses twelve small canvases of the Battle of Gettysburg. In addition, Forbes provided illustrations for several books—three children's books, one of which his wife wrote, and a novel and a war memoir, both by a New York veteran.[6] The quality of the pictures in these five volumes does not match that of Forbes's other illustrative work. His final major project is not at all inferior, however. In 1890 he produced *Thirty Years After: An Artist's Story of the Great War*. In it with his own words and pictures he recounts his experiences in the great war of his generation.

Although Forbes devoted his life to art, he made one noteworthy contribution in a quite different area. He had always liked horses, and he enjoyed painting and drawing them. He also became an avid

3. Jacob Edward Kent Aherns, "Edwin Forbes" (M.A. thesis, University of Maryland, 1966), 15. This thesis has the most biographical detail on Forbes readily available, but it is still extremely sketchy.

4. *Ibid.*, 36; F. Weitenkampf, *American Graphic Art* (Rev. ed.; New York, 1924), 1.

5. Aherns, "Edwin Forbes," 51–53.

6. Mrs. Ida B. Forbes, *Gen'l Wm. T. Sherman: His Life and Battles; or, From Boy-Hood to His "March to the Sea"* (New York, [1886]); Mrs. Helen W. Pierson, *Life and Battles of Napoleon Bonaparte* (New York, [1886]); Josephine Pollard, *Our Naval Heroes: In Words of Easy Syllables* (New York, [1886]); George F. Williams, *Bullet and Shell: A Soldier's Romance* (New York, 1882), and *Bullet and Shell: War as the Soldiers Saw It* (New York, 1883).

An actual sketch, made on the spot by one
of the Special Artists of Frank Leslie's Illustrated Newspaper.
Mr. Leslie holds the copyright and reserves the exclusive right of publication.

"The Struggle for the Guidon," pencil sketch. *Reproduced, with permission, from Print Collection, Miriam and Ira D. Wallach Division of Art, Prints, and Photographs, The New York Public Library, Astor, Lenox, and Tilden Foundations.*

devotee of horse racing. A few years before he died, he invented a starting-gate apparatus that was adopted by some race tracks. Edwin Forbes died in Brooklyn of Bright's disease on May 6, 1895.[7]

The Bohemian Brigade and the Civil War had a great influence on each other, and in a fundamental way the war transformed reporting. Before 1860, American newspapers were identified chiefly with editors and editorials. Existing on the periphery of both the newspapers and society, reporters had largely unsavory reputations as "ne'er-do-well[s]," as "key-hole snooper[s]."[8] The war, however, placed reporters at the center of momentous events, not just crime stories and scandals. Because of the war, reporters became mainstays of American journalism.

Reporters brought war news to the homefront, to a civilian population eager for information about the conflagration and the men engaged in it. Every substantial newspaper assigned reporters to cover the war. In the beginning, southern newspapers, like the northern, dispatched reporters to the front, but in the face of advancing Union armies and massively increasing shortages of essential materials, like paper, they could not sustain their effort. The leading scholar of the Confederate press turned up ninety-four reporters who at one time or another chronicled the war for southerners. In contrast, about five hundred reporters followed northern armies through the South reporting back news of the armies

7. New York *Times,* May 7, 1895, p. 3; Aherns, "Edwin Forbes," 49.
8. Starr, *Bohemian Brigade,* 6.

and the soldiers. The public looked to the press not just for opinion but for information about great events.[9]

The reporting of war news in pictures as well as words helps account for its impact. Artists along with reporters belonged to the Bohemian Brigade. The two groups thought of each other as colleagues: each was involved in telling the story of the war to the readers back home. The reporters wrote their stories. The special correspondents, or special artists, drew theirs.

Pictorial reporting assumed significance because of the illustrated newspaper, which was introduced in the United States by Frank Leslie. Leslie was born in England in 1821 with the name Henry Carter. Trained as an engraver and having worked for the *Illustrated London News,* Leslie arrived in this country in the late 1840s and started out as an engraver in New York City. In the early 1850s he had several different partners in various illustrated-newspaper ventures. Finally, in 1854 he published *Frank Leslie's Ladies' Gazette of Fashion.* The next year *Frank Leslie's Illustrated Newspaper* appeared. Leslie's paper found a place between the staid traditional press and the florid penny press. Still, Leslie devoted considerable space to sensational events and stories; his *Illustrated Newspaper* did have a certain tabloid characteristic. The paper, a weekly, succeeded. By 1860 it had a circulation of more than 150,000, with special issues sometimes selling over 300,000 copies.[10] Leslie's success generated competitors. *Harper's Weekly* came out in 1857, and the *New York Illustrated News* followed two years later.

When war broke out, Leslie and his competitors determined that they would provide their readers with pictures of the conflict. All three illustrated newspapers hired artists and sent them to the South. Leslie himself employed as many as twelve at a time.[11] Most of these special artists were young men in their early twenties who were not yet sure of their life's work. Edwin Forbes worked only for Leslie. The most prolific and best-known special artist, the English-born Alfred R. Waud, covered the war from First Manassas to Appomattox. Beginning with the *New York Illustrated News* in 1861, he moved over to *Harper's Weekly* the next year. Undoubtedly the special artist who went on to the greatest renown as a serious artist was Winslow Homer, who made excursions into the South for *Harper's Weekly.*

The Confederacy did not have the resources, either human or technological, to equal the coverage provided by the three northern illustrated newspapers. A modest amount of pictorial reporting did take place from the Confederate side, however. In the late summer of 1862 the *Southern Illustrated News* was established in Richmond, Virginia. Although consciously modeled on the pictorial papers of London and New York City, it was a poor imitation. The lack of qualified engravers along with dwindling supplies of paper and of the wood essential for the engraving made for an all-but-impossible task. The *Southern Illustrated News* contained only a few illustrations, most of defective quality, and never a single battlefield scene. By the winter of 1864 the newspaper began shrinking in size, and by the end of the year it had disappeared. In addition, Frank Vizetelly of the *Illustrated London News* ranged across the South. Even though Vizetelly sympathized with the Confederacy, many of his sketches involuntarily ended up in northern newspapers. They were confiscated from captured blockade runners and pirated by the northern press, who credited only an English artist.[12]

The war presented these special artists with a marvelous opportunity despite the advent of photography. Although the camera had been present in the Crimean War, the Civil War marked the first conflict in which photography became important. It was the most-photographed war to that time. Nevertheless, technical problems severely restricted its role. The size and weight of cameras and tripods hampered movement. The necessity of having portable darkrooms presented a distinct handicap. The long exposure time precluded photographing anything in motion. Also, costs were quite high for field

9. *Ibid.;* W. Fletcher Thompson, Jr., *The Image of War: The Pictorial Reporting of the American Civil War* (New York, 1960); J. Cutler Andrews, *The North Reports the Civil War* (Pittsburgh, Pa., 1955), and *The South Reports the Civil War* (Princeton, N.J., 1970).

10. Budd Leslie Gambee, Jr., *Frank Leslie and His Illustrated Newspaper, 1855–1860* (Ann Arbor, Mich., 1964), 80.

11. Stuart William Becker, "Frank Leslie's Illustrated Newspaper from 1860 to the Battle of Gettysburg" (M.A. thesis, University of Missouri, 1960), 25.

12. Mark E. Neely, Jr., Harold Holzer, and Gabor S. Boritt, *The Confederate Image: Prints of the Lost Cause* (Chapel Hill, N.C., 1987), 23–30; Frederic Ray, "With Pen and Palette: Artists of the Civil War," *Civil War Times Illustrated,* XXI (April, 1982), 27.

photographers, and before the development of photoengraving, newspapers did not cover these expenses.

In contrast, the special artists used minimal equipment, which permitted great mobility. They usually carried a large portfolio suspended from a strap over the shoulder which contained paper, pencils, crayons, pens, brushes, and at times a few watercolors. They generally used pencils for battle sketches, but for camp scenes they often preferred crayons and charcoal.[13]

Like the regular reporters, the special artists lived with the army and depended upon it for their subsistence. They were the comrades of the soldiers. They knew the rigors of campaigning in the field; they endured exhaustion; they shared the range of emotions that stretched from the tedium of the camp to the terror of the battlefield; they faced the possibility of being captured or wounded or even killed. To convey their impressions realistically to the public, they had to cope successfully with military life in all its guises.

The sketches drawn by Forbes, Waud, Homer, and their compatriots had to undergo a transformation in New York City before they reached newspaper buyers. The engravers redrew every field sketch on wood, cut away the inked sections, and then made a metal impression. The skill of the engraver affected the fidelity with which the sketches were reproduced. In this instance Forbes was fortunate to work for Leslie, who, as a former engraver, understood the critical importance of the engraver's role better than anyone else in the business. He personally supervised the preparation of each illustration for his *Illustrated Newspaper.* Most of Forbes's sketches were faithfully copied by engravers, though they were sometimes adjusted in size or perspective to fit the layout of the paper.[14]

Leslie devised a system that greatly expedited the process of turning an artist's sketch into a newspaper illustration. Larger engravings required numerous blocks of wood, which were bolted together. For his large engravings Leslie had the blocks unbolted and the sections distributed to individual engravers to complete portions of the engraving. Then the blocks would be rebolted. In this way large engravings could be produced in almost the same time it took to complete one small engraving.[15]

Through their work the special artists certainly made the war more realistic for newspaper readers of the 1860s. They also left a significant pictorial record for history. Their illustrations enable those who study the war to understand it more fully. That these sketches, drawings, and etchings grace so many books on the war testifies eloquently to the enduring worth and value of the contribution made by the special artists.

◆

Edwin Forbes brought out *Thirty Years After: An Artist's Story of the Great War* in 1890. *Thirty Years After* is a war memoir, just like scores of others written by both Union and Confederate veterans, especially in the final two decades of the nineteenth century. *Thirty Years After,* however, contains more than just Forbes's reminiscences of his own experiences. While his personal recollections make up an essential part of the narrative, they do not form the central thrust of the book. He used them chiefly to give himself credibility, to give authority to his assessments of the army, the soldiers, and battle. Forbes focused on the army and the soldiers who constituted it. Although he rarely identified a particular army, he generally referred to the Army of the Potomac, his military home for most of his tour. In fact, Forbes often did not specify locations or indicate precise times. Instead, he strove to emphasize the universality of the soldiers' experience. He used pictures and words to tell the story of men at war.

Illustrations surely abound. Almost three hundred etchings taken from Forbes's field sketches, including those in *Life Studies of the Great Army,* dominate *Thirty Years After.* To these Forbes added twenty halftone equestrian portraits from original oil paintings. They include obvious choices like Grant, Sherman, Philip H. Sheridan, and George H. Thomas. But to get his twenty Forbes padded with such figures as Don Carlos Buell, Quincy A. Gillmore, and Joseph Hooker. Although these portraits do not materially aid Forbes in accomplishing his major purpose, he obviously thought they would help him sell his book.

13. Thompson, *The Image of War,* 81.
14. *Ibid.,* 83; Aherns, "Edwin Forbes," 17.
15. Thompson, *The Image of War,* 21.

"Army of the Potomac," pencil sketch. *Reproduced, with permission, from Print Collection, Miriam and Ira D. Wallach Division of Art, Prints, and Photographs, The New York Public Library, Astor, Lenox, and Tilden Foundations.*

Even though Forbes was known as an artist and designated his occupation in the subtitle, thus underscoring his own conviction about its importance, his words do help him. His word-pictures evoke mental images, which the etchings then often confirm. Forbes described the constantly hungry soldiers as "a kind of human locust" (p. 17). He graphically recounted the scene on Cemetery Hill at Gettysburg after Pickett's charge: "A great convulsion of nature could not have made more universal destruction; everything bore the mark of death and ruin" (p. 178).

Picturing a night march during the Battle of Chancellorsville, Forbes employed striking language: "Fires were blazing on every side, which, with the pine trees that had been ignited, so lit up the road that objects were as discernible as in the day; and surging through it all was a mass of earnest, determined men who were intent only on reaching the line of battle where they could be of service to their struggling comrades" (p. 34). On the facing page is one of Forbes's most effective etchings, *Through the Woods at Night*. In a nearly ghostly scene, soldiers march resolutely through the darkened forest with their way lit by a flaming tree.

Forbes wanted his readers to understand what it meant to be a soldier in the Union army. For him the army was a living, breathing organism, whose inner workings he desired to reveal. He would accomplish this goal by illuminating almost every possible area of soldier life. To meet this end he divided *Thirty Years After* into eighty brief chapters, or more accurately snapshots, because the illustrations make up such a critical part of the book. They impart the essence of particular activities, whether feeding the troops or withstanding a charge.

Forbes concerned himself chiefly with the private soldiers, not the generals. Readers will find very little about any general, or for that matter any officers. He does give, however, an illustrated eyewitness account of President Abraham Lincoln reviewing the Army of the Potomac at Falmouth, Virginia, in April, 1863. Forbes succeeded in portraying the reality of military life largely because he understood that the soldiers did not exist in a one-dimensional world. He correctly perceived the astonishing juxtaposition of activities, circumstances, and emotions that made soldiering in wartime a unique experience.

Forbes's soldiers spent much time tending to the same tasks that would occupy a civilian. Activities such as cooking, eating, washing, and leisure pursuits fill many pages in *Thirty Years After*. The etchings provide memorable concrete visual images: lining up to eat (p. 51), washing clothes in a tub and hanging them on a line (p. 170), shoeing a mule (p. 142), whiling away hours reading newspapers (p. 135), playing cards (p. 166), fishing (p. 214), even making and then playing a violin (pp. 266, 267).

The soldier confronted the elements in a way that a population still largely rural or with keen memories of the countryside could identify with. Marches in the rain turned into contests for survival. The cold and wet were exacerbated by roads that became quagmires swallowing up man and beast. In the marvelous etching *A Tough Pull* the viewer can almost taste the dominating mud that clings to everything and has already put down one artillery horse (p. 211).

This kind of exercise could result in utter physical exhaustion, which Forbes vividly depicted. In one etching a tired soldier slumps against a tree (p. 201). In a larger illustration a soldier sits against a tree with his head bowed while his companion stretches out on the ground (p. 203).

Civilian types of undertakings as well as tedium and exhaustion could suddenly turn into what made being in the army different—the terror of combat. Then fury and violence reigned. In *The Halt, for Re-forming the Line,* the surviving infantrymen standing just behind their dead comrades prepare to face the enemy once again (p. 75). An artillery section moves forward into the billowing smoke and the resulting darkness of battle in *Pulling into Position* (p. 179). *A Cavalry Charge* evokes the ferocity of mounted men in collision (p. 11). While the main body hurtles forward, in the foreground the dead riders and horses attest to the horror of battle. *Charge and Check,* though somewhat stylized, presents the face-to-face, personal character of so much Civil War fighting. Union soldiers, with one of their group already killed, defend a cannon at point-blank range against oncoming Confederate cavalry. The charging horses with legs outstretched, nostrils flared, and eyes wide with fear transmit the fierceness and violence of the impact (p. 255).

Forbes realized that the two worlds of tedium and terror coexisted in the closest proximity. His wonderful rendition of a moving clothesline—drying clothes hanging from the rifle barrel of a marching soldier—captures that reality (p. 171). At one battle Forbes observed a field hospital with severely wounded men and blood-stained surgeons almost next to a reserve artillery battery whose troops were sleeping, making coffee, and playing poker. He expressed great admiration for the individual soldier who inhabited and even mastered this strange world. Convinced that these men had determined "to do what they had undertaken," Forbes forcefully delineated his belief in *Infantryman on Picket,* which could just as readily be entitled "A Study in Resoluteness and Solidity" (p. 127).

Forbes knew that battles were dangerous affairs, even for observers like himself. Getting close enough to see what was actually happening necessitated putting oneself in jeopardy. Forbes found the destruction at the point of contact between two armies appalling, in his words "so storm-swept with bullets and shell" (p. 258).

All battles did not present the same scene or spectacle. From Forbes's vantage point Second Manassas offered a grand panorama of rolling hills and fields over which men fought. The tangle of the Wilderness made it impossible "to catch the faintest gleam" of the battle, even though over one hundred thousand troops were locked in combat. To Forbes, Antietam provided "a dramatic and most magnificent series of pictures" as two veteran armies collided with each other throughout the day (p. 258). No matter his perspective on a particular battle, Forbes understood that the average fighting man only knew what occurred in his immediate vicinity. He learned of the general outcome only after the shooting had stopped.

Forbes did not try to put forward every soldier as one of his resolute heroes. He faithfully recorded the presence of shirkers, or in the colorful phrase of his army days, "coffee coolers." These men found somewhere else to be when their units were ordered into action. Then, as soon as the danger had passed, they turned up claiming that they had gotten lost or had ended up fighting with a different outfit. A telling illustration, *Under the Bank,* shows five "coffee coolers" sheltered around their coffeepot while in the background their compatriots march into battle (p. 67). There were also common thieves who when convicted were literally drummed out of the army, as *A Bitter Lesson* strikingly renders (p. 303).

"7th Corps Opera House—Culpepper," pencil sketch. *Reproduced, with permission, from Print Collection, Miriam and Ira D. Wallach Division of Art, Prints, and Photographs, The New York Public Library, Astor, Lenox, and Tilden Foundations.*

One of Forbes's most powerful etchings conveys the awful grandeur of the ultimate penalty for one of the gravest military crimes, desertion. According to Forbes, by 1863 desertion had become a growing problem because of the army's reluctance to enforce the supreme punishment and because of the increasing number of draftees and hired substitutes, but by the end of that year the army was becoming stricter. Once Forbes witnessed the execution of five deserters. His pictorial account is vivid and forceful. Facing the firing squad, the five condemned men sit blindfolded on the edges of their coffins, with their fellow soldiers massed to watch in the background. Forbes's etching captures the definitive moment, with smoking rifle barrels signaling the sentence in the act of being carried out (p. 155).

A Union patriot, Forbes concentrated on the Union army. He did take note of the Confederate enemy, however. To Forbes the Confederates believed in and fought for their cause just as the Union soldiers did. During the early summer of 1863, while visiting Union pickets along the Rappahannock River, he saw Confederates on the opposite bank, some even bathing in the river. This shared humanity led to what he saw as an almost eerie fraternization between pickets on opposing sides. At times they chatted and exchanged coveted items, as in the swap of southern tobacco for northern coffee pictured in *Coffee and Tobacco Trading—A Truce* (p. 163). Then, of course, in nearly the next moment these temporary friends would be trying to kill each other.

Forbes also admitted and admired the military talent of Confederate leaders like Thomas J. "Stonewall" Jackson. After all, Forbes's introduction to the war had been on the losing side in the Shenandoah Valley in 1862. But he evinced even greater admiration for the average Confederate fighter, whose "soldierly qualities were very remarkable" (p. 173). And the "dashing bravery" that impressed him was forcefully illustrated in the stylized *A Gallant Deed of Arms,* which depicts the conclusion of Pickett's charge at Gettysburg on July 3, 1863 (pp. 173, 175).

Forbes's summation of Confederate soldiers touched upon the sectional politics of the late nineteenth century. He told his readers that when they heard a northerner "breathing out particularly hot talk about the South or 'Confederate Brigadiers,' two to one you will find that during the war he was snugly at home making money or earning promotion in politics." These "self-seekers," according to Forbes, could not imagine "the fraternalism that grew up even between opposing armies after hearty fighting, followed by the fellowship of traffic between the lines" (p. 162). Traveling along the road to reunion, Forbes respected the courage and devotion to cause exhibited by the Confederate veterans. They shared much with him; all veterans belonged to the same band of brothers.

For Forbes, however, the war entailed more than the human drama that had produced a powerful bond among participants. The war also had concrete results for the United States. The Union had been preserved, and what he termed "The Reliable Contraband" had become free. Forbes discerned that the black Americans enslaved in the South had been at the center of the difficulties and antagonisms that had brought on war. He states directly that slavery was "the cause of the great rebellion" (p. 233). In *Thirty Years After* he dedicated considerable attention to the people who became contraband of war and refugees on their way to freedom. But like the overwhelming majority of white Americans of his time, northerners and southerners both, he believed that blacks were inferior to whites. He called blacks the "unfortunate race" (p. 233).

Although he clearly thought blacks less than whites and certain of his comments sound condescending to our ears, Forbes recognized their dignity as human beings and also their value to the Union army. He praised blacks for their trustworthiness as guides and for the help they gave to sick and wounded Union soldiers. They were responsible for much of the "daily industry-domestic work" (p. 149). *A Warm Breakfast—Winter, The Chief Cook,* and *An Evening Meal—Summer Camp* picture cooking activities (p. 150). Forbes maintained that only blacks could successfully manage the mule teams so crucial to the supply trains without which the army could not function. An evocative etching, *The Army Mule Team,* shows them in action (p. 243).

Forbes regarded blacks as almost always cheerful, even in "the most laborious duties," and he thought he knew why (p. 149). Two secondary reasons had merit. They were no longer under the control of their former masters, and they could earn a few dollars. But from personal observation Forbes was persuaded that blacks were committed to doing their very best for the soldiers who were fighting to end slavery. He noted many instances of individual bravery, including a cook's service at a cannon at the Battle of Cedar Mountain until killed. And Forbes reported that later in the war blacks gave a "splendid account" of themselves as combat troops (p. 234).

The last chapter of *Thirty Years After* underscores Forbes's conviction that the slaves he encountered during the war recognized their allies. He commented on the "unceasing streams of slaves" entering Union lines wherever Union armies appeared (p. 289). Illustrations on pages 290 and 291 show refugees on foot and in a wagon moving into the Union position. Both the slaves and Forbes comprehended that the Union army furnished the slaves refuge and that their freedom depended upon its success. The final etching, *The Sanctuary,* which represents a scene that Forbes said he had witnessed, dramatizes this truth. In the foreground a black man, woman, and child, with a dog, a family, emerge into a clearing. They have obviously found what they left home for. They manifest a deep gratitude— the woman on her knees with arms upraised in thanksgiving, the man with uncovered head—for what stands in the background, a fort flying the Stars and Stripes (p. 319).

Baton Rouge, Louisiana
April, 1993

Thirty Years After

AN

RTIST'S TORY

OF THE

GREAT WAR

TOLD, AND ILLUSTRATED WITH NEARLY 300 RELIEF-ETCHINGS AFTER SKETCHES
IN THE FIELD, AND 20 HALF-TONE EQUESTRIAN PORTRAITS
FROM ORIGINAL OIL PAINTINGS

By EDWIN FORBES

AUTHOR "LIFE STUDIES OF THE GREAT ARMY;" MEMBER FRENCH
ETCHING CLUB; HON. MEMBER LONDON ETCHING CLUB;
CENTENNIAL MEDAL—HIGHEST ART AWARD

NEW YORK:
FORDS, HOWARD, & HULBERT

Facsimile of 1890 title page

CONTENTS AND ILLUSTRATIONS.

VOLUME I.

————•••————

Equestrian Portrait: HOWARD AT THE CEMETERY GATE, GETTYSBURG.

Equestrian Portrait: MEADE AT GETTYSBURG.

Equestrian Portrait: HANCOCK AT SPOTTSYLVANIA.

CONTENTS AND ILLUSTRATIONS.

VOLUME II.

————•—•————

Equestrian Portrait: BURNSIDE AT FREDERICKSBURG.

Equestrian Portrait: SEDGWICK AT RAPIDAN RIVER.

Equestrian Portrait: THOMAS AT CHICKAMAUGA.

Equestrian Portrait: GILMORE; SIEGE OF CHARLESTON.

An Artist's Story of the Great War.

I.

AWAITING THE ATTACK.

A TRIP ALONG THE LINES DURING A BATTLE.

"WILL you venture down to the front this morning?" asked my companion, who was a special newspaper correspondent. "Except a scattering skirmish fire, an occasional boom of cannon and crash of shell in the woods, matters seem quiet enough." Fighting had been in progress for two days, but now there was a lull.

So off we started, both intent on seeing life along the lines. As we rode toward the front we passed through fields of wheat and rye that had once waved in peace, but were now trampled and destroyed by the army's march. Moving further on, meeting several ambulances going to the rear and a number of wounded men limping toward the hospital, we soon approached the fortified lines and knew that danger was near. Sounds of skirmishing grew louder, and stray bullets whizzed across the field and raised clouds of dust where they struck the ground.

Leaving our horses in care of some infantry posted in reserve in a piece of woods, we advanced slowly toward the line of breastworks in the extreme front. We took all possible cover by creeping though woods and behind fences until we reached the line of redoubts and breastworks facing the enemy's position.

A non-combatant is strangely impressed at the quiet, nonchalant air of the men who hold important position on the line. If it were not for the sharp crack of skirmish fire in front one could almost imagine himself enjoying the delights of a summer camp, although the Napoleon and Parrot guns pointing through embrasures at intervals along the log-breastworks had an air of significance, and the smoke-begrimed muzzles and mud-covered wheels and carriages showed the severe service they had rendered.

We found many of the men asleep along the line; some were playing cards, and others attending to camp duties, such as washing clothes, etc. All seemed free from any care about what might occur; that was somebody else's business.

A sudden rattle of musketry in the woods in front caused a momentary stir and suggested an advance at any moment by the enemy, who was in strong force. We moved cautiously along the line in search of friends (infantry officers) whose brigade held the extreme front, and found them ensconced in a bit of woods on the further side of the hill, which partly protected them from the enemy's musketry fire; yet the skirmishers in front kept the minié balls flying through the bushes and snapping sharply against the pine trees.

Seeking the shelter of a low earth-work, my friend and I smoked a pipe and discussed events, watching meanwhile the scenes along the line.

Within a short distance a party of artillerymen was building a bomb-proof roof in the hill-side as a refuge from the scorching fire of the enemy's guns, for the shell had cut down many of their comrades during the two days' conflict. Their method of procedure was to dig an opening into the hill, brace the sides and end, and cover the roof with logs. In many instances the shelter was covered with earth and sand, and thus rendered safer; one of these places would give refuge to about half a dozen men. Our position was not as pleasant or safety as secure as we might wish, for the enemy soon began to show signs of decided animation. The rattle of musketry became brisk, although the lines in front and the artillery opened fierce fire. My friend and I mutually agreed that our situation was becoming rather more than interesting, and that however much we might desire newspaper information, discretion was the better part of valor; so we made for the rear. In doing this we crossed the line of fire and were compelled to dodge the missiles of the gentlemen in gray, who sat in the tree-tops and leisurely popped away at any one sufficiently incautious to leave cover.

We were much relieved to reach our horses, which we soon mounted, and riding further to the rear found a position on a hill-top where we could rest in safety and watch the progress of the battle, which was now in full activity. The din and turmoil at the front had grown to be simply terrible. The continuous roll of musketry, the crash of guns and bursting of shells made an awful confusion, while the great clouds of smoke and dust that came up from the woods in front of the Union lines, and the fierce Indian yells of the Rebs as they leaped forward into battle, gave to sight and hearing a sickening realization of what it all meant.

After a time the firing of the combatants slackened; the clouds of smoke gradually disappeared, and, except for the sad story which could be gathered as the many wounded came to the rear, it would be a difficult task to persuade one's self that so desperate an encounter had so recently taken place. But hundreds lay dead and wounded, and the dying were praying for the relief that death only brings. What had been accomplished we had to go to head-quarters to learn, but the details of its doing were too plain for misunderstanding and far too terrible for any forgetting.

UNDER COVER.

BEHIND THE BREASTWORKS.

AWAITING THE ATTACK.

3

II.

ARTILLERY IN ACTION.

THE LIGHT BATTERY.

———•———

THE manœuvres and engagements of a great army offer no sight more thrilling than the dash and spirit of the field-artillery. In repose, also, the grouping of the men and horses is in itself a picture. I was sitting one morning by a battery of field-guns watching men take the horses to water and others groom the glossy sides, and was just thinking that they were rather thin from the hard work of the campaign when sudden orders came for a drill.

I followed to the parade-ground and was much interested in the picture and enjoyed greatly the excitement produced upon both men and horses as they manœuvred to the shrill notes of the bugle. An hour of target practice followed, and I found great pleasure watching the bursting shells as they struck the target on the far off hill-side, and threw up a column of dust in the rear. On our return to camp the dinner-call had sounded and we did justice to the frugal meal of "hard-tack" and coffee.

We had idled away the afternoon, and I was sitting on a fence smoking my pipe when there came a distant rumbling. Observing the cumulus clouds above the distant mountain, I concluded that a thunder shower threatened: but I soon heard a rumbling louder and more regular than before; and now the captain came anxiously out of his tent, and the men gathered in groups and looked toward the south. Suddenly a mounted orderly with dust-covered clothing and foaming horse dashed down from headquarters, and, reining up before the captain, handed him an order.

Bustle and apparent confusion now prevailed. Word had been received that the enemy was advancing in strong force, that the fords of the Rapidan had been passed and that our cavalry had been pushed back; but the heavy cannonading told of the Union forces' stout resistance. Soon everything was in readiness, and the battery dashed along the road through clouds of dust, followed by infantry. On, on we went, passing quiet farm-houses whose inmates glanced furtively from the windows and whose cattle dashed about the barn-yard with tails high in air. We soon began to meet wounded soldiers coming to the rear, some on horseback, others in ambulances. Further on we met a strange group coming down the hill. Gray and ragged, with tattered blankets thrown over their shoulders and canteens clattering at their sides, it took but a moment's thought to conclude that they were Rebel prisoners. On close approach we found them to be well-formed, muscular fellows, with an evident air of contentment as though they had accepted their capture as a fortunate occurrence rather than a hardship. But we passed on towards the scene of action, and from the increasing sounds of the field-guns and the bursting of many shell we knew that the conflict was raging. An officer dashed suddenly up with an order from the commanding general, and in an instant the battery was turned off the road, driven at great speed through a waving rye-field and posted on a commanding hill. Thus near to the line of battle hundreds of wounded soldiers met our eye: some, who were able, hurrying to the rear, others more seriously wounded limping slowly and sighing with pain at every step.

Far off in the front, through dust and smoke I saw the Union line of infantry posted

along a length of fence, and on a long rolling ridge sweeping round to the right the musketry rolled heavily, and our line was evidently being sorely pressed. Reinforcements of
infantry were sent in at intervals, and the crash and clangor of opposing guns increased in
volume. Dense clouds of mingled dust and smoke arose and fierce yells filled the air as the
Rebs charged our line in front, and soon a mass of men in gray, with flags flying through
their lines, were seen advancing on our right-front. Then our battery came to the defense.
The guns were loaded with canister and sighted, and with a roar that shook the earth were
discharged. Again they were loaded, "double-shotted" with canister, and the captain's voice
rang out, "*Fire by battery! — Fire!*" Immediately after, the great mass of men in gray
seemed to melt from view, the flags sank, and the force that within so short a time had seemed
irresistible had been repulsed with terrible loss of life.

Our battery soon advanced to a more commanding position and opened fire on one of
the enemy's batteries that had made sad havoc along our line. Shells were dropped among
their guns, and one fired a caisson which exploded with a tremendous crash, and so badly
crippled the enemy's battery that it was compelled to retire from the fight. Shortly after, the
struggle ended and the enemy retired from our front in defeat.

Our officers and men now buried the dead, cared for the wounded, and repaired as far
as possible the damage done. Soon the moon came peacefully up through the smoke of
battle, fires were lit, coffee and "hard-tack" were taken from the haversacks, and by the light
of burning fence-rails the much needed food was taken. At tattoo, lights were put out; and
now no sound broke the stillness save the tread of the sentinel at the guns, or the stamp of
the artillery horses as they stood munching their corn or wheat.

BRINGING UP A BATTERY.

"JUST IN TIME!"

7

III.

A WEEK WITH THE CAVALRY.

OR picturesqueness of scene and romantic beauty the cavalry affords greater variety than any other part of army life. The brilliant array of gay trappings, the movements of the spirited horses, and the many incidents in camp life and on the march, combine to make a picture that time cannot efface from memory.

It was in the spring of 1862, while with the army of Gen. McDowell at Fredericksburg, that news came from the Shenandoah Valley of the defeat of Gen. Banks at Winchester by Stonewall Jackson, who was just then rising into fame. Orders came from Washington detailing Gen. Bayard's cavalry and a large force of infantry to the Valley with the idea of intercepting the enemy before they could escape southward with plunder. The columns started, passing through Warrenton Station and Manassas, the cavalrymen riding and walking alternately. The main body reached Manassas on the second day and after a short rest pushed on through Thoroughfare Gap, a gorge in the Bull Run Mountains through which the Manassas Gap Railroad passes on its way to the Shenandoah Valley. Debouching into the Loudon Valley, which lies between the Bull Run Mountains and the Blue Ridge, the column took a meandering course over hills and through intervales, being stared at in amazement by the inhabitants. The white people glared at us with lowering brows, but the negroes greeted us with furtive smiles and grimaces.

We passed through Manassas Gap without adventure, but when we arrived at Front Royal (in the Luray Valley, paralleling the Shenandoah), we found all the paraphernalia of war: columns of infantry were marching along the main street and groups of officers were seen scattered about the town. On a clear sunny morning we came in sight of the Shenandoah Valley, a fair land resting in peace and plenty, which one could not imagine was so soon to be made desolate. Intelligence was received that Jackson's army was still in full retreat down the Valley and that his trains were passing through the town of Strasburg on the Valley Pike, about nine miles distant. Gen Bayard was ordered to push forward with the cavalry and make an attempt to capture the enemy's wagon trains.

On reaching the ford of the Shenandoah River, where the railroad-bridge crossed it, we forded the stream, climbed the hill on the opposite bank, and sighted the town of Strasburg. Viewing the ground with field-glasses, we discovered the Confederates in full march toward the south. The trains of white-topped wagons were lumbering along the pikes; on the hill-tops near the town long lines of infantry and cavalry were marching; and north of the town, in the fort built by Gen. Banks, the enemy's artillery was posted to guard the passage. Scouts were sent towards us to gather the significance of our appearance, but no further moves were made except the sending of a shell at one of our staff officers who ventured too near their lines.

While examining the enemy's position with my glass, I discovered in an open field below the town, a body of men dressed in blue, drawn up in a line. Close inspection proved them to be Union prisoners that had been captured from Gen. Banks' column. The poor fellows could see plainly our advance on the hill-top, and perhaps had hopes of rescue, but it would have been indiscreet on the part of Gen. Bayard to attack without infantry, so they

9

were doomed to further bondage.   Quite remote in the distance beyond the retreating enemy,
rise of smoke and boom of cannon told us that Frémont had come from West Virginia, but
like ourselves, had arrived just too late to join forces in cutting off the enemy's retreat.   His
advance and our advance were not yet in strength enough to act.   A small force of Union
infantry came up late in the afternoon and fortified the railroad-bridge over the Shenandoah,
but it was not until the next morning, when more of our troops had come up, that we were
ordered to advance into the town where we met the advance of Frémont's column.   The enemy
meantime had escaped, passing between the divided Union forces.

On riding into the town of Strasburg, I saw on the porch of the village church a
group of Union soldiers, among them a Zouave whom I had known before as one of Banks'
body guard.   He greeted me with a hearty hand-shake, and related how a part of the very
prisoners I had seen through the field-glass had escaped.   They had been placed for safe-
keeping during the night in the village church, and taking advantage of the darkness a
number had secreted themselves under the floor of the pulpit and escaped thus during the
confusion of the retreat, the Rebel guards being too hurried to count them.

The pursuit of the Confederates was energetically continued by Frémont.   He placed
Bayard's cavalry in the advance with his own mounted force, who pressed the enemy's rear
guard at every opportunity.   At Mt. Jackson we found that the bridge over the North Fork
of the Shenandoah had been burned by the enemy and were delayed until a pontoon could
be laid.   This was soon accomplished, and we crossed the river and pushed on to Harrisonburg, the cavalry skirmishing briskly on the way, and a field-battery occasionally brought into
play.   I had the pleasure of accompanying the "Jessie Scouts" (a Missouri company named
after Gen. Frémont's wife) during this part of the march, and no days during my army life
were as full of excitement and incident as those.   We often were within short gun-shot of the
enemy's rear-guard, but the scouts were utterly fearless of danger and seemed to live a
charmed life; harrassing and skirmishing with the enemy, but elusive as the wind.   Beyond
the town of Harrisonburg the cavalry advance under Col. Percy Windham was ambuscaded
through gross carelessness, being forced into the woods without precaution.   I escaped the
slaughter, however, by having stopped on the road-side to read a Richmond paper I had
secured in the town.   The ambuscade was avenged in the afternoon, for a force of one
hundred and ten infantry Bucktails under Col. Kane attacked Jackson's rear-guard under Gen.
Ashby, and after a most desperate fight defeated them and killed their daring officer, but
with a loss to the Bucktails of more than half their number.

Frémont finally caught the fleet-footed Jackson below Harrisonburg, fought an incon-
clusive battle with him at Cross Keys, and, owing to the disobedience of his orders to a brig-
adier of McDowell's force to burn the Shenandoah bridge in *front* of Jackson, he was morti-
fied to have the Rebs slip off by night, cross the river, and burn the bridge *behind* them.   As
Jackson afterwards said to one of   Frémont's officers captured in Pope's
campaign, "If as good work had   been done in the Luray Valley
as Frémont did in the Shen-   andoah, not so many of us
would have got away for   McClellan at Mechanicsville."

Altogether, it was a   very dashing and exciting
week that I passed with   the cavalry.   It satisfied
my desire for adventure,   and I stayed near headquarters during the re-   mainder of the campaign,
marching with the main   column.

A CAVALRY CHARGE.

IV.

THE PONTOON TRAIN.

THE ENGINEERS.

———•———

LTHOUGH perhaps not the most attractive, the Engineer Corps, which in all preparatory work is the most scientific, is in its special department one of the most necessary branches of the service of the great army in the field; and, while not generally engaged in the intense action of combat, its danger is not slight and its work is indispensable. The corps includes as its working force the sappers and miners and pontoniers, or bridge-builders. In time of peace their labors are of permanent importance, and in time of war they select and lay out the camp, construct or plan for the destruction of works of attack or defense, and have especial charge of the multifarious duties connected with the movements of forces.

When an advance was to be made towards the enemy's line, the Engineer Corps often worked well to the front and removed with dispatch all obstacles that would impede the march. Bridges were rebuilt in a twinkling, and when a wide river was reached the work of laying pontoons was commenced. This was often accomplished under severe fire, such as no timid man would care to face.

One of the finest sights during the march of the great army was the pontoon train. The huge scows resting on their heavy wagons went tossing over the rough roads, pulled by six-mule teams which were urged on by frantic and sometimes profane drivers. Often a wagon would get stalled in the mud where a stream crossed the line of march. It would then be necessary to detach the teams from the rear pontoon wagons and with them make an effort to drag the stalled pontoon to solid gound. Sometimes they had to attach a long rope to the tongue of the wagon, upon which hundreds of infantrymen would seize, and help the mules to drag it from the mire.

On nearing a stream, a road was chosen where the approach to cross would not be too steep. The wagons were drawn near the bank and the pontoon boats were slid off from the rear of them into the water. This work was often accomplished under the enemy's fire from an opposite bank of the river; but our men worked with a will, loading the boats and pushing them off with a dash and a cheer to clear the enemy away.

Then the real work of building a bridge would begin. Boats would be pushed out, turned lengthwise with the current, and placed at regular intervals across the stream, anchored at both ends. Then a set of men would quickly attach stringers from boat to boat and another set would hurry forward with planks to place over them, thus forming a floor. In an incredibly short time the bridge would be completed and the main body of the army would march across amid great cheers. On reaching the bank the troops would deploy across the field and make lively work for the enemy if their passage had been opposed.

A night march over a bridge is highly picturesque and full of incidents of interest. Bright fires would blaze in the fields near the bridge-heads, and by the light the infantry and artillery would march across apparently in great confusion; but the great mass of men appearing so much out of order to a spectator were under complete control, and could be called immediately into rigid form at an officer's command. The ammunition-trains would make great clatter in crossing, and mules would often get balky and delay progress. A sudden storm would produce great excitement; rain would pour in torrents and in a few hours a placid stream would become a raging torrent. Extra anchors and guy ropes had to be put out to prevent the bridge from being swept away, for the water would often rise above the banks and sweep around the approaches. At times the engineers' efforts would avail nothing, for the bridge would break loose at one end or a part be forced from the line elsewhere. Then repairs had to be made; and no praise is too great for the brave men who went cheerfully to work and skillfully made good the damage.

When an army had crossed a pontoon-bridge and pressed on in pursuit of the enemy, the bridge would be taken apart, the boats and the tackle loaded on to the wagons, and the pontoon-train would in a few hours reach the head of the column again, in full readiness to facilitate further advance of the army. At times a railroad-bridge would be destroyed by the enemy's rear guard and the engineers would obtain a duplicate bridge from the rear and quickly get it into place. These duplicate bridges speeded the army's progress to such a degree that the Rebs made many jokes about them, and on one occasion when a Southern soldier was informed that a tunnel had been destroyed which would delay Sherman's progress, he replied, "O no, it won't, for Sherman carries duplicate tunnels with him." When time did not admit of the use of a duplicate bridge, the engineers would hastily construct a bridge of trestle-work out of logs cut from adjacent woods.

I always found a night march with the Engineer Corps quite an exciting experience. The enemy's rear guard seemed to find a malicious—though perhaps natural—pleasure in placing all manner of obstacles in the way of the Union advance. Trees were felled across the roads and impassable labyrinths of interwoven boughs would have to be cleared by the engineers' axes.

The Engineer Corps was often called upon to lay out a line of breastworks to cover the front of the army from a surprise. It is not easy to realize how severe this labor was and how hard the soldiers worked at it. A ditch had first to be dug in the front with pick and spade; then the trees were felled by the axe, cut into lengths, and used as a backing for the bank of earth thrown up from the ditch. Traverses were built to protect men and guns from flanking fire, and the front covered by an abatis made of limbs of trees lying lengthwise with sharpened ends placed toward the enemy. Another fence which is sometimes placed in front of a fortified line is made by sharpening heavy logs and burying butts in the ground with points forward. This can be removed only by the axe, and if attempted under fire great loss of life is the result.

The Engineer Corps also has its share of destruction to make. Railroad-bridges are burned and canal-locks blown up, or the channel of a river is obstructed to prevent the enemy's advance. These men were seldom idle; in winter camp or summer march there was always something for their well-trained heads and skilled hands to do. Their loss of life was not as great as in other branches of the service: but they were exposed to much hardship and frequent peril; they did a very noble and indispensable duty, and no army could avail much without their assistance.

THROWING UP BREASTWORKS.

CROSSING THE RAPIDAN.

SHERMAN AT ATLANTA.

V.

THE EVER-HUNGRY SOLDIER.

A KIND of traveling human locust dressed in faded blue, is a phrase that might have been truthfully applied to the Union soldier; always hungry, never satisfied, and willing to join a foraging party on the shortest possible notice. At times he literally cleared parts of our country of all bounties acceptable to man and beast; and yet depredations were laughed at and forgiven, for the little obtained by the brave "boys in blue" was but slight recompense for the great service rendered to the land.

Many were the ludicrous scenes in those memorable campaigns. At the back door of every cabin or farm-house on the line of march could be seen groups of irrepressible Yankee soldiers with one question: "Got any pies for sale, Aunty?" and when such things were obtainable, eager hands stretched forth to receive them. Often hoe-cake and biscuits were offered instead of pies, and seemed just as desirable to the hungry men. They always paid liberally for such supplies, and many poor people made considerable sums of money in thus catering to their wants.

A party of "the boys" on scouring through the barn-yards would often chase up a nimble porker, whose ridiculous efforts to escape would greatly amuse them; but a final corrall in some fence corner and a quick thrust of the bayonet would end the noise and life of the unfortunate pig. Or perhaps a proud-stepping old rooster who had been a neighborhood tyrant would come in their way. Age was no objection to such healthy appetites, and the wringing of the old fellow's neck was only a question of very limited time. A bee-hive was a strong attraction to the soldier's "sweet-tooth," but a capture of it sometimes resulted in more bodily pain than had been counted on.

The remains of a pillaged vegetable garden suggested the visit of a cyclone; everything would disappear in a twinkling, and the men always seemed to confiscate the onions with especial relish. But first of all delights was the sudden sight of a cherry-tree in full bearing. How with a bound and a cheer the soldiers would run to it! In scarcely more than a moment of time all small limbs would be broken off and feasted upon in the ranks when on the march. The sight of fresh meat always increased the already ravenous appetites. When, after pitching camp at evening, the regimental butcher would select a fine steer from the division herd, and with his Springfield rifle plant a bullet in the forehead, great expectation prevailed. The skin would be removed in the shortest possible time, and almost before the meat was cool it would be distributed, and the odor of beef-steak would soon fill the air. Berries in their season were a luxury always accepta-ble. Many a veteran soldier has halted during the heat of battle to snatch and eat a handful of blackberries; or in a crowded under-growth, with bullets whistling by. would

The Army Butcher.

discover a patch of huckleberries, and at a taste of them memory would go back to the old outing-parties and the juicy home-pies made from the culled fruit.

Luxuries for the mess often came from the river or sea. When an old net was obtainable, streams would be drawn, and the suckers, bull-heads, and black bass secured would make a welcome variety to the scanty fare. If near the shore, oysters and clams would be sought for, and were gratefully devoured by the men who were subject to so much hardship. Game could sometimes be procured, and an old shotgun if obtainable was a great prize. With the colonel's permission to fire near camp, the fields would soon be beaten and rabbits, quail or perhaps a wild turkey would be added to the bill of fare. But many times the troops were limited to plain scant rations, and anything eatable was accepted then. Green horse-corn was often gathered from the fields, thrown on a fire of burning fence rails and scorched to a good deep brown. Without salt or other condiment it would be devoured with all the zest of a great luxury.

When Sherman marched to the sea his orders were, "The army will forage liberally on the country during the march. To this end each brigade commander will organize a good and sufficient foraging party under the command of one or more discreet officers, who will gather near the route traveled, corn or forage of any kind, meat of any kind, vegetables, corn-meal, or whatever is needed by the command, aiming at all times to keep in the wagons at least ten days' provisions for his command and three days' forage. Soldiers must not enter the dwellings of the inhabitants, or commit any trespass; but during a halt or camp they may be permitted to gather turnips, potatoes, and all vegetables, and to drive in stock in sight of the camp. To regular foraging parties must be intrusted the gathering of provisions and forage at any distance from the road traveled."

How well the troops obeyed this order, their good condition on their arrival at Savannah bore evidence. General Sherman relates that although the foraging was attended with much danger and hard work, there seemed to be a charm about it that attracted the soldiers, and they thought it a privilege to be detailed on a party. He said that he was often amused at the strange collections that were secured of mules, horses, and even cattle, packed with old saddles and loaded with hams, bacon, bags of corn meal and poultry. While walking up to a house on a plantation where a bivouac was made, General Sherman passed by a soldier who had a ham on his musket, a jug of sorghum molasses under his arm and a big piece of honey in his hand, from which he was eating. Catching Sherman's eye he remarked *sotto voce* to a comrade, "Forage liberally on the country!"

One could conclude in a measure how much food it took to supply an army by watching the enormous trains of laden wagons. I heard it stated that the wagon-train of the Army of the Potomac would cover a distance of sixty miles if stretched along a single road. To see the enormous piles of hard-tack and pork barrels at the railroad depots near camp convinced one of the truth of the old adage that "an army marches on its stomach." When supplies failed, only those in command knew how plans miscarried.

Got any pies for sale Aunty?

The hungry edge of appetite

ROADSIDE COMMISSARIES.

19

VI.

THE DRUMMER-BOYS.

THOSE omnipresent youngsters whose pranks gave so much life to camp or march deserve more than a passing tribute to their characteristic personality. Through rain or sunshine, at rest or in action, they seemed imbued with the same good-nature; and whether beating the drum or marching with it slung over the shoulder, they were the most picturesque little figures in the Union army.

Many of them were boys of twelve or thirteen, youths in years, but after a season of army life, men in experience. Parents no doubt sent them forth (or learned of their running away to the army) with grave apprehensions of the dangers they would be exposed to, but if they could have had an occasional glimpse of them in their newly acquired self-reliance and persistency, part of their sympathy might have been bestowed on those with whom the boys came in contact.

I am sure that many of the housewives of the country through which we marched long remembered the modest and innocent-faced youths who so often pestered them in their hunger. Nothing seemed to escape their prying eyes; no well was deep enough to make butter secure from them, and no cellar was sufficiently dark to keep the goodies it contained from their grasp. In camp, any mischief that was set on foot could be safely attributed to the drummer-boys and their confederates the fifers. A stern hand was necessary to make them obedient to military discipline, and a week in the guard-house or half a day's penance carrying a log, proved to them that a soldier's life had restrictions as well as pleasures. And yet they served an important as well as pleasing purpose, for what like their marching rattle-clangor or their sudden camp-calls stirred the soldier's pulse! And the march on the parade-ground during dress-parade or brigade-drill often inspired hearts that were despondent. Both drummers and fifers were in their special element at a grand review, when they appeared with white gloves and shining brasses. None were so proud in all the glorious array. When the order to "fall in" was given, they stepped majestically forward, and as the regiment approached the point of review, where perhaps the President or commanding general was posted, they glanced toward the reviewing officer with an expression of self-consciousness which suggested to a looker-on that the parade would have little importance were it not for their presence.

Painters of military pictures are fond of placing a broken drum in the fore-ground of their battle-scenes; but no representation could be more incorrect, for during a battle the musicians and drummers are detailed to the rear for hospital service, and may often be found behind some fence enjoying a quiet cup of coffee. They were sometimes made use of by the surgeons to bring the wounded men out from under fire on the battle-field, or to carry water to those sick with fever and whose patience in suffering was remarkable. With quick steps and bright faces they did good service and brought hope and cheer to many sufferers. They had their hours of drill under a drum-major, and in some quiet spot near camp would practice the calls and marches. But their unfailing good-nature lightened their many burdens and a volume of anecdotes might be related of their original ventures and ready wit.

An incident occurs to me now that happened in Virginia, after an order had been issued from headquarters which forbade foraging. In the early part of the war it was looked upon as trespassing, and those in command failed to appreciate that all civilians outside of our lines were our bitter enemies. One commander thus conscientious met a drummer-boy carrying off a rooster by the heels. "Did you not know," said the officer, "that foraging had been forbidden?" "Yes," answered the boy sheepishly (but keeping a tight hold on the rooster) "I know I have done wrong." Then he looked up with a saucy twinkle: "But, General, he got up on a fence and hurrahed for Jeff Davis, so I killed him." The general's face relaxed; he laughed, and said, "Well, go on to camp with your chicken, but no matter whom the next one cheers for, you must not touch him."

Ah! well, the soldiers would have missed other comrades far less than the lively little drummers, and many marches through scorching sun and suffocating dust would have been much harder to bear had it not been for these little musicians. Lagging foot-steps often quickened and weary faces brightened at the sudden sound of drum and fife, and many a "God bless you, boys; you give us cheer" went out to them in the long march. There is many a duty of war that tries the courage and nerve of the soldier more than the battle-field, with its wild excitement. Marching is one of them; and when it is remembered that these little chaps were hot and tired and dusty and drooping, as well as the men, it may be seen that it often required genuine heroism in them to unsling their drums and tune up their fifes for the inspiriting of the veterans' long line of march. They have been celebrated in song and story, and to those who returned to civil duties, memory of army life must seem like a dream. The scenes in which they mingled are now read as history by our children, and when we think of the drummer-boys, may we say fervently:

> "Sweet is the dew of their memory,
> And pleasant the balm of their recollection."

A Morning Lesson

Rappahannock Station Va
Feb. 13th 1864
from life

23

VII.

WINTER HUTS.

THE COMMISSARY'S HEADQUARTERS.

 O THOSE reared amid comfortable surroundings, and who had left bright fires and home luxuries for the field of battle, life in an army hut must, for a time at least, have seemed a strange existence; but after the hardships of campaigning, the exposure on the picket-line, or sentry and fatigue duty in winter, the little shelter became a haven of rest. Much of original skill was displayed by the soldier-architects in the designing and erecting of these structures. Their materials were more than limited, and as for tools, the dull army ax was about the only building-instrument that could be made available.

A winter camp was generally located on a well drained hillside, convenient to water and accessible to supply teams. After selecting a site the limits of the camp were designated, streets laid out and arrangements vigorously carried forward that the men might get under cover before the inclement weather began. Ax-men were detailed to the nearest pine woods for logs, while others scoured the country in search of further building material. Sometimes an abandoned house would be discovered, which the men would swarm over and take away piece by piece, until at the end of two or three days nothing would be left of it but the foundation. Everything that could be called a board was of value, and window-frames, doors and sashes were treasures indeed, and seized upon with the greatest eagerness. Even the foundation was not always left to mark the spot where the house had stood, for the stones were available for chimneys, and were often carried away with the rest.

The walls of the huts were made of pine logs joined together at the corners, and their interstices plastered with yellow mud. Space for a doorway was left at one end, and a chimney at the other. This was usually made of stones plastered with mud, and extended on the top with one or two barrels, the latter improving the draft, and, in the soldiers' eyes, adding to the style of architecture. The roofs were often made of canvas, although some of the men were ingenious enough to build them of boards, which gave much more warmth and were rain-proof.

The commissary's headquarters in the illustration gives faithful delineation of a style of structure to which the soldiers were most partial. It was furnished quite luxuriously with home-made chairs and benches, a bunk to sleep in, and a fireplace from which came a gentle warmth. The walls were more or less tastefully decorated with pictures cut from the illustrated newspapers, and a visitor, glancing at the interior, would conclude that there were some genial spots in a soldier's experience.

Exterior comfort was also considered in neatly laid walks before the door, made of barrel staves. This made a dry spot to sit upon, and the soldiers were often seen together there chatting in the sun. Washtubs was also improvised, by cutting barrels in halves and attaching handles to each section. Protection to horses was a necessary consideration as well as to men, and the arrangement of pine boughs against the chimney in the picture was a stable contrived for the sergeant's favorite horse.

It was interesting to watch the groups of men that continually gathered about these headquarters. The greatest number were seen when rations were issued to the mess. Then pork was weighed out, and hard-tack, coffee and other supplies distributed. Now and then a soldier would appear, to obtain a barrel for a chimney-top, or a hard-tack box to make a seat for his hut.

Notwithstanding the great effort made by the men to have their huts habitable, they experienced much discomfort at times. Roofs would leak, and it was not an uncommon sight to see them blown off altogether; then the rain would pour in and cause much consternation until damages could be repaired. Or perhaps an easterly wind would blow down a chimney and so fill the hut with pine smoke that the occupants would be driven into the open air. Then they would scheme anew to remedy the difficulty, and after placing a board across the barrel and trying other experiments, the quarters could be again occupied.

The winter evenings presented varied scenes in the huts. Many times the men would be sitting before the fire discussing the coming spring campaign, or retailing bits of camp gossip gathered during the day. Again I would find them enjoying a quiet game of euchre or draw-poker by the dim light of a tallow dip furnished by the commissary; while by the same insufficient light a soldier with thoughtful face would be laboriously penning a letter to the "old folks at home." Story-telling would often be in order, and the best romancer in the regiment would at times regale the boys with bits of real personal history, and again would trust entirely to his fertile imagination.

Evenings were also spent in song, and the sound of the manly, mellow voices fell sweetly on the ear. They were often accompanied by the insinuating strains of a violin or the twanging of the banjo. Popular military songs of the period were indulged in with great spirit, and the recollection of their effective influence has always remained vividly in my mind.

"Home is where the heart is;" and the soldier's home for long months was in his hut. When the spring campaign opened, it was with a pang that the hand of destruction was laid on the shelters, and when the order to "fall in" was given and the column made its way over the hill to the ford to meet the enemy, regretful glances were cast backward at the disman-tled winter-town, soon to be occupied by crows and turkey-buzzards, who always flock to a deserted camp to feed upon the refuse matter.

Memories cluster thick and fast about them now, I know, to those who have been spared to live the scenes again in recollection; for at army re-unions I listen to stories galore, that were told in those winter camps.

COMMISSARY SERGEANT'S HEADQUARTERS.

VIII.

A SCOUTING PARTY.

ANT of occupation or dullness of time were complaints that rarely came from the army scout, as the demand for his services at head-quarters was constant. To penetrate the enemy's lines and locate his out-posts and main body would often be a sudden and peremptory order. Then the necessity of burning a bridge to impede the enemy's progress would unexpectedly present itself, and the frequent intelligence received of the activity of bushwhackers and guerrillas would cause the scouts to be despatched beyond the lines to abate, if possible, that never-ending annoyance.

The scouts connected with the army were an active and wiry body of men, who were expert horsemen, splendidly mounted. They usually traveled in small parties to escape observation, and were dressed in gray homespun to look as much as possible like the inhabitants of the country where active operations were carried on. They were always well armed with carbines and revolvers.

I had the pleasure of accompanying several scouting parties during the war, and remember most vividly my exciting experiences with that branch of the service. During the many campaigns in the Shenandoah Valley I scoured the country on both sides of the pike from Harper's Ferry to Port Republic in company with scouts from the various commands; and later, under Gen. Grant, during the campaign from the Wilderness to Petersburg had a number of adventures with the scouts of Sheridan's cavalry.

Shortly after the battle of the Wilderness a party of six scouts were sent by Gen. Grant to locate the enemy's right flank, and to discover whether the bridges over the North Anna River were held by a strong force, and also if Lee's army, which then occupied Spottsylvania Court House, was receiving heavy reinforcements from Richmond. I received permission to accompany this party and started with them at midnight from camp near Todd's Tavern. We moved to the left in the direction of Port Royal. On the first day we did not meet any force of the enemy and about noon entered the town, consisting of but few houses, a blacksmith's shop and a tavern. Ascertaining from contrabands that a small force of Stuart's cavalry was posted a few miles to the south, beyond the Mattapony River, we succeeded in slipping past by crossing a ford below them. We proceeded at a trot in the direction of the North Anna River, with an advance guard of two men three hundred feet ahead, meeting with no adventure until five o'clock. Then our guard come back at a gallop, with pistols drawn, and reported having come face to face with three Confederate cavalrymen at a turn in the road a short distance ahead. Preparations were at once made to receive an attack from the body to which that advance guard of three probably belonged; but after waiting about five minutes, our own advance was sent cautiously forward again and found that the enemy had disappeared.

Later in the afternoon we saw clouds of dust in the south and west, and moving cautiously that way, we were able to get a view of large bodies of troops moving in the direction of Spottsylvania. A battle was evidently in progress at that place, as we could hear the steady growling of guns in the distance. We esconced ourselves in a piece of woods on a hill-top three-quarters of a mile from the road where the enemy's troops were marching, and watched them with intense interest till sundown.

Feeling unsafe in such close proximity to the armies, we accosted an old contraband, evidently a slave, and asked if we could reach a certain point by riding over the farm where he was. "No, sah!" he replied. "Massa wouldn't let nobody ride ober his farm, but you might go down the road by the ole mill and git thar that way." Our ideas of "Massa's" rights, however, differed from those of the old negro and we started across country. Toward daylight we neared the North Anna River and learned from negroes that the stream was held by a force of cavalry, and that the railroad-bridge was strongly fortified and guarded.

On approaching the enemy's position carefully, we were able to see, with the aid of a field-glass, men at work on the earthworks. At intervals we could hear the rumbling of trains and the screech of a locomotive whistle, showing that Gen. Lee was still in communication with Richmond. We posted a sentinel near the edge of some woods and rested within them until nightfall, when the commanding officer wisely determined to return to the army.

Starting, we avoided as much as possible the main road and moved cautiously northward. Toward midnight we saw the glare of camp-fires on a hill a mile or two distant, and were obliged to make a detour to the eastward to avoid possible capture. Toward daylight we struck the road leading to Fredericksburg and came in sight of a party of the enemy's cavalry, who made a dash to capture us. Two of the scouts were slightly wounded, but hard riding saved us, and we reached the right of the Union lines near Spottsylvania just as Gen. Grant's army was moving by the left flank in the direction of the North Anna River.

The country lying between the Blue Ridge Mountains and the Orange and Alexandria Railroad was thoroughly scouted during the war, as large parties of guerrillas under the redoubtable Mosby made life miserable for the Union forces in that section of Virginia. In the West, scouts of the Union army did splendid service, often penetrating hundreds of miles into the enemy's lines and returning with information of great value to the commanding generals. During the Atlanta campaign Gen. Sherman relied greatly on the work of scouts, and had large numbers of them out in the enemy's country in front. In West Virginia and East Tennessee the scouts were natives of the mountains, true Union men, whose spirit for our success was intensified by sufferings endured and outrages inflicted by the hands of their Secession neighbors. Brother often fought against brother, and family feuds commenced then have been continued to the present day. West of the Mississippi the scouts were generally recruited from the men of the plains, Indian fighters and hunters, and in some cases half-breed Indians were enlisted in the service of this corps. Although not consolidated into one command, this branch of the army performed deeds of bravery which will live in memory as long as the war itself. All historians should seek to do full justice to this brave and daring body of soldiers.

ON THE ALERT.

MCCLELLAN AT ANTIETAM.

IX.

A NIGHT MARCH.

HILE IT IS always preferable for a great army to advance on an enemy by the light of day, there have been some most wonderful marches made in the dead of night. Many Union soldiers can recall to mind the varied scenes of adventure when they tramped in darkness through unknown country, occupied by the enemy in such strong force, and so well fortified at every available point, that it seemed like an impossibility to make an attack that would result in anything but defeat.

None had more interest for me than a march I made in 1863 with the Army of the Potomac under command of Gen. Hooker, when it left the winter camp on the north fork of the Rappahannock, opposite the town of Fredericksburg. This town was then occupied by the Confederate army commanded by Gen. R. E. Lee; and upon orders from Washington active preparations were made to turn their position and drive them out of their fortified lines.

The whole Union army, except three corps under Gen. Sedgwick, marched up the north fork of the Rappahannock and, crossing on pontoons at Kelly's Ford, moved rapidly to Ely Ford on the Rapidan. Fording this stream (about four feet deep) the troops advanced quickly and took Chancellorsville, thus placing themselves on the enemy's rear and flank. Holding this menacing position, Gen. Hooker gave orders to fortify a strong line in the dense woods surrounding Chancellorsville, where he awaited the enemy's attack. Meanwhile, Sedgwick's command had made a strong feint below Fredericksburg by crossing the river on pontoons and displaying a large force in front of the Confederate entrenched lines, on the hills in rear of the town. Two corps were then detached from Sedgwick's force and marched in the direction of the United States Ford to form a junction with our main body under Gen. Hooker. Heavy skirmishing and some fighting had already taken place, which suggested a determination on the part of the enemy to retain possession of their stronghold.

I accompanied the detached column along the north fork of the Rappahannock late in the afternoon, and approached the ford, at which point on the river two pontoon-bridges had been thrown across. As we marched along, we could hear artillery and musketry fire from the opposite side of the river, but did not suppose the contest would be intense before we could reach the field. Just before dusk, however, a tremendous volume of sound came from the woods where the two armies confronted each other. It commenced with crackling musketry fire, as if advancing skirmish lines had become engaged, and soon swelled into a continuous roar which made the ground tremble with its power. Now and then could be heard a separate cannon shot, as if but few guns had secured favorable position. As the musketry fire became louder, we knew that the Union lines were being forced back, and clouds of dust and smoke rolled up from the woods where the two gallant armies were struggling for victory.

Our pace was quickened, and troops hurried forward in route-step to succor the hard-pressed Union lines. From the high bank on our side of the river we could get a view of the field of conflict, on our approach to the ford. Looking over the stream we saw a densely wooded country stretching for miles toward the south and west. In the open fields of the foreground were ammunition and supply trains, reserve artillery, extra pontoon-trains,—in fact,

33

all the impedimenta of a great army. It was a thrilling scene as it lay bathed in the warm glow of a May sunset. Clouds of smoke rolled up from the woods, which in many places had taken fire, and as we stopped to gaze for a moment we might conclude, were it not for the noise, that the sight before us was the conflagration of a great city.

We descended the hill to the river, and crossing on the pontoons, were soon on our way towards the front. We passed through the wagon-camps on a flat near the river, and ascending a gentle slope were soon in the dense woods beyond. Darkness had now fallen, and the din of the conflict increased, though we concluded that the enemy's advance had been checked, as the reports of firing came no nearer. Sounds rose and fell as the opposing forces changed position, coming clearly and distinctly from a wooded ridge but with muffled tone from the valleys. Suddenly there came a burst of artillery, and a tremendous roar continued for one hour. Then word was received that the enemy's advance had been checked.

Suddenly we met straggling parties of demoralized troops hurrying towards the rear, and found on inquiry that the Eleventh Corps, holding the right flank of our army, had been surprised and put to rout by Stonewall Jackson, who had been making one of his famous forced marches for the purpose. These men were panic-stricken, rushing about at random with no directness of movement, their only thought being to get away from the bullets. Guards were thrown out on both sides of the road to put an end to the disgraceful confusion, and when the way was cleared we pushed forward toward the firing.

I shall never forget the scene at this point, at nine o'clock. Fires were blazing on every side, which, with the pine trees that had been ignited, so lit up the road that objects were as discernible as in the day; and surging through it all was a mass of earnest, determined men who were intent only on reaching the line of battle where they could be of service to their struggling comrades. Marching hurriedly forward, they soon came to a road leading from Ely's Ford to Chancellorsville, and deploying to right and left the lines were very shortly in such a position that the damage done by Jackson's masterly surprise was almost made good, although a last desperate attempt was made at eleven o'clock to take possession of a plateau surrounding the Chancellorsville House.

The incidents on the road during the remainder of the night were full of absorbing interest, for troops were continuously pushed forward. The moon looked placidly down as the column of men, broken here and there by batteries of artillery and ammunition-wagons, hurried toward the front, and through the woods on all sides could be seen large bodies of men in reserve, grouped around camp-fires, preparing coffee and other much needed food. Thousands were wrapped in gray blankets, sleeping peacefully, dreaming perhaps of a far-off home, while only a mile away the roar of the musketry rose and fell in continuous sound.

Soon after midnight there was a cessation of battle-turmoil; but the rumbling trains and weary troops steadily made their way through the smoky wood until the sun lit up the eastern horizon.

Thus the great night march was ended, and the last of twenty thousand men who had marched bravely during the night came straggling by. Their eyes were so heavy that they could scarce keep them open, but so high were they in spirit that a passer-by would think they were marching to a scene of pleasure instead of perhaps to a field of death.

THROUGH THE WOODS AT NIGHT.

X.

CHRISTMAS AT THE FRONT.

"PEACE ON EARTH, good-will toward men" could not ring out its grateful cadence in the scenes of conflict through which our army was passing; nor even during the ordinary camp rests, when most of the soldiers, if they had anything in the nature of a special banquet in honor of the ancient festival of good cheer, had to get it by special foraging in the enemy's country. Yet, although there were no home-greetings, tender memories of Christmas-tide filled the hearts of the soldiers and took them back in thought to where little ones sang in anthem the story of old. Remote from scenes most dear and happy in the consciousness of a country's defense, our brave men brushed away a tear and sought to enjoy the holiday as best they might.

I was just feeling a sense of my own loneliness one Christmas day when an officer of the Signal Corps invited me to take dinner with some friends of his on the picket-line. It was quite early in the morning when we mounted our horses and started from camp. After riding some miles, we came in sight of the picket-reserves; then rode on and found that the main picket-line extended across a valley through which flowed a creek. Nearing a point of crossing, we passed a picket-post on a sand-bar in the middle of the stream, and halted a while to admire the beautiful surroundings. The hut, which was prettily fashioned of pine boughs, sheltered three or four sleeping men, while the cook was getting a frugal dinner ready on the camp-fire in front. Near-by, the officers' mess was being prepared, and we were cordially invited to partake of "chicken fricassee, camp-style." The odor of the cooking was appetizing, and our long ride had given us an appetite, but as we were expected elsewhere, we were obliged to decline and soon took leave of the hospitable officers.

We rode down the line and found the post, commanded by my comrade's friend, on an old farm road. The men were camped in the farm garden, where they had thrown up a shelter of boards against the fence as a protection from the cold wind. We dismounted in the barn-yard, and entrusted our horses to an old negro servant who promised them a feed of corn. We were most cordially received, and the dinner was soon placed before us on a table improvised from the cover of an oat-bin.

We found that living on the outer picket-line was much better than in the main army camp, and were surprised at the real luxuries placed before us, most of which had been obtained from the farmers at very small cost. The bill of fare consisted of rabbit-stew, fricasseed chicken, griddle-cakes with honey, and excellent coffee. To this we did full justice, and, with the addition of a little "commissary," had a more enjoyable feast than we had eaten in months. The rough fellows often detailed as cooks, and especially the "darkeys," who attached themselves to the various commands as camp-followers and servants of all kinds, developed much culinary talent at times, and the clearness of the coffee and toothsomeness of their simple dishes would put to shame many a professional cook. It is fair to allow, however, that perhaps the admirable hunger-sauce of outdoor life had something to do with these savory concoctions.

After an hour or two of social chat over our pipes, we rode further down the line and stopped at various points to talk with friends who were on duty. None seemed to have fared

37

as sumptuously as ourselves; most of the men were cooking salt pork, though one party had secured a turkey from a neighboring farmer and looked lovingly towards it as it roasted before the glowing camp-fire. Some of the men were fortunate enough to have received boxes from home, and their faces grew bright as they lifted out roast turkey, chickens, bread, cake and pies that kindly hands had prepared. An occasional bottle of "old rye," secreted in a turkey or loaf of bread, would give rise to much fun and expected enjoyment. The provost guard, however, seldom overlooked a bottle, and confiscated any contraband liquor; and his long experience had bred in him a sort of special sense for any such little infractions of the rule, which was inflexible even for Christmas, and if got the better of at all had to be by a skillful and imperceptible breaking.

But little more of interest came in our way on the agreeable trip I have mentioned, and we returned to camp much brightened by the scenes which so pleasantly broke the monotony of soldier life on that Christmas day at the front.

Something Good

A CHRISTMAS DINNER.

XI.

THE ARMY HERD.

"BEEF ON THE HOOF" was the soldiers' name for the fresh beef furnished them, and the herds of cattle from which it came were no inconsiderable portion of the army's supplies. The Commissary Department usually furnished a certain number of steers to each moving column, and it was a pleasant sight to watch the droves with their escorts as they traveled along the road. A stalwart white ox, with eyes too gentle to suggest slaughter, would sometimes be in lead, and around his neck would be hung blankets, a cartridge-box and other accoutrements of the guard. Often a soldier would sit astride the animal in lead and guide him with a long pole, while the rest of the herd would be kept in order by a series of vigorous shouts.

When a herd reached camp at night-fall, it would be driven into an adjacent field, where it was carefully guarded during the night and where it could rest and feed till the column moved again.

Sometimes fresh beef rations would be issued to the men while in the midst of battle. I recall to mind an instance where during an engagement I was watching an army butcher slaughter an ox, when a sudden charge was made by the Rebs which quickly caused a scattering of both spectators and men engaged in the work. The herd of cattle stampeded and dashed back through the ammunition trains and lines of troops, causing a great panic for a time.

Cattle were collected by foraging parties whenever practicable, and during Sherman's "March to the Sea," immense numbers were secured in the rich country through which he traveled. During the war a supply depot for cattle was established at Washington, just outside the city limits. Great numbers of cattle were sent thither from different localities, and drafts were made from the great herd and sent to the different armies in the field. Sometimes they would be captured by the enemy's cavalry, and many a drove of well-fed oxen intended for Uncle Sam's boys would go to sustain the strength of the "fighting Johnnies," who were always blessed with vigorous appetites.

They were not peculiar in that, however, and I have already noted the importance to all army operations of the "commissary of subsistence." One can well believe what is said of the ancient Romans, that their success in war was not altogether the result of their indomitable courage and splendid discipline, but that these were sustained by the fact that they paid more attention than any other nation of their times to the organized and efficient serving of the commissariat of their army. If it is true that man must eat to live, it is indisputable that man must eat to march and fight.

I once saw a herd of beautiful cattle being driven through the streets of Baltimore. The leader, a handsome red ox, was mounted by a Zouave who sat astride with his Springfield musket across his knee. "A picture of war and peace!" I thought:—the dashing Zouave with bronzed skin, strong, characteristic face and gaudy uniform; and the patient beast, whose eyes wondered mildly at the sights of a great city.

BEEF ON THE HOOF.

XII.

THE MOVING COLUMN.

HE most interesting war-sight to an observer is a great army on the march. I learned one morning that the whole army had been ordered to move forward, so I mounted my mare *Kitty* and rode out to see the great column pass by.

The first object that came in sight in the distance was a division of cavalry, the advance guard, which presented a splendid appearance. The horses had evidently had hard service, but looked tough and business-like. Neither had the soldiers a superfluous pound of flesh upon them, but both officers and men looked bronzed and hardy, and, like the horses, appeared able to endure continued hardship. Flags and guidons were flying and sabres clattering, and men were chatting and laughing. In rear of the cavalry several batteries of horse-artillery rumbled along. The powder-and-smoke-blackened muzzles gave evidence of recent service, as did the limbers and caissons covered with mud and dust; blankets and other traps were fastened to the latter, and here and there a bag of oats or bundle of hay for the horses.

Just behind, the headquarters flag appeared to view, and I knew that the commanding general, Grant, was approaching. I had not seen him in some time, so awaited his coming with pleasure. He sat his horse with easy grace, his right hand resting upon his thigh. He wore a slouch hat ornamented with a cord, a double-breasted military coat carelessly thrown open, and a vest which had lost two buttons. He was, as usual, without belt or sword, and had the inevitable cigar in his mouth, unlighted. Anxieties and responsibilities had left telling traces, for the general was much thinner than when he left winter camp a few months previous; but the resolute face, which time proved so true an index of character, remained the same. After Gen. Grant came the headquarters staff, followed by a cavalry escort.

Then came the infantry, and as they surged along I was struck with surprise at the youthful appearance of the troops. Many of the enlisted men were hardly more than boys; but notwithstanding their few years they looked strong and muscular, their blankets and knapsacks slung over one shoulder and canteens clattering a refrain to their steps. Their bright faces bespoke the best of cheer, and a ringing laugh echoed along one part of the column when some witty fellow had made an amusing remark.

The staff officers rode backward and forward with anxious oversight, while the company officers made effort to hold the men to their gait. The general color of the troops' clothing, originally blue, was a greenish yellow; the sun and rain having faded the uniforms, and the yellow dust of marching settled thickly in the fabric. A Zouave regiment soon appeared, and the gay uniforms of the officers and troops gave new brightness to the moving column, although their flowing, baggy trousers were mostly tattered. One Zouave who wore an old white "stove-pipe" hat was the subject of much merriment; he had evidently lost his fez in the last encounter, and in the bereavement had donned some old farmer's ancient head-gear. Quite a number were barefooted, and gingerly picked their way over stony places, and the poor fellows were laughed at by inconsiderate comrades when a misstep caused them to wince with pain.

After I had viewed thus for hours the varied elements of the army on the march, a low, rumbling sound broke upon my ear, and sharp glances and quickened footsteps told of the men's realization that their front was already engaged with the enemy. The column was now shifted to one side of the road, and a couple of batteries dashed along, the speed of the horses increased by the slash of whips and cries of drivers. The gunners ran frantically by the side of their pieces or clung excitedly to the ammunition boxes. The column was soon doubled up, the rear division taking to the fields beside the road. Fences across their course seemed to disappear at a touch, and corn and wheat fields were swarmed over as if by a legion of locusts. Ambulances were scattered through the column to pick up the sick, and the pale faces that glanced out from some of them told how severe a strain the march had been in many instances. Several times I saw men fall out of the ranks too foot-sore to proceed a single step further, and after receiving the captain's admonition to return to duty as soon as possible, would retreat to the shelter of a fence-corner and fall into the sleep of sheer exhaustion, oblivious to the clatter and noise.

The sun was scorching, and the dust suffocating as it drifted to leeward and settled a foot deep over grass and weeds, and lay like heaps of winter snow on the fence rails. A grateful though brief respite was given to the troops, and as the column halted, the men dropped down in the dust by the road-side to snatch a moment's rest. Orders to "fall in" were soon given, and the weary column was again under way. Ammunition wagons were hurried forward, and the negro drivers lashed their animals and yelled as if to hasten the speed at every jump. The baggage-trains were turned off the road and parked in the fields to await the outcome of the struggle. One unusual picture presented itself: two infantrymen languidly mounted on an old gray horse; one was wounded and the other sick, if a pale, sad face was any criterion. A drummer-boy was acting the Good Samaritan by carefully leading the horse and conveying the suffering soldiers to a place of refuge. Meanwhile, the infantry still surged along, officers urging their men to increased speed. When the chief part of the column had passed, stragglers that always follow an army and foot-sore men tramped on, wagons guarded by infantry, reserve artillery, army forges and pontoon-trains, followed in irregular line. Occasional groups of men limped by, different ones being supported by a hay-fork or a crutch made of a forked stick. The road now became littered with blankets and knapsacks flung away by the troops when they could no longer endure their weight in the weary march. Some parts of the road were blue with overcoats cast away, no doubt without a thought of the protecting warmth they would lend at night-fall.

Interspersed through the column were negro servants of officers, many of them very grotesque. They were all proud of their new-found freedom, and stepped gleefully chattering along as if to the "Happy Land, far, far away." Some of them had confiscated old mules and horses, over which they had slung kettles and camp utensils in ridiculous fashion, and seated astride some of the animals were the pickaninnies, trusting to an unknown future with their happy parents. And so the last scene of this wonderful pan- orama of human beings passed by, and the resident whites and negroes of the locality ventured out from their hiding-places and picked up the too-plentiful cloth- ing, as if to say, "There is no great loss without some small gain."

With the Moving Column

TYPES FROM THE MARCH.

47

HOOKER AT LOOKOUT MOUNTAIN.

XIII

THE SOUP-KETTLE.

WINTER CAMP.

T WAS a cold and dreary day that I rode through camps scattered over miles of hillside, and as the wind moaned through the pines and the chilling blast swept my face, visions of home and its cosy comforts came back to me. But before I could long indulge in regrets, peculiarities of the different camp-homes so interested me that thoughts of my own hardships were put to flight.

It never occurred to me before that there could be class-distinctions in camp-life, yet that such a thing was possible was at this time clearly defined. One regimental home would have an air of neatness and comfort which bore evidence of efficient officers, and their care of the men; all would be sprucely dressed, healthy in appearance and alert and intelligent in their movements. But in immediate vicinity, and with the same opportunities of comfort, I would find a carelessly constructed camp, with men poorly dressed, sluggish in movement and despondent in spirit.

"This is like all life," I said; "even where conditions are the same, some will thrive and pronounce the world a success, while others will falter by the wayside and discover nothing within grasp."

It was early in the day and all were astir in the camp-streets, and it took but a few glances to conclude that preparations were being made for dinner. Some were cutting wood, others were building fires, and the cooks were concocting the simple but savory soup. The fires were usually made of pine; but when hard wood was obtainable it was preferred, as it lasted longer. Beans were the basis of soup, as a rule, and these with a piece of salt pork always made an appetizing mess to a soldier. Beef soup was sometimes served, when an addition of desiccated vegetables ("desecrated" the boys called them) could be had. Occasionally a company secured a cook who had served in a restaurant, and his services were greatly appreciated, for he could often make a most acceptable mess from very simple ingredients. The cooks were amusing characters, who held rather rigid sway and whose word relative to the composition of a soup was law. They used for soup-making heavy sheet-iron camp kettles, which were slung over the fire on a pole, each end of which rested on a forked stick.

I stopped at one of the camps just as the dinner call sounded, and was amused at the quickness with which the men responded to the lively notes of fife and drum. All houses on the company-street were soon vacated, and a general move made towards the soup-kettles.

Some of the men came with coffee-cups and others with tin pails made from tomato and fruit cans. The latter were sold in great quantities by the sutlers to the soldiers during the winter season.

I watched the hungry but orderly line that formed in front of the fire, as they patiently awaited their turn. First came a fair-faced boy of perhaps eighteen summers, full of life and with the rosy glow of health. Next came a more sedate man, but none the less hungry if one could judge from the anxious look on his face as he watched the filling of his can. A good natured Irishman some distance in the rear kept all the men laughing. "Say, Bill," he called out to the cook, "Skim the top for thim fellers but kape the grounds for me. Sich boys can live on thin soup, but we men nades something thicker." "Oh," said a slow German near the end of the line, "Give us some kraut and Limburger, and shust one class of pier." "Shut up, Dutchy!" cried out a New Yorker, "this ain't the Bowery. Take what you can get, and be thankful." And so talk was exchanged until the whole line had been served and the last man had taken his departure.

I followed on to one of the nearest huts, which I found most comfortable, and tenanted by three men who were at dinner. They sat near a center-table made of boards taken from an old barn door. On it was set the soup and wheat bread which the commissary served during the winter, some hard-tack, and some cake sent from one of the soldiers' homes the week before. They were all young, and a jolly party, who had little thought of what privations or disaster the next campaign might bring them. There was often much of quiet enjoyment about the soldiers' dinner in winter camp, and thoughts of the pleasant times must have come back to the boys in the hot summer march. Then hard-tack and raw salt pork became luxuries, and a hurried bite under fire was often all they could get; and water,—ah! how they longed for just one swallow of water as they tramped through dusty road and field amid singing bullets and bursting shells! Sometimes they had to drop and sleep without supper; and those poor fellows used up by the way fared badly enough. But whatever of comfort or discomfort was theirs, they were usually in cheerful mood; and even when they grumbled, at bottom one could find, by a little probing, the solid sentiment—"*The Union must be saved!*"

"Used Up."

"FALL IN FOR SOUP!"

XIV.

MARCHING THROUGH THE RAIN.

 HO THAT rendered service in the great war will ever forget the discomforts of long marches in the rain or tramps in the deep mud!

The roughest experience that I can recall was one day's march when orders came to flank the enemy's position. The Union army had for some time been trying to dislodge the enemy, but found entrenchments so strong that this could not be done by direct attack, and the commander-in-chief decided that a flank movement was the only way by which the Rebs could be forced out of their impregnable lines.

Word came at midnight that a move must be made, and we were ordered to withdraw cautiously from our breastworks, which in some places were only a few hundred yards from the enemy's line. The men were ordered to make as little noise as possible and to prevent the rattling of accoutrements. Officers were told to give command in low tones so that the opposing pickets should not suspect that a move of great importance was taking place. The advance skirmish-line, which was in close proximity to the enemy, was left in position; but was ordered to withdraw at the first gray light of dawn. The movement commenced at midnight and was successfully accomplished, as the night was cloudy and an impenetrable darkness overspread the country. The men crept along toward the rear, feeling their way through tangled woods and swamps with an instinct that came of years of severe experience.

At daylight drizzling rain began to fall, and a cold east wind gave promise of an uncomfortable march; but after a halt was made and a hearty breakfast eaten, the column started in good earnest, determined to gain a position which would make the enemy loosen his grip. The rain soon fell heavily, and our men marched steadily through its down-pour, protecting themselves as best they could. Some covered themselves with rubber ponchos, and often one would share his with a less fortunate comrade by stretching the rubber covering across two short poles and marching underneath the shelter of this improvised umbrella. Some would cover themselves with blankets, but these, not being waterproof, gave only partial protection. The column after a time presented a soaked and bedraggled appearance; the road became slippery, and the mules and horses as they plunged along spattered the mud in showers. Fine uniforms were covered, and the entire column partook of the clay-color of the road. When descending into a valley the men would be compelled to wade through water which within a few hours had increased from a rivulet to a torrent. Sometimes the water would reach the waist; but the troops would plunge through, shouting and laughing at the mishaps of those who slipped and for a moment disappeared in the muddy stream. Some of the soldiers sought to better things by throwing up temporary bridges of logs; but the greater proportion did not seem to think it worth the effort, and accepted conditions as they were. At times when the ground was too soft to march upon, delay would be prevented by building a corduroy road, which is a laying of logs crosswise.

The column was halted about midday, and the cavalry in advance was pushed forward to learn if the enemy had prepared to resist our movement. Meanwhile the men were huddled together along the roads and in the fields, protecting themselves as well as possible from the driving rain. Officers sought the shelter of old barns and farm-houses whenever possible, and all hands made a quick cup of hot coffee and snatched a bite from the haver-sacks. A message soon came from the advance cavalry that the way was clear, and after an hour's halt the column pushed on. I sat on my horse by the roadside for an hour and saw the troops go by. The formation was in open order, each man marching at his own ease and carrying his gun as he could. At times the column would take to the fields, and throwing down the fences would make a wide-beaten road, brushing aside the corn and trampling the wheat and rye into a miry mass. The men at last marched quietly and soberly, there being an entire absence of the laughter and banter heard in fair weather or even in the early part of the day. The mounted officers sat their horses glum and reticent, huddled in their ponchos, and showed but little activity,—except that when a canteen was passed about occasionally, that smelt suspiciously strong, they awakened into new life.

In rear of the infantry column came the artillery, literally smothered in mud, clouds of steam arising from the heated bodies of the horses as they tugged away to what seemed their utmost at the harness; and yet the poor creatures made renewed effort to cross the soft spots, when the drivers urgently cracked their whips and made hortatory remarks! Back and forth on the flank of the column staff-officers were hurrying, to urge the men into rapid and continuous movement so that the line should not be broken and distance lost. Although in sympathy with the brave men who suffered so much discomfort, my sense of the ludicrous was aroused at the grotesque appearance of the officers' contraband servants; cooking utensils were slung over their backs or upon poles, and some were leading horses and mules which were laden with full paraphernalia of a camp-kitchen. They seemed demoralized and generally despondent, given to sighs and groans as they marched along. Last of all came the wagon-trains, escorted by infantry-guards, the mules doing splendid work under the incessant lashing and urging of the dusky drivers.

But here I took a short cut across country and soon reached the head of the column, when I found the troops going into camp, in rain-soaked fields, on a ridge of ground that crossed the line of march at right angles. Information had been received that the enemy were posted a short distance in front, and had the day been fair our troops would not have gone into bivouac but into fight. The commanding general, however, knowing that the ammunition was liable to damage in such a storm, did not think an attack advisable. In less time than one could imagine possible, the fields were dotted with the little "pup tents" and the smoke of hundreds of camp-fires drifted across the ridge. Rain-soaked and wretched, our brave boys lay down to rest, yet willing in their weariness to spring into battle at the first alarm and "follow the flag."

ACROSS COUNTRY IN A THUNDER STORM.

XV.

THE RESERVE LINE.

O A PERSON unaquainted with military movements or engagements, it is natural to conclude that all interest should center in the line of battle, but while the desperate work which decides an army's fate is done there, so much of smoke and confusion exists that there is not the opportunity for careful study of individual things that there is in the rear.

So, one afternoon, in the heat of a great battle, I mounted my horse and rode back along the reserve line to witness whatever scenes of interest there might be. I first came upon a park of ammunition wagons with the kind and caliber of contents marked plainly on the canvas covers and ready at a moment's notice to dash forward and distribute supplies to those sorely pressed at the front.

Near-by was a cavalry brigade; the men were in most cases dismounted and held the bridles of their horses as they grazed on the grass or picked at the sheaves of wheat in the field throughout which they were scattered. Picturesque groups of officers were gathered here and there under the shade of trees, for the heat of the sun was intense. Further on I found the ambulance corps posted, and watched their continuous dispatching to the front with the necessary appliances for the wounded. Riding on a short distance beyond, I came to a line of ambulances moving slowly to the rear, and, following them as they turned up an old lane, I found a field-hospital with its terrible scenes of suffering. It was an apple-orchard in rear of an old farm-house, and beneath the shade of trees and under tents hundreds of wounded men were lying. I was much impressed at the stillness of so many sufferers, and thought that their patient resignation bore strange contrasts to the descriptions I had read of the "shrieks of the wounded and groans of the dying."

Surgeons were grouped about an operating-table improvised from an old barn-door, and as I rode close upon them I saw that an infantry soldier was raised up and placed before them. From the blood stains on his pantaloons he had evidently been wounded in the upper part of the leg, and his pale face bore an anxious expression as the surgeons prepared to examine his injury. One of them calmly thrust his finger deep into the wound, felt about, withdrew it and spoke in a whisper to an assistant at his side. "Will it have to come off, doctor?" the wounded man asked anxiously. "I'm afraid it will, my good man," he replied kindly. The poor fellow closed his eyes and with a sob said "All right; I expected to give my life if need be, and if I only lose a leg I pay the debt easily. Go ahead."

Following the ascent of a hill I came to a battery of reserve artillery, and from this position I had quite a view of the battle in progress. Groups of interested spectators were scattered about the guns, some sitting on the wheels, others standing on the axles. Officers in front were watching the ebb and flow of the battle through glasses. Some of the men were sleeping under a temporary shelter of boards which they had thrown up as a protection from the burning sun of that hot day. Several men were making coffee and two or three groups of men sheltered under the shady side of a caisson were engaged in playing poker. This amusement seemed in strange contrast to the death struggles taking place not a mile distant, and I wondered how the indifferent fellows could have so little apprehension of their fate. "Sufficient unto the day," perhaps, "is the evil thereof."

The Reserve Line was usually a place for rest and refreshment, but it must be always with a keen outlook for possible flankings or surprises from the rear. The men, unless posted for that purpose, left care-taking to their officers, and enjoyed their ease.

————•————

HEN the day's march was ended and camp had been pitched in a pleasant grove, at times when the enemy was remote enough to dispel all ideas of danger, there was much pleasure in the soldier's evening meal; but when in close neighborhood to the foe, ceremony was a thing unthought of, and the whistling bullets and shrieking shells made supper a very brief and urgent indulgence. It was a matter of good fortune if the men were able to finish the meal at all, at such times, whether in the advance or in the reserve; for often a charge from the enemy would cause a sudden scattering and abandonment of food, mess-kettles, coffee pots, etc. And the triumphant Johnnies never ignored the most frugal meal, but made immediate appropriation of all food and camp-conveniences that came in their way.

The cook's position in preparing a meal was not an enviable one, and his consideration of personal safety were often a source of amusement to the soldiers. When the battle became warm he would nervously gather brush and fence-rails for the fire, but keep an anxious look-out toward the enemy, and was ready at the sound of a shell to dart to the rear or jump behind some friendly rock or tree. Perhaps after much perturbation a fire would be started, and then would begin an anxious search for water. When this was found, coffee and bean soup would be made, and distributed; then the men, with cup in hand, would seek cover behind trees or under the lee of breastworks, and there

munch the hard-tack and enjoy the soup and coffee in comparative safety. When the meal was finished the old pack-mules would be brought forward, and without the formality of washing, pots and kettles would be made secure to them and then would be sent to the rear.

The scenes of hasty suppers were less frequent at the reserve line than in the advance, of course, but when they did take place they were the more lively from being unexpected.

A hot day

A hasty supper

NOONTIDE AND EVENING.

59

XVI.

THE PRESIDENT'S REVIEW.

———— • ————

URING the winter and spring of 1863 the Army of the Potomac was camped on the north bank of the Rappahannock River, opposite the town of Fredericksburg. It had to all appearances recovered from the disastrous battle of the previous December, when, under the leadership of Gen. Burnside, it had attempted to drive the Confederates from their strongly fortified position on the south bank of the stream. Gen. Hooker had since succeeded to the command; under him the morale and discipline had improved, and in April of '63 the army was in better condition to assume the offensive than it had been at any previous time. It had been reorganized, and the different corps under their able commanders were ready to advance upon the enemy on receiving orders.

It was announced early in April that President Lincoln would soon review the army, and great preparations were made for this important event. A spirit of rivalry arose among the commanders of corps and divisions as to how their men should appear; and brigadiers and colonels of regiments and captains of companies and the rank and file joined in the strife. Clothes were brushed and repaired, shoes polished, brasses brightened, and white gloves were received with great satisfaction to lend finish to the uniforms.

All desirable preparations had been made, when word came that President Lincoln had arrived at Gen. Hooker's headquarters near Falmouth, and that he would review the whole army on the following day. The soldiers fell asleep full of anxious expectancy, and at dawn the camps were astir with busy preparations. Breakfast was hurriedly disposed of, and by eight o'clock everything was in readiness for the march to the parade-ground.

This was a level stretch of country several miles in extent, north of the town of Falmouth and in direct sight of the enemy's camp: and towards it as a common center columns of infantry marched slowly along. Mounted officers preceded them, and the men who came under my notice trotted along in route-step, chatting gaily and making comments on the events of the day. Bodies of cavalry, with bright colors and fluttering guidons, wound slowly over the rolling hills, and here and there batteries of artillery lumbered along. The cannoniers sat with folded arms upon the ammunition boxes, consciously proud of the splendid appearance of their guns.

When I reached the reviewing ground a wonderful sight was presented. Seventy thousand troops of all arms were drawn up in long lines, and under the soft grey light of an April day formed a picture that I shall never forget. The President soon arrived, and, after passing up and down between the lines, was escorted by Gen. Hooker and staff to a position on a gentle slope near an apple orchard, where he awaited the movements of the troops.

I placed myself where I could see Mr. Lincoln to advantage. He was very tall and his horse being rather small his feet appeared to almost touch the ground; his black frock coat and high "stove-pipe" hat seemed in strange keeping with the soldiers' uniforms, and his pale, anxious face in great contrast to the thousands of sun-burned ones about him. From the position he had taken, the whole body of troops could be seen at once, and his kind face lit up with pleasure from time to time at the great picture before him. It was a beautiful sight to see the great army stretched for miles across the gently undulating hills, waiting for orders to march in review; flags and guidons innumerable fluttered in the breeze, and mounted officers could be seen dashing about in all directions, engaged in giving orders.

But the signal to march (a cannon-shot) was given at last, and the head of the column, preceded by the commander-in-chief and staff, appeared in sight, moving to the sound of the headquarters band. Crowds of spectators, composed of civilians from Washington, officers' wives and friends, sutlers, wagoners, officers' servants, and those detached from duty, were ranged in lines and kept in position by Rush's Lancers as the column passed through. The infantry, marching in "company front," presented a magnificent appearance. They were bronzed and hardy-looking, and marched with mechanical precision; and for hours the men poured by, under the critical eyes of the President and the General in command. The President was again and again saluted and made pleasing acknowledgment by the raising of his hat. As each corps commander passed the reviewing-stand, he would wheel to the right and with his staff fall in behind the President.

Not the least interesting feature of the review was the tattered and smoked battle-flags; they were carried in nearly every instance by a splendid specimen of the American soldier, who seemed conscious of his precious burden.

The cavalry corps, under command of General Pleasanton, followed the infantry, and were a grand sight as they too marched in company front. The bright trappings of the men and horses, the gay regimental flags and guidons, gave a brilliancy and color that the infantry did not have, and the animated movements of the horses, with the blare of bugles and noise of tramping were sights and sounds not easily forgotten. The artillery came next, with heavy rumbling sound, nearly two hundred guns passing by; both men and officers were in the best of condition and the batteries were finely horsed.

When a regiment had passed the point of review, it hurried off in "double-quick" that the progress of succeeding troops should not be impeded; the artillery also made way at a trot, and by noon the last of the long columns that had formed the grand pageant could be seen disappearing over the hills in various directions. None were left but a few camp-followers and idlers, who gathered in groups and discussed the day's exciting scenes. The President rode through the camps in the afternoon, accompanied by Gen. Hooker and staff, and great enthusiasm was manifested among the soldiers. In the evening a reception was held at the General's headquarters, and the President returned to Washington the next morning, after expressing great admiration for the splendid array which had passed before him.

A Final Review at Post Lincoln
A R Waud

LOGAN AT VICKSBURG.

XVII.

COFFEE COOLERS.

HE absurd names that were given to individuals and things during the war were legion, but none of them caused more queries from those out of the Service than the one which gives title to our chapter and the picture of the thing itself "Under the Bank." If I were called upon to define the name "Coffee Cooler," I should say: He belonged to the genus *tramp*, shirked all work, avoided all danger, and could invariably be found where duty *did not* call; and yet, when conflict was ended, he "could a tale unfold" that would make one believe that shot and shell possessed no terrors for him, and that in the foremost line of action he had struggled fearlessly forward to victory.

During the winter he became an invalid; carrying water and cutting wood were duties left to his comrades, and under the doctor's care frequent draughts of "whiskey and quinine" were most acceptable.

In the spring, however, he burst forth like a butterfly from its cocoon, and, if not able to sip real nectar from the flowers, stood in readiness to devour all luxuries of the season that might come within his reach. And his spirits were most buoyant, for he knew that the danger of the coming campaign awaited not him,—only the brave boys in the front. It was his policy to seem eager to advance into action; but no comrade ever saw him in a battle; and he bore no scars, save the sting of bees that he had received in robbing a hive of its stores. He would boast of his bravery like Falstaff; but when artillery rumbled his utterances ceased, and as the column closed up he became much agitated. When the steps of the brave men quicken at the cheering words of the officers, and they shift their loads as if they had suddenly become lighter, then the "coffee cooler" becomes at once much afflicted. He is overcome with an unquenchable thirst, and in spite of the sergeant's protest stops at every spring to drink. Suddenly his shoes hurt his feet, and he limps painfully along, warily watching his chance to slip away unnoticed. After a time he drops groaning by the roadside, and after removing his shoes, searches with apparent carefulness for a stone-bruise or other injury; but as his regiment disappears over the hill, he hurriedly puts on his shoes and walks without difficulty across the fields to a cosy farm-house which his quick eye had seen before dropping out of the line.

The case of one such army tramp came to my notice, and I learned that after reaching the farm house he worked upon the sympathies of the people who lived there until he was well fed and his haversack stored with the best the larder contained. Thus feasted and supplied he sallied forth and soon fell in with kindred spirits—skulkers from commands. They immediately joined forces and sought the seclusion of a neighboring wood, where they made arrangements for a feast. Two of the party were sent to capture chickens and anything else the country afforded, while the rest set to work gathering wood to make a fire. The fragrant odor of coffee soon gave evidence that they had been successful. (It was a "cold day" when they did not have at least some ground coffee in their haversacks, and the fact that when caught these fellows were nearly always gathered about a steaming pot of the grateful beverage, gave them their nick-name of "Coffee Coolers.") Presently the foragers returned on the double-quick, laden with chickens, sweet potatoes and green corn. The chickens were soon picked and cooked, the corn and potatoes roasted, and the hungry shirkers devoured them with the zest and merriment of a royal banquet. Then followed a smoke, and the burning brand was passed from pipe to pipe amid many jokes. The evening was spent in jollity, and the distant sound of musketry caused but little thought of their falling comrades at the front. The camp-fire in time died down, and our heroes wrapped the drapery of their blankets about them and lay down to pleasant dreams.

Just at daylight, however, the sleeping party were suddenly lighted upon by the provost-guard, who without ceremony suddenly aroused them with the butts of their muskets. Numerous and elaborate were the excuses offered; but none availed them, and they were turned over to the tender mercies of the officer of the guard, who already had a hundred stragglers in charge that he had gathered within an hour. Formed in column, they were all marched to the provost-marshal, and from him were distributed to their several commands. That "the way of the transgressor is hard" was now illustrated; for amid the jeers of comrades the "coffee coolers" were subjected to various punishment. Some were bucked and gagged; some compelled to carry logs on the shoulders for hours in the sun, and others were placed in the extreme front line of battle.

I remember an instance where thousands of stragglers were scattered for miles through woods during a great battle. Orders were sent to the provost-marshal to sweep the country in the rear and force every man back to his regiment. A brigade of infantry was taken from the trenches in front, and marched about three miles to the rear, where it was stretched across country in open order with a frontage of about one mile. Advancing, they gathered in all delinquents, and deaf to all entreaties marched them forward. When the line halted and the catch was counted, there were found to be about three thousand of these skulkers. Men who were detailed to this service sought not the responsibility, for the pleading of the really sick, and the pitiful efforts of the frightened to justify their absence, appealed to sympathy and fellow-feeling. Many declared that they would rather remain under hottest fire than be detailed to such duty.

After all, the pleasure gained by the straggling "coffee coolers" scarcely compensated for the anxiety experienced and the penalties paid. Had they held firmly to the flag, their safety would have been as fully insured and they would have enjoyed the pleasant consciousness of duty done.

Going To Provost Head-Quarters   Under Guard.

UNDER THE BANK.

XVIII.

CAVALRY ESCORTS, ORDERLIES, AND FORAGERS.

O PLACE in the vicinity of headquarters had more of life and brightness than the camp of the cavalry escorts. It was usually pitched in the nearest woods, where both men and animals might be protected from the hottest rays of the sun. The little shelter-tents were scattered about in picturesque confusion, and groups of horses could be seen picketed where the shade was most dense. The camp was a busy one during the day, everyone seeming to have important work to attend to. Some would be bustling about cleaning the horses, others would be occupied in repairing saddles and equipments; while a short distance away a squad would be engaged in saber exercise. I never tired of looking at this drill, and often wondered, as I watched the glistening swords, how they could be handled in such unison of action.

Other duties fell to the cavalry escort while in camp, such as going off to guard ammunition or supply trains from depots to the army, being sent with dispatches to distant headquarters, or being detached as orderlies to accompany officers on special duties. In active service the duty was more severe and dangerous, the orderlies being often sent into the thickest of the fight; but, on the whole, the duty at headquarters was not objected to,—on the contrary, it was often preferred to the life with the main cavalry command.

URING a campaign there was often much delay in getting food for the cavalry horses from the rear. Grass alone when obtainable was not nutritious enough to keep them in good working order, and in the event of a railroad bridge being burned by guerillas, or a loaded wagon-train being captured by bushwhackers, cavalrymen would be compelled to resort to extreme measures to sustain their horses. The country would be scoured in all directions, and barns and corncribs emptied in short order, the supplies loaded upon wagons and brought into camp. Groups of horsemen could often be seen riding across country with bundles of hay or bags of corn slung across their saddles. Sometimes receipts for the produce taken would be given; but in war "necessity knows no law," and in urgent circumstances no ceremony was observed.

Foraging parties were often attacked by the enemy with a hope of securing supplies, and hot fights would ensue, for a soldier never loosened his grip on bounties except under compulsion. In danger, the loaded wagons would be hurried towards camp, the guards and foragers posting themselves in flank and rear of the train.

Men, like horses, were often short of rations, and pigs, poultry and small game were never ignored. They often made a ludicrous appearance on the return to camp, with the bound chickens squawking and struggling to get loose, and the ducks quacking lustily. A stone jar of honey often found a place on the saddle, and was a great treat at the mess. Discipline was lax on these expeditions, and great mirth prevailed with such fun as boys— or, what is the same thing, soldiers let loose—could find on the road. Those who were detailed to the foraging parties were much envied by the less fortunate ones who were kept at regular duties.

The Cavalry Camp.

A Dispatch Bearer

An Orderly Sketch from Life

Cavalry Foragers.

SOME HORSEMEN.

71

XIX.

RE-FORMING THE LINE.

IRCUMSTANCES afforded me a fine opportunity of watching minutely the preparations of the Union army previous to the battle of Antietam, also the grand advance and the terrible struggle of those brave men who dashed defiantly forward into a volcano of Southern fire.

The infantry was first ordered forward, and under the shelter of the trees of a wooded ridge of ground the men were formed in lines. The artillery was then posted in advantageous positions to cover the advance; while the cavalry found shelter from the opposing artillery fire until the outcome of the contemplated move could be determined. A body of infantry skirmishers covered the front, and at the word "Forward!" advanced and sent a responsive fire to every puff of smoke from the enemy's skirmish line. The latter fell rapidly back toward the main position in a sunken road on the ridge. The main body of the Union forces formed in three lines, and moved slowly forward. The battle-worn and tattered flags floated in the sunshine, and the clanking accoutrements, rustling and tramping feet, and officers' voices in command, mingled in one deep, strange sound, comparable only to the continuous roar of sea-surf at an incoming tide.

As soon as the enemy's main line caught sight of our advancing host it gave greeting with a withering artillery fire; solid shot and shell ploughed lanes through the living mass. The scattering fragments of the shells that burst above the heads of our men did more execution than if they had exploded on the ground, and every solid shot, fired with a ricochet, bounded like a baseball, sending up a cloud of dust wherever it struck and sweeping every thing in its course to destruction. Despite this deadly work, how grandly our line advanced, and how calmly they closed up the gaps and moved on, leaving a blue trail of the fallen dead behind them!

But the enemy's infantry fire soon became so severe that our advance line began to waver and show broken places. Looking through my field-glass I could see the mounted officers galloping up and down behind the troops, and the line-officers engaged in steadying the men as the showers of bullets swept across the ground in their front. In examining the enemy's position on the crest of the hill I could see their battle-flags quite plainly through the smoke; and, just appearing above the edge of a sunken road seemed to be a line of heads. Puffs of smoke played along them, varying at intervals in volume. Musketry fire could be plainly heard, the sound rising and falling from a terrific roar to a scattering fire.

But soon a murderous crashing volley told of reinforcement to the enemy's line, and our own men halted and took advantage of the slight protection of a ridge of ground to regain their formation. Then came the order to advance again, and through smoke and an avalanche of fire they dashed defiantly up the ridge and poured a volley into the faces of the enemy, and then fired steadily at will.

Through my glass I soon saw hundreds of wounded men coming to the rear, some limping alone, others moving in groups, but all making for the same quarter, where they hoped to find relief. I saw also that our own lines began to lessen and great gaps appear. The Confederates had done deadly work, and off to the right of our forces several of their batteries had secured an enfilading fire along our front. As the grain bows before the scythe, so were our men in front felled to earth by the bursting shells sent at this murderous angle.

Scanning the enemy's front near the batteries, I saw a body of our infantry posted behind a rail-fence, and from this position pouring a destructive flanking fire in return. I could see the wounded hurried back, and here and there a straggling grey Reb retiring from rock to rock or wisely making a screen of the bushes.

But our line of battle soon retired from its advance, and fell sullenly back to a retired position where they could halt and re-form. "Where is that gallant army," I asked myself, "that but one short hour ago dashed so fearlessly into action?" But a glance across the field in front of the enemy's line told the sad story, for there lay brave men stretched in hundreds, sleeping their long last sleep; and many wounded had gone to the rear, some on foot who were able to walk, and those who were disabled had been taken in the ambulances. I looked at the sadly broken lines of the men who remained, with the thought that they would falter from further duty; but when I saw the blackened, resolute faces, and the quick, firm steps as they closed up the line, I felt that they possessed more than bravery—the soldier's steady courage.

Reinforcements soon appeared, and our men, refreshed, started forward with renewed determination. The line breasted the hill once more, and with a rush dashed upon the enemy's front, covering the last few hundred yards at a double-quick, and halting but an instant to discharge a volley in the face of the foe. Then the bayonets came into savage action, sweeping the enemy before them, broken and scattered. Those who escaped rushed back through an orchard in the rear, and, taking shelter behind some farm-houses and out-buildings, kept up a dropping fire on our troops: but it availed nothing, as the enemy's center had been broken, and they fell back in confusion.

The whole of this battle was most gallantly and stubbornly contested on both sides, and after many bitter conflicts seemed to end as a stand-off; yet it sufficed for its main purpose,—to check and turn back the daring Lee and his brave army from Pennsylvania and the North. The special point of interest for us in the present chapter is "The Halt for Re-forming the Line."

The Bivouac of the Dead

THE HALT, FOR RE-FORMING THE LINE,

XX.

RECONNOITERING.

IT MAY seem, to those who have only read of battles, a simple matter to find the position of an opposing army; but those practically familiar with military tactics know that it is a most difficult thing to determine, so that an advance may be properly made against it. If the enemy are stationed in a country with which their own troops are alone familiar, the friendship of the residents (who, as voluntary spies, bring them reliable information) is invaluable. An advancing body can judge only from inspection, and a reconnaissance in force is often a necessity.

I took part in a reconnaissance in the June of '63, during the Gettysburg campaign, and have a most vivid recollection of the characteristics of the movement.

The Army of the Potomac, under command of Gen. Hooker, had marched from its position near Fredericksburg and was encamped near the town of Aldio, watching the movements of Lee's army, which had left Fredericksburg and was crossing the Blue Ridge Mountains to the Shenandoah Valley on its way to another invasion of Pennsylvania. The enemy's cavalry, commanded by Gen. J. E. B. Stuart, were posted as a screen, east of the Blue Ridge Mountains in the Loudon Valley. They were quite active, and in a series of fights had given our cavalry many a hard scrimmage.

It became necessary to have more information of the enemy's plans than the scouts could gather, and a reconnaissance in force was determined upon. Gen. Pleasonton, commanding our cavalry, was ordered to advance upon the opposing cavalry forces and drive them back until their infantry supports were uncovered. A division of infantry was detailed to assist in the movement, and one morning at daylight the advance started from Aldio. We took the road towards Ashby's Gap, the cavalry deploying and advancing slowly, and after a march of several miles it came upon the enemy's cavalry force, which was posted behind stone fences and heavy woods on both sides of a road in which a section of artillery was also placed.

A heavy line of our infantry skirmishers advanced upon them, and we shelled them vigorously with a light battery which we had posted on the pike. They fell back slowly, giving up the point of vantage reluctantly. They were intimidated at the sight of our infantry, who would have considered it little more than pleasant exercise to attack cavalry in such a country.

I followed the troops as well as I could, while keeping to high ground as much as possible so as to see the varied incidents of interest. I remember watching an advancing regiment of Union cavalry which was evidently preparing a trap for the enemy. They were in regular line-of-battle; and behind them, screened from the enemy's view, was a gun from a light battery. The intention was to get near enough to make the masked gun effective before the enemy could discover the trick.

From my position on a hill I could with a glass see every move of the opposing lines. The enemy was posted on the edge of a distant wood, with skirmishers scattered along the stone fence in front. Our regiment approached slowly through an open field, unconscious of danger, when suddenly a body of Confederate cavalry dashed out of the woods in column formation. Yelling like Indians, they made for a direct attack, and to all appearance the Union chance of repulse was slight; but when they were within about two hundred yards of our lines, our cavalry in front of the "twelve-pounder" wheeled to right and left, the gun was quickly unlimbered, and a double charge of canister poured into the exultant Rebs. In an instant, those who did not fall scattered like a flock of birds before a blind, and the Union line in rapid advance soon drove them towards Ashby's Gap in their rear.

During the advance the long line of cavalry skirmishers in the front moved slowly over the country, seeking cover behind fences and buildings whenever possible, firing at everything visible along the enemy's line. The main body of the Union cavalry, several thousand strong, followed closely, deploying on both sides of the main road, on which artillery moved. The infantry kept close behind, ready at any moment to reinforce a weak point. A rattling fire was kept up all day, until the enemy made a stand at the foot of the mountain at Ashby's Gap. Just before sundown a charge was made which convinced the Rebs that our cavalry was in the best of condition. A band of music was posted on a hill, and to the inspiring notes of "Yankee Doodle" our whole line moved forward. With drawn sabers they dashed upon the enemy and forced them back into the Gap, where was posted a corps of infantry, ready to receive the Union line. So strong was this force, that no further attack was made. The Union troops camped on the field, attended to the wounded, and gathered up the spoils of the running fight at leisure.

The next morning just at daylight, a retrograde movement was begun, and the Union troops fell slowly back toward the main camp at Aldio. The enemy followed closely, pressing our rear at every opportunity, and shelling our rear-guard at every possible point. I halted at a village on our route and saw the column pass by. Looking down the main street toward the enemy I saw a section of one of our batteries posted on the road firing back at the advancing foe, while the main body of our mounted force passed slowly along. Many wounded men were mounted in the column, and the ambulances were full of the more helpless ones. One cavalryman had a dead comrade hanging over the saddle, conveying him to where he could pay him the last tribute of a Christian burial.

Toward evening the Union force arrived at the old camp again, and the enemy thought it advisable to withdraw toward their main body.

The reconnaissance had satisfied Gen. Hooker that the passes of the mountains were occupied by infantry, and that the enemy's main body were bound for Pennsylvania. This decided his next move, and in a few days the whole army was marching up the Loudon Valley toward the Potomac River. They crossed at Edward's Ferry, and from that point advanced to gain the glorious victory of Gettysburg.

The Last Act of Friendship.

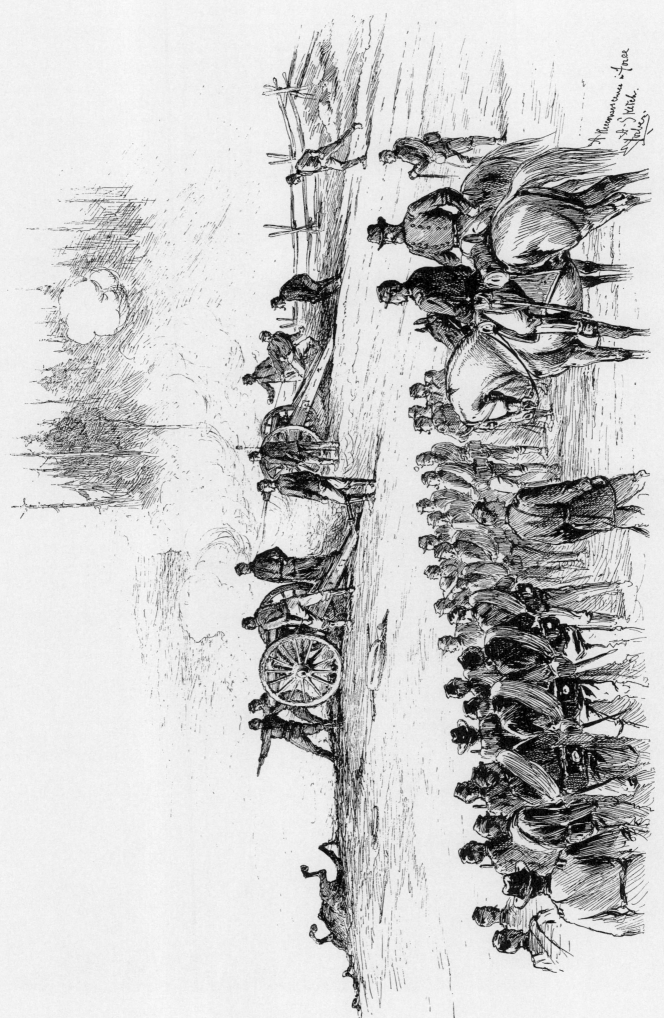

A RECONNAISSANCE IN FORCE.

CUSTER AT TREVILIAN STATION.

XXI.

THE NEWSPAPER CORRESPONDENT.

Watching the Battle.

WHEN time shall have made the history of the great war complete, people who read the records will fail to appreciate how much historians will be indebted to the newspaper correspondents. Leading journals sent talented men to the front, some of the larger ones having several correspondents with each army in the field. I remember one instance where there was a correspondent with each corps, and a manager at the general headquarters whose duty it was to supervise the collection of news. Each correspondent was furnished with a good saddle-horse, to facilitate quick movement from point to point. Their duties were to gather all facts, rumors and matters of interest pertaining to army life, to keep informed of all movements, and during a battle to push well to the front to obtain material for graphic descriptions. During the winter a correspondent's work was easily accomplished; he gathered what information he could of contemplated movements, picked up camp-gossip and incidents, and reported the deaths of soldiers who died in hospitals. But when the spring note of preparation sounded for the army to gird itself up and prepare for a coming campaign, the correspondent as well as the soldier was aroused into active duty.

I had found in winter camp a pleasant comrade, who was an army correspondent for one of the New York papers, and we resolved that when the army should be ordered to move, we would together—for a time at least—follow its fortunes. When orders were finally given, they were at short notice, we learning only at sundown that camp was to be broken the next morning; but we were at headquarters by daybreak, and in the saddle for the march.

The columns moved along the roads to the south, and the wagon-trains were parked in long lines near their old camp-ground, ready to start as soon as the way was cleared. My comrade and I hurried forward along the side of the column, and soon reached the head of the line. We found the main body of cavalry moving rapidly after the advance guard, who were approaching a ridge on the crest of which the enemy were known to be posted in full force. Leaving the main road, we kept forward; but on high ground as much as possible, to obtain view of all that took place. As we were wondering just when hostilities would commence, a cannon boomed and a shell whizzed over the heads of a cavalry squadron that was moving slowly to the front. The small cloud of light smoke that drifted from a hilltop in the distance defined the enemy's position.

Two light batteries soon came galloping from our rear, took position on a hill, and unlimbered. The guns were quickly sighted and at the word "Fire!" two shells were sent toward the enemy, who by this time could be plainly seen on a distant knoll. One burst in the air, without destruction, but a puff of smoke among the enemy's guns and the muffled report that followed proved that the other was well placed. The enemy, however, soon returned sharp fire, and the shells came so suggestively close that we moved to the right along the ridges, where we could watch the battle with comparative safety. Soon a body of Union cavalry skirmishers, followed by heavy mounted columns, advanced across the level bottom-lands toward the Rebs. We adjusted glasses and watched with intense interest the game of war that was being enacted at our very feet. The enemy opened severe musketry fire from bushes along the ridge, and our skirmishers halted and waited for the main line, which was advanc-

ing at a trot, evidently determined to make a bold dash at the foe; but they received a volley of shell from the distant battery on the hill, and we shuddered as the great number of
men and horses fell.   Nothing daunted, those not disabled galloped up the hill and drove
from the underbrush a swarm of grey coats.   Meanwhile the Union infantry had deployed
and made ready for an advance on the enemy's main position; and simultaneously the whole
line moved forward and was soon heavily engaged.   In the end, the ground was left in possession of the Union forces.

Now the anxious work of my friend began.   We mounted our horses and started for
the field-hospitals, where, by making himself known, he was able to obtain a list of names
of the wounded as they were brought from the field.   Then, hurrying to the front, we rode
over the battle-ground, where many items of interest were obtained.   Detailed parties for
burying the dead were next visited and names secured of the killed with details for classified
lists.   We found them already at work disposing of the silent figures; the old and the young
men lay together in the trenches.   Sickened at the ghastly sights, and faint from long fasting,
we sought our haversacks, and, buying each a cup of coffee from a soldier, disposed of our
not over-plentiful repast.

Making haste then to temporary headquarters in a grove, my newspaper friend sat
down upon a stump to write an account of the battle.   He interviewed as many as possible
of the officers and men who had taken part in the engagement, and, industriously writing all
through the evening by the light of a camp-fire in front of the general's tent, he finished his
story by midnight.   I separated from him at this time; but, although he had been at it
since daybreak, his work was not done, for he mounted his horse and visited the hospitals to
obtain a final checking of his lists of the names of the dead and wounded.   This work was
completed by two o'clock in the morning, when he made his way through the sleeping army
to deliver his material to the manager, to be forwarded to the home-office by special messenger.

A correspondent was often compelled to carry his own despatches to the nearest post
or telegraph station, and would ride at break-neck speed to be the first to deliver the intelligence and "get a beat" on other correspondents.   Duty often took them through dangerous
guerrilla country, and on many occasions they barely escaped.   Quite a number of the brave,
bright fellows lost their lives on the battle-field, others returned home with shattered health,
and a large number were captured and confined in Southern prisons.   The smoothly-written,
crisp columns that appeared in the newspapers were no criterion of the dangers that their
writers were exposed to; and while tributes are paid to gallant leaders and courageous soldiers, the bravery and endurance of the newspaper correspondents should not be forgotten, nor
their work be unappreciated.   For four long years the feverish inter-
est of the nation hung upon their words, and, aside from
the official documents and reports, the most valuable
material of the history of those times is to be
found in the work done by these alert, hardy
and heroic soldiers of the pen.

WRITING IT UP.

NEWS FROM THE BATTLE.

XXII.

UNBRIDGED RIVERS.

A Heavy Load.

HILE the main Union armies were always furnished with pontoon bridges for rivers, difficulties were often met which made these time-savers unavailable. Sometimes the roads approaching the river could not be passed by vehicles like the pontoon wagons, and occasionally the streams along the line of march would be too many for their use. In such instances fording became inevitable; but it had to be cautiously approached. Once I had been riding with the cavalry advance, and, after having been fired upon by bushwhackers and meeting several other adventures, we reached a hill overlooking a stream with wooded borders that had to be crossed. The enemy was posted on the low banks opposite us, and the ominous line of yellow clay breastworks, which "the boys" learned to know so well, gave evidence of fortification. It ran along the bank and through the low growth of brush, which was quite thick in places, and afforded protection to their skillful sharp-shooters, whose keen aim reached some of our men as soon as they appeared in the open space in the region of the ford. First, three companies of our men dismounted, pushed forward toward the river, and lay down behind the bank of an abandoned canal. From this point they kept up a sharp carbine-fire on the enemy's works, so that it was unsafe for the Johnnies to show their heads

Watching the enemy's operations through a glass, I saw a group of mounted officers behind an old farm-house, a short distance above the fording-place on the other side, despatching messengers to the main body, half a mile back from the river. Several had made safe passage, running the gauntlet of our skirmish-fire at full speed, when two officers dashed into sight from behind the house and made for the rear. One was mounted on a grey horse and the other on a bay. Side by side they raced, with bodies bowed down on the necks of their flying horses, and each moment of life seemed a marvel as they escaped the shots of the Union carbines, fired by plainsmen long experienced in fighting Indians. Suddenly the officer on the grey horse collapsed, fell from his saddle and quicker than thought was laid out flat on his back, dead: his arms close to his side, his cap and saber near him in the yellow road. His companion deftly slackened speed and caught the grey horse by the bridle, and then, lying close, rode rapidly on to a place of safety.

A Dead Shot.

He straightened up in the saddle as he disappeared into the wood, and in almost a moment of time a section of battery dashed out from the same place and opened a revengeful fire, as if to recompense the death of a favorite officer. A Union battery soon sent and maintained a spirited responsive fire.

But now came the forming of Union cavalry under the cover of woods on our side of
the stream. Columns of them moved into the open, and made straight for the ford, in the
midst of carbine-fire from dismounted Rebs on the opposite bank, and lively shell from the
battery on the edge of the woods beyond them. Many men and horses sank as shells exploded
and bullets took effect, on the hither bank and in the water, but the main body ploughed on
through the river, causing the spray to fly in all directions, and then steadily pushed up the
farther bank, a formidable mass of mounted men. They were soon face to face with those
who manned the breastworks, and drove them toward the rear. Our cavalrymen pursued, and
captured many prisoners. The Rebs in the wood beyond retreated as soon as they saw the
ford carried, and our cavalry pursued in hot haste.

The head of our infantry column now appeared. I rode down to the bank and laughed
heartily at the grotesque appearance of the troops, most of whom had taken off their trousers
to make the passage of the deep stream; and, holding clothing, guns and cartridge-boxes on
their heads, breasted a current which almost swept them off their feet. Some were in fact
carried down, but were rescued by a line of cavalry posted below for that purpose. Despite
all misfortunes, the men seemed to enjoy this novel experience, and chatted merrily and
laughed loudly when a comrade slipped on the rocky bottom and drifted down stream. The
cavalrymen rescued the "dough-boys" (as they deridingly called the infantrymen) amid shouts
of laughter, and dragged them one by one to a place of safety.

When the infantrymen regained footing on solid ground, they made a ridiculous appearance as they tried to pull their clothing over their shivering legs. Those who had not taken
the trouble to prepare were as bedraggled as so many "drowned rats," and sought in vain
to wring the water from their uniforms. I have often recalled the comical scenes of this incident, and without much imagination I hear again the peals of laughter along the column;—
so did tragedy and comedy tread close on each other's heels.

The Rescue

FORDING THE RIVER.

XXIII.

THE "BUMMER."

———•———

Marching through Georgia.

HIS characteristic name was peculiar to the Western armies, and particularly to the men of Sherman's force who left Chattanooga in the spring of 1864 on that magnificent and triumphal march to Atlanta and the sea. The genus "bummer" was not perfectly developed until Atlanta was deserted and the march into the unknown country began. Then necessity, or "natural selection," brought into full existence these daring spirits, who swarmed in front and on the flanks of the moving columns that swept with irresistible force through Georgia and the Carolinas, spreading consternation through the crumbling "Confederacy." The march proved that, when the shell was once penetrated, the great Rebellion was without reserves of either men or material of war. The only apprehension of difficulty that Gen. Sherman seems to have entertained in this venture, was that supplies might not be obtainable; but the country was rich in produce, and the organized foraging parties nearly always returned laden with bounties for both men and beasts. In obtaining these supplies, it was desired and ordered by Gen. Sherman that men should keep within specified limits, and the greater portion of them did. Many, however, overstepped the bounds, and their lawless and reckless conduct gave the name of "Bummer" to all foragers. An officer could not be cognizant of all that occurred in a scattered command, but all possible effort was made to prevent men from looting private property. Charges were made, however, of robbery of family silver and other valuables. Mills, manufactories or stores of material which might aid the Confederacy were to be invariably destroyed, and columns of smoke along the line of march were significant of how well these orders had been executed.

There was little or no fighting to be done; the march was the main thing, and the feeding of the multitude the one necessity. It is not strange, then, that out of the myriads in a great army, which of course includes all sorts and conditions of men, there should be many who, when the bands of discipline were a little relaxed, should take advantage of it, and, whether intent on fun or on devilment, make the most of their brief chances. Not a few traveled ahead or alongside, independent of the army, so long as it was safe, and like our friends the "coffee coolers" enjoyed a lively vacation from duty, showing devotion only to booty. It was this class who did the real damage to private property.

Many of the bummers' pranks were harmless and amusing. When on the march a town was sighted, a rush forward would be made and a motley crowd of "boys in blue" would clatter down the main street, some on foot, some on horseback, with guns prepared to meet Wheeler's or Hampton's cavalry. Hooting and yelling like Indians, they would make for the town-hall or court house, and, removing the secession flag from the staff on the roof, would hoist the national colors. Then some wag would improvise a court, and sitting in the judge's chair presided with mock dignity while a delinquent bummer charged with some grave offence would be dragged before him to receive sentence. At Milledgeville, Georgia, a mock Legislature was convened, and the Ordinance of Secession of the State was repealed with great solemnity.

On arriving at Savannah the bummer settled back into soldierly regulation again, and for weeks experienced no excitement except the perils of the breastworks and trenches in rear of the beleaguered town; but when the enemy evacuated and retreated through South Carolina he again appeared in full bloom, and, in front of our pursuing army, caused wide-spread consternation. The capture of Charleston was but an incident of the march, and the army swept again inland toward Columbia, on its way to join Grant in the siege at Petersburg. Supplies were less plentiful in the Carolinas than in Georgia, but the bummers with renewed vigor set to work to procure the best the country afforded.

Parties often appeared arrayed in grotesque costumes that had been confiscated from

country houses. One fellow appeared wearing a gingham sunbonnet; another, a military costume of the war of 1812; and another was dressed in an old blue coat and cocked hat with tarnished gold braid, and in his hand carried an old-fashioned saber that may have belonged to one of Marion's men.

But with the surrender of Gen. Johnston, the bummer's occupation was gone; the rigid lines of military discipline were again tightened about him and the happy-go-lucky days of adventure must now become a memory. On to Washington the army tramped, and at the grand review which terminated its existence, not one of the regular-stepping, bright-faced troops suggested the reckless bummers of a few weeks before. All walked proudly erect as they passed the reviewing stand, and cast longing glances at their grand old commanders.

A CAUTIOUS HALT.

"THEY'RE JOHNNIES, SURE AS YER BORN, BOYS!"

XXIV.

THE VIDETTE.

On the Lookout

IFE on the outer lines was solitary and dangerous, and yet the safety of the whole army often depended on the vigilance of the posted videttes. I have watched them many times when they were almost within touch of those of the opposing side, and did not envy them their responsibility. In glancing along the line I saw them seated like equestrian statues, but the slightest crackling of brush or rustling of leaves would start them into life and fill them with apprehensions of danger. Truly have the videttes been called the "eyes of the army."

Never having been able to see the videttes except from a distance, I decided one day to ride over to the outer line and gather what information I could of their duties and movements. I rode forward and after passing various bodies of cavalry posted along the front of the army, I came in sight of a position supposed to be held by the enemy. Looking across a beautifully diversified country as far as the eye could reach, I saw a line of solitary horsemen posted at intervals in the open ground. I took my glass to study a mounted figure who had position on a road about half a mile distant. He sat gracefully upon his horse, grasping with his right hand a cavalry carbine, the butt of which rested on his thigh, and with the left he held the reins with easy freedom. His glance seemed directed toward the enemy, and yet he sat as if in a reverie. What was the train of thought! Did memory take him back to the old farm-house to which his brother was just guiding home the gentle cows, and his kind old father waiting with pail in hand ready to take from them the rich yield of milk? Perhaps visions of his silver-haired mother passed before him, as she prepared the evening meal and faltered with a sigh at the vacant place at the table, where for long years she had laid a plate for him; or, tenderer still, did visions flit before him of her with whom he lingered to gain the last sweet promise, and recollections of her tender eyes wake the tears in his?

But now the horse began to move slowly to and fro, dropping his head to nibble the luxurious grass along the fence, and the soldier roused himself as he discerned a cloud of dust rising in the road that came from the wood. Curiosity waked me up, too, and touching the spurs to my mare I rode over to the horseman and spoke to him. He nervously drew up the idle reins and rode a short distance forward. I followed, and we soon saw something moving forward from under the shadow of the trees; and I was sure it was dressed in gray. My comrade assured me, however, that a horseman would not advance so slowly. A moment more, and we were able to distinguish a vehicle of some kind, drawn by a single animal, and at last a farm-cart, drawn by a diminutive old gray mule and containing a family of negroes, came fully to view.

Such a picturesque group I had seldom seen. Old "Uncle's" head was covered with an ancient gray slouch hat, and his black face was fringed with a snow-white beard, while his old clothing was so patched that the original fabric was lost sight of. "Aunty" had a pert turban, but poor clothing; and the pickaninnies were scantily covered with ragged slips made of muslin. When within speaking distance of the vidette, the old man pulled his rope lines and brought the little mule to a full stop. Doffing his hat he gave a low bow and said "Good-day, sah," but looked timidly at the formidable figure in front of him who moved forward to question him. We learned that he had taken advantage of the presence of the "Lincum sogers" to escape from bondage with his family, and that he had been traveling two days. When asked if he had seen any of the enemy's troops, he answered, "Oh yes, mistah. Heaps o' sogers back dah, about ten miles. Mistah Johnson's men. I can't tell how many, mo'n I eber seed befo'. Calvery; de big guns on wheels; an' lots o' sogers dat carries dem guns an' dese yere tings wha' yer sling ober yer back. Yes, infantry, dats wha' de call 'em. Dey was a right smart lot o' men, too, an' had flags an' drums an' mo' wagons dan I ever seed in all my bo'n days."

The vidette asked him if he was sure those soldiers were not marching when he saw them. "Oh no, massa," he replied, "dey was all about de fields, cookin' an' eatin' an' sleepin' in de little white tents; dey was movin' bout in de *camp* pow'ful smart, but dey *wasn't* movin' on *dis road* when I lef' dem day befo' yistiddy, *I'm shuah!*"

Directing the oddly fashioned and assorted outfit toward camp, where it would be taken care of, our cavalryman moved toward the side of the road, dropped the reins on the horse's neck and allowed him to resume feeding. He then opened his haversack, the contents of which had been long neglected, and made a meal of raw pork and hard-tack. He looked regretfully at the remains of the three days' rations, and saw that his supplies had diminished more than prudence would dictate; but it seemed a soldier's fate to devour supplies in advance and then be compelled to suffer an involuntary fast.

The sudden sound of two carbine shots, however, caused my soldier friend to quickly sling his haversack in place, and, seizing the reins and spurring his horse, he darted into the road and looked anxiously for the cause. A cloud of dust rising in the distance roused his suspicions, and he glanced anxiously to right and left as if to note any movement of the line of our videttes. Soon two horsemen appeared on the road leading from the wood opposite, and, moving out into the field, appeared to be in consultation. I began to think it time for a non-combatant to move towards the rear; but I did not retire so far but that I could watch movements with my glass. Soon, a few shots were heard and a well-defined line of the enemy's advance of cavalry came into view. The Union line of videttes opened fire, and then reloaded and discharged their carbines continually as they fell back to the main body. Heavy columns of the enemy's cavalry debouched from the road, and the Confederates soon opened fire with light batteries.

The fight had evidently begun, and our vidette and his comrades had vanished from the front and were making the best possible resistance in the regiment to which they belonged.

THE REFUGEES.

THE MOUNTED SENTINEL.

McPherson's Death, before Atlanta.

XXV.

GOING INTO CAMP.

The Pup Tent.

OW WELCOME was the news as it passed along the moving column that the day's march was nearly finished, and that the tired men would soon find rest in camp! Often they had marched from daylight, taking only such intervals of rest as a blockaded column allowed, or the half-hour's halt at midday for dinner gave. Lagging as their footsteps might have been, they would become much animated as camping-ground was neared, and in anticipation of the evening meal would step out of the column and confiscate all fence-rails available. They made a ludicrous appearance as they trudged along, with a gun on one shoulder and a fence-rail on the other.

I saw a column leave the road just at sunset, and as it marched along a ridge of high ground the men and horses were cast in silhouette against the bright back-ground. I saw different brigades march to allotted positions, and the work of pitching camp soon began. Knapsacks and traps were unslung, and in a short time the hill-sides were covered with little "pup" tents. The noise of axes—faint at first, but swelling into a muffled roar, in the hands of a multitude—soon filled the air, and camp-fires began to blaze along in all directions. As it grew dark, the tents looked like thousands of Japanese lanterns, and I rode along the ridge to take notes of the firelight pictures.

Stopping at a large farm-house, surrounded by a grove of oak trees, I found that the commanding general had established headquarters there. Wall tents were being pitched on the lawn in front, and the headquarters cook was unloading the mess-cart a short distance in the rear. Aides and orderlies were hurrying to and fro, and a general air of business pervaded everything. Farther on, the artillerymen were going into camp; and the horses, after being unhitched and unharnessed, were tethered to a long rope stretched between two trees in rear of the batteries. Some of the men were grooming and feeding the horses, while others were scattered about, busy at various camp-duties. The country was covered by a dense cloud of smoke, lit up by the glow of the fires, and the many sounds from the camp mingled in one great roar. The braying of the mules impatient for their feed rose clear above the din, asserting their importance—which, indeed, was freely recognized. Riding through the wagon-camps some distance in rear of the main line, the quartermasters by the light of the camp-fires sought to restore order. The feed-boxes for the mules were placed upon the wagon-tongues, and three animals, perhaps, hitched each side. Impatiently eager, the beasts would jump from one side to the other like goats and kick at intervals as mules only know how. The negro drivers hurried about, emptying oats as fast as possible, so as to lessen the noise of their lively animals.

Turning again toward the front I found a large body of infantry building a breastwork in anticipation of a dash of the enemy, who were not very far in advance. Large fires were burning at intervals and by their light the men were busy felling trees and cutting them into lengths, while others placed them in position along the line marked out by the engineers. Hundreds of men were engaged in digging a trench in front of the works and throwing up an embankment behind it, to which the logs served as a backing; while others were out in front, converting the unused branches into an abatis. Jubilant spirits prevailed, and the jests

97

and laughter in the face of so much danger seemed strange. The officers were anxious and active in giving directions, and by midnight a fortified line covered the sleeping army.

I started back to headquarters with an officer of engineers, and found the strange quiet of the night in deep contrast to the evening scenes. The guns along the ridge looked sombre and grim, and the sentinel at the end of the line of pieces stood like a statue with his drawn sabre resting carelessly in the hollow of the arm. The horses in the rear were munching hay and cornstalks, and the battery-men were fast asleep under their slight shelters. The infantry camps had lost their life and brightness, and all the men were sleeping, except the guard who paced with muskets at "a shoulder;" under all, the low rumble of late wagon-trains could be heard, as they toiled along the pikes, toward the general camping-ground.

On reaching headquarters I found the general in a room on the ground floor looking over maps and papers, and questioning an individual who had come for a "g'yard" (guard) to protect him from soldier-marauders who were making too free with his pigs, chickens and hay. Some of the officers had not retired and we gladly accepted an invitation to join a party who were taking a late supper. It was washed down by the inevitable "commissary," and the jug made its appearance from under the camp-bed at regular intervals afterward. But, tired and sleepy, I at last lay down on the floor of the verandah and, wrapped in my blanket and with my boots for a pillow, slept soundly until daybreak.

GETTING READY FOR SUPPER.

GOING INTO CAMP AT NIGHT.

99

XXVI.

ROADSIDE REFRESHMENT.

The Wayside Spring.

N THE spring and fall of the year, when streams were swollen and springs overflowing, it was an easy matter to supply the army with water; but on the long march in midsummer-heat, with the thermometer in the nineties, the scarcity of it brought the men much suffering and taxed their mettle to the utmost.

I remember one torrid morning, when hardly a breath of air was stirring, that tents were struck before daylight and the head of the column turned into the road just as the red sun came up through the camp-smoke. It had been intensely hot for two weeks, and this particular morning seemed to be the culmination of the fiery ordeal. The soldiers looked exhausted at the start, and tramped wearily along, wiping the perspiration continually from their dark and dusty faces; even the wags—generally irrepressible, in the face of death itself—were silent under this strain. The horses in the column were drooping and spiritless. As the sun rose higher and the heat increased, the troops straggled along the road in open order, to escape the clouds of suffocating dust. They began to hitch at the knapsack straps, continually seeking to readjust them so that the weight might seem less. Overcoats and ponchos were thrown along the road, and here and there a soldier would halt and with impatient mutterings toss his knapsack over into the bushes; one crying out, "I will not die like a pack-mule; and no future need of these things will be worth the misery."

A suffering from thirst soon began to be felt, for the wells and springs had not been frequent enough on the route to supply water for the parched mouths and throats. When one appeared, men broke from the column, and the place was soon surrounded by a surging throng. Frantically they rushed forward with tin cup and canteen in hand, hoping to get a drink before the spring was emptied. This would be very soon done, then the poor fellows would scrape up the water as it trickled through the earth, not appearing to mind the muddy mixture that it often held. One wit looked into his cup rather doubtfully and said "It can't be helped, boys; we're made of dirt, so here goes!" and he quaffed the contents amid great laughter. When an old spring-house was found, a guard was stationed with musket in hand at the door and the thirsty crowd was kept in subjection. A limited number of men were allowed inside to fill the canteens that were handed in, and by careful dipping would keep the water clear. Many kinds of filters were made and sold to the troops, and those who possessed one were considered fortunate.

An instance of a hot march occurs to me, on which the simple character of the great commander General Grant was brought into prominence. It was during the movement from the disastrous battle of Cold Harbor to the crossing of the Chickahominy. I had halted at General Warren's headquarters, which were pitched behind an old farm-house on the roadside. While busy sketching, I heard a soldier remark, "General Grant has just dismounted on the road in front." Not having seen him since the battle of Spottsylvania, I was anxious to see how he looked after the strain of the late terrible fighting; so, slipping my sketch-book into my pocket, I started around the house and came upon the general, just as he moved into a crowd of men, who were struggling about a well to get a chance at the bucket as it came up.

When the men saw who had arrived they saluted respectfully, and the general quietly said, "Can I get a drink of water here." A soldier near him dipped a smoky tin cup into the water and extended it to him. At the same instant, an orderly from General Warren's tent hurried up, and holding out a tumbler, said, "Here's a glass for you, general." "No, this will do," said Grant, and drinking the cup dry handed it back to the man with a simple "Thank you." The soldiers looked at him wonderingly as he moved towards the tents, yet with a satisfaction that told of faith in the simple, quiet commander. Except for the three stars on his shoulder-straps, Grant might easily have been taken for a carelessly dressed quartermaster.

The suffering of the horses and mules on a hot march was equal to that of the men, and when the road was crossed by a stream the patient creatures would hurry down the incline and, plunging their noses deep into the water, would take long draughts, lifting their heads at intervals to get breath. They left the stream with much reluctance, and were it not for the sharp cracking of the long black-snake whips in the hands of the drivers, it would have been difficult to urge them along.

Dust-covered and weary would be the column when ordered to camp, and much diminished in numbers. Many that started in the morning would have become used up and dropped by the wayside, and few of them would get to camp before midnight. A force of over two thousand men, which I accompanied, started from camp on a morning in June; but when they halted at three o'clock they numbered only three hundred. Some were exhausted in the close atmosphere of the pine woods; many died of sun-stroke; and those that dragged wearily into camp during the night did duty with impaired health for weeks. Marching in the summer weather was oftentimes as fatal to the soldiers as a series of battles.

A Soldiers Drink.

A THIRSTY CROWD.

103

XXVII.

THE ADVANCE GUARD.

———•———

In the Front.

HE DUTIES of the advance guard are in every feature precisely the opposite of those of the rear guard. While the latter must always act strictly on the defensive, harassing and impeding the enemy's approach, the advance guard must be ready to attack the retreating foe and make effort to bring it to a stand, so that the main body of troops may come up and take it at a disadvantage. In a forward movement, a detail was usually made up of infantry and cavalry, with perhaps a section of a battery. These were placed under command of a capable officer, who ordered them forward to clear the road of small bodies of the enemy, to remove all obstructions, repair broken bridges, and perform any office that would facilitate the advance of the forces.

I was once in company with such an advance when the opposing commanding officer in our front was the redoubtable "Stonewall" Jackson. His rear guard made it very lively for our "boys in blue" as they trod persistently on his heels. Jackson either in advance or retreat was very much like a hornet. He could not be felt of without someone getting hurt.

We left camp and pushed warily down the pike at early dawn, our commanding officer being especially cautious because of the recent loss of a number of men. A small body of our cavalry were in the extreme front, followed by three squadrons; and when about a mile distant from camp they were fired on by what appeared to be half a dozen mounted Rebs, who were of course looked upon as a rear detail of the rear guard probably just beyond them. The way being clear and open, gave opportunity to the cavalry. Orders to draw sabres were given, and to the inspiring notes of the bugle the three squadrons charged down the road at a gallop. A terrible confusion very shortly ensued, for too late our commander discovered that he had been drawn into a skillfully laid ambuscade. The few Confederate cavalrymen had been placed as a decoy; and, our cavalry on dashing forward were suddenly tangled up in a labyrinth of telegraph wires adroitly stretched across the road, and invisible in the dim morning light. Horses and men went down in a struggling mass, and then desperate work began. A large force of the enemy's infantry had been posted in the bushes of some high ground on the right of the road, and when our cavalry struck the wires these opened a withering fire at close range. A dreadful scene followed; the writhing snarl of men and horses were on the ground, bullet-struck about as fast as they struggled up, while those that were in fields to the left returned all possible fire. Word of our position was sent back and two regiments of infantry soon advanced at "double-quick" to the rescue. These were thrown out to the right and rear of the enemy's force holding the hill, and shortly drove them on the run down the pike, our attack on their flank being too sudden for them to change front.

Taking care of the killed and wounded next occupied all thoughts, and after an hour's work they were all disposed of. No trace of the struggle remained save the carcasses of twenty horses, which were drawn to one side of the road.

The order was now given for an advance. There was no further danger of ambuscade, as the sun was quite high, although the enemy made it hot for our advance guard at every rise of ground. At one point of the road, trees were felled across and a number of farm wagons intermingled to form a breast-work. Our cavalry charged up to it, sending carbine and revolver fire direct into the faces of the defenders, but were driven back with loss. Our men remained quiet until reinforced, then charged again; upon which movement the Confederates started and ran to the next rise of ground, where they had a section of a battery posted. Quite a number of our men and their horses lay dead in front of the obstructions in the road, and at least a dozen of the enemy behind them, all shot in the head. Blood was plentifully spilled about, and large pools had formed on the ground under the horses.

Our wounded were taken to farm houses and barns in the neighborhood, and the advance steadily pressed on. The enemy were soon on the go again, and our cavalry, reinforced by a full brigade, went down the pike at a trot, as it was expected that the Rebs would burn an important bridge a few miles in front if they could cross in time. I rode with the column, and soon saw a cloud of black smoke, which told that the bridge was burning. Order was given to advance at a gallop; and the cavalry dashed through a village and on to a hill beyond, where we saw the burning bridge, and knew that the Union troops were foiled. The enemy had guns posted on the opposite bank, and a shell was thrown among our mounted men, the bursting of which scattered them like a flock of birds. Riding up to a group which was gathered around a prostrate form, I found a surgeon examining an arm which had been torn to pieces by the shell just thrown.

Some one cried, "Look out! They are going to fire again!" Glancing across, I could see their guns plainly, and thought best to get out of their range; so, galloping down the hill to the rear I was moving to a place of safety on the right. Then I heard the boom of a gun, shortly followed by the shriek of a shell. This passed about a yard behind my horse, and fortunately fell to the ground without exploding. I rode on into a place of comparative safety, where I could watch the fight. Two of our batteries were brought up and sent to the right, where they could enfilade the enemy's position, and the other was posted on the rise of ground near the burning bridge. Heavy fire was opened, and through my glass I soon saw the Rebs "limber up" and gallop to their rear with Union shells bursting over their heads. Our guards could now do no further duty until a pontoon was laid; so I returned to camp for supper, and, after completing the sketches I had made, lay down with blanket and poncho on the open ground to sleep. During the night a heavy rain fell, and when morning came I was completely drenched. But my fatigue, after that day with the advance guard, had made me happily insensible to it all, and I had slept like a dormouse.

CLEARING THE WAY.

"FORWARD!"

XXVIII.

ARMY BREAD.

"Home-Made" Bread.

"HARD TACK" for summer rations and bread for winter was a pretty general rule for the "boys in blue." The hard-baked condition of the former made it but slightly susceptible to atmospheric changes, and difficult of penetration by insects. If an occasional white maggot appeared, however, it was brushed off indifferently, and the hungry soldier's appetite was in no degree lessened.

The bakeries in winter camps served excellent purpose. They were portable affairs, made of sheet-iron, and sheltered by roughly-built sheds. The bread was made by professional bakers, who furnished supplies under contract, and the loaf-laden wagons were always a welcome sight in camp.

I knew of a baker who made a barrel of flour into buns, and sold them to the soldiers for five cents each. The mixture had been fermented to such a degree that the buns when baked were like a puff-ball, and with slight pressure of the hand would become but a mouthful. Feeling a contempt for a fellow who would exact such a price for so inferior an article, I asked him what he made out of the barrel of flour; and he unblushingly replied, "O, a hundred and fifty dollars." In addition to the bread furnished by the bakers, car-loads came from the base of army supplies, but no quantities received ever exceeded the demand. None but one who has visited a supply-depot could possibly have an idea of the immense quantity of bread and hard tack that was constantly forwarded. Thousands of boxes were stacked to a great height, and train would follow train, loaded with nothing but bread. Waiting wagons would soon be filled and wend their way back to camp, then return and reload, until the temporary supply became exhausted.

If the army was moving through a grain-producing country in the summer, bread was then easily obtainable for the soldiers, and men were sent to take possession of all the wheat, rye and corn possible, and other detachments were sent to take control of the grist mills. Often after a short ride barns would be found upon plantations, full to overflowing of the country's produce; and with the assistance of the negroes, who always lent a willing hand, wagons were soon loaded to the top. Then a merry journey to the nearest grist-mill followed, and no delay was made if the old-fashioned overshot wheel was found turning. The men detailed to work the mills had often been "dusty millers" in former times, and went to work with a zest and dexterity that came of experience only. As fast as the grain was ground it was poured into bags, which were generally placed in wagons and conveyed to camp; but in lieu of these the backs of mules were sometimes laden, and men, who counted the labor no penalty, would often shoulder them and carry them to camp in high glee.

Baking was done in various ways. The Dutch oven of a neighboring farm-house often proved a "treasure trove," and when thus favored the services of a soldier who had been a baker were secured, and a large quantity of bread would be hastily made. When the piles of brown loaves came in sight for distribution, cheer after cheer rang through the air. When ovens were not available, men were left to their individual devices, and then appeared in wonderful array "flap-jacks," "Johnny cake," and "corn pone." The chief quality to recommend these was solidity, for yeast was an unknown quantity; but they were palatable "for a' that," and many mock ceremonies took place, of a host dispensing luxuries to honored guests.

Receipts were frequently given for grain taken, but not during Sherman's campaign, when "all was fish" that came to the soldiers' nets. The feeling was by that time aroused that the Union forces had been too considerate of the enemy's possessions.

The Southern commissary departments did not issue as bountifully as our own, probably not because of a desire to stint, but because supplies and facilities were limited. While our boys sometimes grumbled that bread was not cake, the "Johnnies" munched cheerfully the "rations on the stalk" as they called the green corn. Perhaps they fought more bravely because of their limitations; I am sure if my own conditions were similar I should want to commit murder in some direction. Southern leaders thought our soldiers too much pampered to insure good results, and "Stonewall" Jackson boasted that he "could whip any army that drove a herd of cattle." Had his information been more complete he might have threatened an army which was fed on *soft bread*. However, no beef-on-the-hoof or Union hard tack was ignored that fell into the hands of the "boys in gray," and they had not lost their bearings entirely when one of our generals in the Shenandoah Valley, whose supply-trains had often been raided, was wittily dubbed by them "Jackson's Commissary."

But, food or no food, the fact is that both sides were American soldiers, and neither will deny that the other did stout fighting.

A Fresh Batch.

The old Grist Miller

Bread for the Starley

CRUMBS OF COMFORT.

III

HOWARD AT THE CEMETERY GATE,
GETTYSBURG.

XXIX.

A NIGHT IN SUMMER CAMP.

"TATTOO."

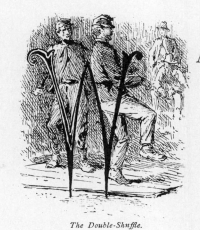

The Double-Shuffle.

ANDERING into camp one night just as the sun was setting, when thousands of tents dotted hill and valley, the settled peace and quiet that had followed the day's activity seemed restful after my many hours of hard riding. No movement of any kind was taking place, except the arrival of a belated army-wagon, laden with forage or commissary stores, or the return of a general officer and staff from a friendly visit to a neighboring camp. It was supper-time. The smoke from the many fires hung over the camp in the still air, and slowly drifted in horizontal lines into the groves of tall pines near by. Groups of men were scattered about in the company streets, cooking queer messes in saucepans or utensils improvised from tomato cans; and, sitting in front of the shelters, solitary soldiers could be seen devouring, with the never-failing soldier's appetite, concoctions of their own that would puzzle a professional cook.

When supper was finished candles were lighted, and the scene became one of beauty and brightness. The lights shone through the canvas covers with a warm glow, and a casual observer might conclude that a festive illumination was taking place.

I heard the notes of a violin not far distant, and, passing into one of the streets from whence the sound came, I found a company of soldiers in great glee. A barn-door had been secured and laid flat on the ground to serve as a dancing floor; and upon this jigs, reels and breakdowns were being danced with wonderful facility by some of the soldiers. Others, less accomplished, laid boards on the ground and stamped applause to each performer with gusto. Moving on, I found men reading and writing in some of the tents, and in others they were playing poker and fast losing their hard earnings. There were many sharpers in the army, who enlisted for what they could make by their wits—soldiers "for revenue only." Most of them had all the tricks of the art of gambling at their finger-ends, and victimized their confiding comrades in great numbers. Fortunes were won by these harpies, both in bounty money and regular pay of the soldiers.

In an adjacent camp I found another musical party, singing songs to the accompaniment of a harmonica, skillfully played by a drummer boy. The popular patriotic airs were sung in chorus. Then a soldier who possessed a fine voice was called on for a solo, and after an affected reserve that would do credit to a society belle, the fellow stepped forward and sang with genuine pathos "Mother, I've Come Home to Die." Then followed "John Brown's Body," the chorus of which was taken up with tremendous volume; then "I Am Lonely To-Night," and others.

Officers were gathered in tents in social groups, and from the frequent passage of the company cook with hot-water kettle in hand, I think they must have had refreshments. Pushing aside the flaps of one of the tents, I was greeted cheerfully, and accepted an invitation to join the party. By a little crowding I was accommodated with a seat on the camp-bed. Several line officers were on the bed and others scattered about on the camp-chairs.

A witty story-teller kept us all convulsed with laughter, and the colored cook appeared at regular intervals with the hot-water kettle.

At nine o'clock Tattoo was sounded. The regimental band, with small drums, fifes and a large bass drum, sauntered into the central street, and forming themselves into a circle, played the signal for retiring.

All now sought their quarters for the night, and after a very short time no sounds could be heard except the tramp of the guards, as they marched back and forth and kept a sharp lookout for any stray soldier who was courageous enough to attempt to run the guard. The company fires died, the heavy smoke drifted away, and the rising moon looked down upon the weird stillness of the canvas town. Here and there the silence was broken by a soldier confined in the guard-house, who vented his discontent in violent and profane words, but the voice was soon stilled by the gruff command of the sergeant. Then might be heard at intervals the relief guard going the rounds, and a novice would be much interested to see them approach the sentinel on duty and pass the countersign. It was not an unusual occurrence for a commotion to take place in the night in the wagon-camp, and the loud braying of the mules would echo through the camp until the negro drivers lashed them into silence. But in the early morning hours deep quietude settled everywhere, and no sounds arose to disturb the sleeping army.

SUPPER TIME.

TATTOO IN CAMP.

XXX

A MORNING CALL.

The Battery Guard.

S THE passage of years makes more remote the events of army life, the veteran's memory grows stronger in recollection; but no reminiscence, however treasured, will take him back in thought and feeling like the familiar sound of the old bugle-calls. From a keyless instrument the notes were necessarily of simple character, but clear and sweet; and the rollicking calls of the cavalry and artillery, and the sober but not less musical calls of the infantry, will always arouse the old spirit of the war-days.

And who that has lain blanket-wrapped in camp or on battlefield will ever forget the sweet " Reveillé " that floated like a dream to the weary sleepers, often coming as a harbinger to a bright, jolly day in camp, but many times as a forerunner of desperate conflict!

I have often recalled the scene of one picture, when the army was lying in line of battle confronting the vigilant enemy, from whom we were expecting an attack. Our troops were drawn up on a long range of hills, where quite an open country with fences and occasional groves of trees stretched in front. We had full reason to suppose that the enemy was in strong force and made ready to give them a soldier's reception.

During the early night troops were placed in position; batteries were posted on every hill, with infantry supports in the rear, and cavalry was massed on both flanks of the line to prevent a surprise in that direction. By midnight everything was in readiness for an attack that the coming dawn might bring. The great army, which covered a line eight miles long, and which by daylight had swarmed about like one great hive of bees, was now lost in sleep. Long lines of infantrymen in gray blankets lay in rear of stacked muskets; some had secured cornstalks enough for bedding, but the great majority were stretched on bare ground, with knapsacks and fence-rails for pillows. The artillerymen were sleeping around the rear of their unlimbered guns, except the solitary guard, who moved quietly to and fro and kept an anxious eye toward the enemy. In rear of the guns, limbers and caissons, with horses attached, stood ready for any unexpected movement.

The excitement of apprehension had driven sleep from my eyes, and I watched by the camp fire and listened to the night sounds. From far off in the front came the steady, plaintive call of a whip-poor-will, who had evidently been roused into unusual activity by the great army, and this, with the ominous cry of a screech-owl, made the darkness seem weird and strange. The hours passed slowly. At last, with the first gray streaks of dawn, a few faint musical notes came from far down the line. It was the Reveillé! Other and still other bugles followed in quick succession, until the whole air was alive with the inspiriting blasts, and in almost an instant—with the instinct of watchfulness—the sleeping host was aroused, awake. Then, as far as the eye could reach, multitudes of men arose, rolled their blankets and packed their traps. Men and horses next had to be fed. Thousands of camp-fires soon blazed in every direction, and fragrant coffee simmered merrily in kettle and can. A great canopy of smoke hung over the country, and the sun in crimson glory rose above the bustling throng.

But scattering shots of musketry, far in front, had already caused the coffee to disappear in urgent haste, and in time more brief than could be imagined the scene of apparent confusion had become one of order and quiet. The gunners at the batteries took position; the drivers mounted their horses; the infantry stood rigidly exact, with anxious ear strained toward the enemy.

Soon, a scattered skirmish-fire commenced, and just as the sun rose the battle began. Ere long, wounded skirmishers began to come back, and were indifferently glanced at by the men in position, for such sights were common ones now. Some were leaning on their guns; others were supported by branches of trees; one used a pitchfork for a crutch, while an officer was carried in a blanket by four of his men. The enemy's batteries had sent disastrous fire among our troops. Here and there a solid shot would be thrown, whose action of ploughing a trench in the earth and then bounding out was more destructive than the conical missiles from the rifled guns, which bored into the ground and burst.

But while the Rebs were doing their worst our batteries were not inactive, and the interchange of compliment became so animated that I thought best to seek for my art-material in a quieter spot. So, dashing toward the rear, I ran the gauntlet of the flying missiles, and did not halt until a mile away. Many brave fellows of whom I knew not fell on both sides that day; and the Blue and the Gray in a common sleep await the Reveillé of the Resurrection.

Sounding the Charge

REVEILLÉ ON THE LINE OF BATTLE.

119

XXXI

BUILDING BREASTWORKS.

———•———

Digging for Dear Life.

URING an aggressive campaign there was little of leisure for man or beast. From daylight till sunset men were flitting about with anxious faces, mind and body taxed to the utmost. Men and mules were kept at work; if not in actual march or fight, then in continuous preparation, and in the unceasing labor even the mules seemed sometimes to take on an air of responsibility. But the most dangerous and severe work was in the extreme front, and nothing but the most determined effort and rapid execution accomplished the purpose or preserved the lives of the laborers.

A day's experience at the great Battle of the Wilderness illustrated the brave spirit and unflagging industry of the officers and their men. The armies of General Lee and General Grant had grappled in the woods surrounding the Wilderness farm, and after a few hours of desperate fighting settled down and fortified the lines. I rode out on the right, and watched during the early part of the day the work of fortifying our front. The main line was laid out on a rise of ground commanding an open field, heavily wooded on the enemy's side. The Rebs, after a hard struggle, had driven our men back and had made two unsuccessful attacks on our present position. Minie balls from sharpshooters on the edge of the woods and in the tree-tops whistled by, uncomfortably close, so I dismounted in a patch of woods, and running from behind one tree to another, secured a position finally where I could get a view along the line of battle. The men were digging with pick and spade for dear life, and had already thrown up quite a formidable work, so that, thus protected, they had suffered comparatively little loss. Squads of men were felling trees behind the ridge, and, clearing the trunks of branches, hurried forward with them to the earthworks, where they were used as a backing. In an incredibly short time a splendid breastwork covered our lines on both flanks as far as the eye could reach, and the confident demeanor of the men spoke of the security they felt in the protection. Two brass twelve-pounders, double-shotted with canister, were posted on each side of the road that ran through the works toward the enemy.

The skill of our skirmishers was now brought into play, and a steady rattle of musketry was heard along the line. The usual train of poor wounded fellows began to pass to the rear, but the scene was oddly varied by a squad of queer prisoners. Those of one group had in the lead a stalwart, red-whiskered fellow, who carried a patchwork quilt (used, presumably, for a blanket) under his arm. Behind him came a youth with light-gray jacket and trousers, and a gray infantry cap trimmed with light blue. The next one to him wore a striped worsted sailor cap. And the last in order was an old man with long, white hair, who was evidently a recruit, for he still wore a citizen's hat—an old-fashioned stove-pipe. They stepped along to the rear cheerfully and briskly, as if not at all averse to entering our lines.

A number of shells were soon sent over by the enemy, but did no damage, unless to the trains in the rear.

I ventured along the line, keeping under cover as much as possible, and was greatly interested in watching the different groups along the works. At one point the " head-log " was just being put into place. This was usually a tree-trunk eight or ten inches in diameter, and was made secure about four inches above the top of the works, so that men could fire through the opening and have the heads protected. Further on, a tangle or abatis was being constructed. Parties of men were cutting down pine trees and lopping off the branches, and others, seizing these, would hurry forward and place them on the ground, points outward, thus making a formidable obstruction to an enemy's approach. The men not employed seemed to have no apprehension of danger, and notwithstanding the threatening noise, were grouped about under shelter of the breastworks—cooking, playing cards, and many even sleeping peacefully. At intervals a man would be struck by a ball and start hastily for the rear, and not until some one was wounded did the thought of danger come to them. Even the direct aim of the sharpshooters did not intimidate them, and they stood on the breastworks and walked in front of them as if possessed of a charmed existence.

Stretched in the rear were the picturesque little shelter tents which lent protection from the sun's hot rays. Muskets were not stacked in their front, but stood leaning against the rear of the works, so that in the event of an attack not an instant would be lost.

The enemy made one dash for our breastworks during the day, but were driven back by hot fire. During the rest of my stay matters were comparatively quiet. Slipping back to my horse, I felt much relieved as I rode out upon the open ground near the Wilderness Tavern, which was General Grant's headquarters. From this point I obtained sight of the reserves and trains. The open space was full of army wagons, and columns of infantry like great blue snakes were winding in, marching from rear to front. Ambulances were coming and going, and ammunition-wagons were passing along the roads in all directions. I reached my own headquarters just in time for the evening meal, and ate of a variety of food in the comfortable dining-room of the farm-house to the accompaniment of rattling musketry. But, however acceptable the food might be, there was less of relish as a glance through the window at the ambulances creeping along the roads in the valley toward the rear told of the wounded and dying.

Building Breastworks

THE LULL IN THE FIGHT.

XXXII.

PICKET DUTY IN THE RAIN.

The Piping Times of War.

NOUGH privation and regrets of home come into the every-day life of a soldier without the loneliness and exposure suffered on the picket line, and it is not to be wondered at that so many died of homesickness in the variety of trials that they were subjected to. The greater part of the Union army was made up of boys direct from comfortable homes, and to one who saw what they endured it was a marvel how they lived through the ordeal.

The "fair weather" soldier was common in the army, and under favorable conditions was a "jolly good fellow," and grew fat in prosperity and on good rations; but when taken away from a settled camp he became irritable and complaining, and on picket duty his discontent knew no bounds.

I was once riding in a cold winter storm when the rain swept in gusts across the country, and found the reserve picket line, wrapped in overcoats and ponchos, and crouched about a scanty fire, the very personification of misery. They were scarcely recognizable as the jaunty, chipper soldiers of the day before. Another group had found refuge under some rails that they had placed slantingly against a fence with a couple of ponchos thrown over, and sat huddled up in solemn silence, the picture of despair.

I was curious to learn how some of them accepted conditions; so fastened my horse to a fence and walked out to the advance line. The first one I came to stood in surly position with his back against a pine tree, and with the lock of his gun tucked under his arm to protect it from dampness. The rain trickled from the brim of his hat, and his face was pinched with cold.

"Good day, my friend," I said. "This is the tough part of a soldier's life."

"Soldier's life!" he muttered, with an oath. "What made me a soldier, and why am I here? I will tell you. When I saw the quick-stepping boys, with bright brasses, going to the front, and saw the flags wave and heard the bands play, I felt that it would be fine fun for me to go too; but where are the pleasures [with another oath]? This is one of them, I suppose. Living on poor army rations is another; and being shot at, of course, another. Ah, well, if I had known what I know now I should have staid at home and enjoyed my warm bed and decent food."

I tried to cheer him by saying that the sunshine would soon raise his spirits again, and walked on to the next picket. I found a mere boy, whose cheerful face was in great contrast to the one I had just left. He had a bright complexion, with slight down upon the face, and a winning smile. "A mother's boy," I thought, as I approached him. I asked him how he stood the storm, and he replied, "Oh, first rate!"

"Wet?

"Yes, I'm wet enough; but I don't care for rain or snow. I expected to go through fire and water if need be for the good cause, and this isn't so bad if one will only keep cheerful about it. I shall be glad to get back sound and well; but if I knew I should leave my bones out here—why, we all had to look that in the face when we started. The fun about offsets the hardship; but, even if it didn't, we came for *business*—and [with a chuckle] this seems to be part of it."

Leaving this young philosopher, I passed down the line and found many kindred spirits, but here and there a weak-backed, discouraged man.

And yet the trials that all these and thousands of other fellows suffered were only of the day; for when the sun broke through the clouds everything was transformed. The fires at the reserve post burned up brightly, the men crawled out from their temporary shelters, and even the chronic grumbler to whom I first spoke I saw walking erect, his gun over his shoulder, whistling "The Girl I Left Behind Me."

A Cosy Shelter.

INFANTRYMAN ON PICKET.

127

MEADE AT GETTYSBURG.

XXXIII.

OFFICERS' WINTER QUARTERS.

" Chuck on Some Logs, Pete!"

THE building of camp-houses for officers was done with great care, and they were provided with many more comforts than those of the private soldiers. The most common form was the "Sibley tent." A circle of logs, set deep in the ground in upright position, was first made. Then the lower edge of the tent was attached to the upper ends of the logs, which stood four feet above ground. The apex was held up in place by three long poles whose upper ends were crossed, and the lower portions extended down the outside of the tent into the ground.

In the interior, a large fireplace was built on one side, also a stone-and-mud chimney; and on the opposite side a rough door was fitted to an opening which had been left for the purpose. These structures were quite roomy and surprisingly comfortable. Bunks were made by driving four posts at the corners, left about a foot above ground, and straight pieces of board fastened and extended from one to the other. Pine boughs were laid lengthwise, and covered with quite a depth of pine needles gathered from the woods; and when over the whole a blanket was spread a most comfortable bed had been completed. These bunks were ranged around the sides; swords, saddles, and other accoutrements were hung on the log wall; and a glance inside, when the glowing wood fire was burning in the great fireplace, proved that bright scenes and agreeable conditions were sometimes a part of army life. Here, when off duty, officers found time to lounge and read, others to write, and many to form groups for card-playing. I always found their quarters pleasant calling-places, and soon forgot a day's hardships in their good company.

Another style of officers' huts was log houses roofed with "A" tents, having also large chimneys at the rear ends. The headquarter-huts were generally built in rows on each side of the commanding general's quarters, the latter being of larger dimensions than the rest. Houses of the line officers were built at the ends of the company streets, commanding a view of the regimental camp.

A commanding general could sometimes secure an old mansion, and thus temporarily enjoy home comforts. The parlor was generally used for an office, and the other rooms occupied as sleeping apartments by the general and his staff officers. When thus comfortably housed there was no exposure to storms; as there was in the huts, whose canvas tops often leaked, the men, indeed, being sometimes awakened by a stream of cold water running down their backs or into their faces. A gale of wind, too, occasionally carried off the canvas roof, and the rudely aroused inmates would rush off for help to repair the damage before the storm should destroy their meager but much-treasured possessions.

But some officers were compelled to use the "Wall" or the "A" tents without the log walls. These were not nearly as comfortable as the log-houses, for the wind came under the edges, and it was almost impossible to keep warm in bad weather. A bright log fire modified discomforts somewhat, though in cold weather the faces burned while the backs froze. But comforts, however slight, were accepted gratefully by all, and the jest went round, and songs were sung by many brave, bright fellows who now fill soldier's graves.

The above group of sketches will show, more clearly than descriptions can do, the divers modes of utilizing tents—whether merely as roof or as house entire. It is astonishing, when men get down to it, to see how little is really required for comfort, even among the civilized and well-reared.

AFTER DRESS PARADE.

XXXIV.

NEWSPAPERS IN CAMP.

———•———

News at the Front.

PRIVATE soldier's world, in an active campaign, does not extend far beyond the lines of his own brigade, and except in his immediate vicinity of action, details of a battle in which he had participated were as new to him as to his relatives in the far-off home. Imagine, then, with his horizon bounding such narrow limits, how eagerly he longed for the arrival of the newspapers which would bring him news of "The Last Great Battle"—of which he had been a part, yet about which he knew but little—as well as of the world in general.

The sale of popular newspapers in the army was immense, and men who furnished them made fortunes. The work of distribution was in the hands of general agents, who received them in bulk from the North. They placed them with sub-agents in the field, who made final distribution with a large corps of mounted newsboys.

In winter-camp, a log shanty was built near the railroad station, and here were sold papers, stationery, and the demoralizing dime novel, which came into being about that time. The weekly story-papers seemed an especial prize to the "boys," and passed through many hands; when finally read, the pictures were cut out and stuck up, more or less ornamentally, on the walls of the log-shelters. During an active summer campaign the work of distribution was difficult and dangerous, the papers having sometimes to be brought from the rear on horseback through a country infested by bushwhackers. Perhaps the army might be engaged in battle and stretched over miles of ground. Fear of rivals would prevent the newsboys from waiting until the ending of the engagement, and out upon the danger-line they would go, to sell their stocks as soon as possible. Among the batteries where shells were bursting they would halt, and, surrounded by crowds of clamoring soldiers, would sell their papers and make change with the coolness of veterans—which indeed they quickly became. Or they would pass along the lines of infantry lying on the ground in the rear, and in a few hours get rid of their supply.

At the battle of Antietam, I was scanning through my field-glass the long lines of Union skirmishers which had been pushed up under shelter of broken ground and scattered rocks, when I noticed one of the men lying on his back, under shelter of a low bank, calmly reading a newspaper, regardless of the enemy's bullets which continually drove up the dust and made the chips fly from the rocks within a few feet of him. I marveled at his coolness as he turned the paper inside out. He scarcely moved his head when a comrade beside him dropped his gun and, lifting his wounded right arm carefully with his left, crept with bent body to the rear.

I was once making effort to reach the front in anticipation of a great battle, and had to ride forty miles. While pushing along, keeping a lookout for bushwhackers, I heard the sound of galloping horses in my rear. On looking around I saw two mounted boys, riding along with a "dare-devil" air. On coming up to me the larger boy cried out, "Say, Mister, can we ride with you? We're afraid of being picked up." I laughed at the idea of the slight protection that I could offer, but cheerfully accepted their company in my own loneliness, and soon learned that they were on the way to camp to sell newspapers. We rode along without any exciting adventure, except the sight of two or three of the enemy's scouts, who were evidently watching the road with the expectation of capturing a wagon train. We moved on until within ten miles of camp, when the boys became impatient, and said they must hurry on to reach camp before dark. So, bidding me good-bye, they hurried off on a lively gallop, and were soon out of sight. I quickened my horse's speed soon after, and at the end of four miles came in sight of a pontoon train, guarded by infantry, also on its way to camp. I was glad of the protection of the pontoon guard, and rode with them until safe within the Union lines.

The boys passed out of my mind; and I should probably never have recalled the incident, but one day the next winter as I was riding through camp, a little fellow on horseback hailed me and said, "How d'ye do? Don't you know me?" I told him that I did not, and he said: "Why, I'm one of the newsboys that rode with you last summer on your way to the army; and I just want to tell you what happened to us. You remember when we left you and hurried ahead? Well, after riding a little way, we came up to a pontoon train and rode with it awhile, but soon left it and rode ahead with a sutler, who was anxious to join his regiment. We pushed along, but had not ridden more than half a mile when a party of Moseby's men jumped out of the woods, and, seizing the sutler's horses by the head, hurried us all into a patch of woods near the road. The Mosebies sat perfectly quiet on their horses, and watched the pontoon train pass; and I saw you riding near the first wagon."

I asked about the fate of the sutler, and he continued: "Just as soon as the train was out of sight, the Rebs set to work and plundered the wagon of all they could carry. They took the sutler's horses and then left. They did not take *our* horses, as the Captain said we were poor boys, and he wouldn't put us on the ground."

"You were fortunate," I replied.

"Oh, yes," said the boy; "we didn't lose anything. We helped ourselves to a pair of new boots out of the sutler's wagon."

I laughingly bade the fellow good-bye, and as I rode back to headquarters I thought, "he surely believes that 'everything's fair in love and war.'"

ARRIVAL OF THE NEWS-BOY.

XXXV.

A DEFEATED ARMY.

A Friend in Need

WHEN victory has perched upon an army's banners, no words can describe the animated spirit and proud carriage of the men. Even when many have fallen, the survivors feel that the sacrifice has not been in vain, and the wounded bear their pain with joyous resignation. But when a proud host is vanquished the troops fall into a marked listlessness and helplessness of demeanor.

This feeling of despondency was fully shown after the battle of Groveton or Second Bull Run. Desultory fighting had been going on for some days as the Army of the Rappahannock fell back toward Washington. Officers and men were losing confidence in the commanding general (Pope), as they felt his inability to take advantage of his superior position. The Union army was between the two main bodies of General Lee's forces, and our men felt, and freely said, that if properly managed we should have been able to destroy the enemy by massing on either of the widely-separated wings. The opportunity was lost, however; and, in spite of what seemed to be insurmountable obstacles, General Lee with the main body of his army passed through Thoroughfare Gap in the Bull Run Mountains, and by forced marches joined the detachment under General Jackson at Groveton, at which point Jackson had held the Union army at bay for two days. The reunited forces now presented a defiant front.

As I sat on my horse on Bald Hill, near the Henry House, I realized that the Union situation was a discouraging one. Every attack upon the enemy's front had been repulsed with bloodshed, as they were protected by the embankment of an abandoned railroad. Our regiments had been decimated, and thousands of dead and wounded were lying in the hot sun between the opposing lines.

About fifty guns along our front were shelling the enemy's lines, when a terrible fire opened on us from the enemy's right, which enfiladed our batteries and the masses of infantry supporting them. The effect was terrible. Solid shot ploughed through the ranks, and as shells burst among the men who were in column of division, closed in mass, great open spaces appeared where they fell. Ambulances soon began to appear, and hundreds of wounded who could help themselves came drifting to the rear.

And now the enemy took advantage of the opportunity by an advance from their center and right flank. In the open ground near the center long lines of gray could be seen coming slowly forward toward our line, firing at will; and in the woods along the ridge on our left a terrific roar of musketry could be heard, which suggested a flanking movement by the enemy. We hurried troops forward in resistance, and shortly, on the two sides, fifty thousand men stood face to face, pouring volleys of musketry. The heroic resistance of the Union line availed nothing, however, and it was compelled to retire slowly. At sundown our force made a final stand near the Henry House. It was useless. Sullenly the whole line retreated, and, after crossing Bull Run at various fords and bridges, was soon on its way back to Centerville.

I stood by the side of the pike in the gathering darkness, and watched the dispirited throng as it passed. Disorganized infantry regiments mixed confusedly with batteries swept by Ambulances and wagons surged along filled with moaning wounded men, who heard in their pain the shrill yells of the drivers and sharp cracks of their whips as they urged their tired and overladen beasts to a place of safety. Groups of wounded on foot came slowly along the edge of the main current, and rendered one another such assistance as was possible. Here and there a wounded officer appeared tenderly cared for by his men, those seriously wounded being carried on stretchers or in blankets. With heavy hearts and languid feet the troops moved on, until far into the night, the march being lit up by camp-fires on all sides; but by midnight there were few passers-by except stragglers and the belated wounded who enquired for the location of their regiment, and limped their way onward. Last of all came the rear guard, moving quietly, halting on each rise of ground, and forming into line on either side of the pike to resist any possible advance of the triumphant enemy.

Tired and despondent myself, I now rode through heavily-falling rain into Centerville, and, tying my horse in an old shed by the roadside, I crawled for shelter under the body of a wagon which lay upturned on the ground. It was so very dark that I could scarcely discern objects, and was surprised to find several soldiers already under the wagon. The one alongside of whom I lay told me that he had been severely wounded in the face. I gave him my rubber poncho, and told him how sorry I was that he had been so unfortunate. He replied: "I don't mind being wounded so much, but to be hit in the face will so disfigure me that the girls will never look at me again."

I left the poor fellow before daylight and did not have opportunity of seeing his face, but I have often recalled his odd reply, and wondered if his apprehensions were well founded or if his wound became a badge of honor more sightly to "the girls" than a handsome, unscarred face would have been, had he stayed at home.

After the Battle.

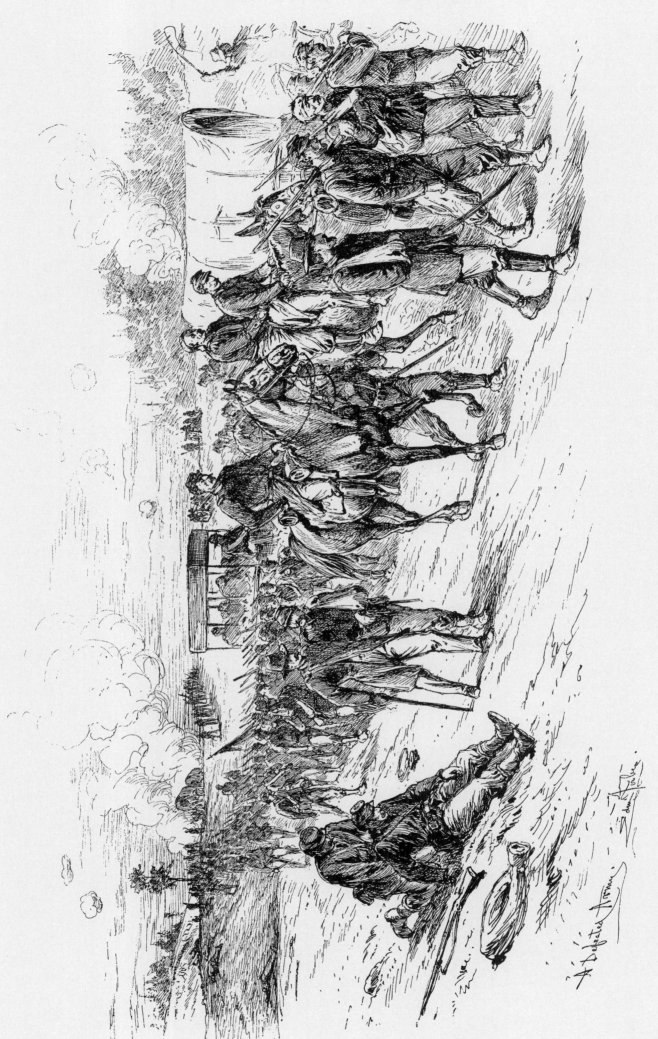

ON THE RETREAT.

XXXVI.

THE ARMY BLACKSMITH.

An Efficient Rear Guard.

HOES for horses in the army were as much a necessity as for men, and the work done with hammer and anvil was as important in its place as that accomplished with cannon and musket. Without it artillery horses would be of no service, cavalrymen would have been compelled to do duty on foot, and no such wonderful raids as those of Sheridan, Wilson and Averill would ever have been heard of. Wagon trains could not have moved from place to place, and without supplies of food and ammunition campaigns could not have been carried on.

The blacksmiths' forges were distributed among the cavalry, artillery and wagon trains. They were mounted on four wheels, similar to the artillery caisson. On the front wheels rested a box, containing all tools and necessary supplies; and on the rear wheels a furnace and bellows were mounted. The wheels were connected by a bar and coupling pin, and to the bar was attached a screw vise.

During the march the forge was at the rear of the column, but as soon as a halt was called the blacksmiths commenced work in earnest. They were generally brawny fellows, dressed in worn blue suits and the traditional leather apron, and could be found by the roadside under shade of trees ready to commence business. First the fire was made in the furnace; then the anvil, mounted on a block, was placed on the ground, and hammer, nails, horseshoes, etc., were at hand.

Quite a picture was often formed when the cavalrymen and artillerymen stood about the forge in their bright uniforms, awaiting their turns. Perhaps an old mule would be driven up by his master, and, like all his kind, having a decided prejudice to being shod. He would stand flapping his ears lazily, apparently indifferent to all surroundings, but cunningly making up his mind to resist all attentions when shoeing time came. So, when the blacksmith approached, he pricked up his ears and turned back his eyes, and when attempt was made to examine his feet he squealed and lashed out his hind legs, soon clearing a circle about him. Such a situation seemed discouraging; but the blacksmith and his helpers, wholly undismayed, fastened a strap to one fore leg, a rope to the other, and, despite the animal's frantic struggles, soon had him panting and groaning on the ground, one fore leg bent and strapped up taut. He was then turned on his back, and a long rope passed around his hind legs and neck to prevent him from kicking. One might conclude that with these preliminaries the creature would be rendered helpless, but the possible ventures of an army mule were limitless; so, as a further precaution, the rope fastened to his fore leg was held taut by the soldiers, the one around the neck and hind legs was drawn in opposite directions by some of the lookers-on, and the head was held to the ground by the negro driver with a tight clutch of the ears.

Having their victim thus pinioned, the smith and his assistants would set to work, amid the laughs of the men and the groans of the vanquished mule, to whom no means of defiance remained except the rolling of the eyes and the switching of the tail. When the work was done and the mule released one would naturally look for a desperate resentment, but so humiliated did the poor thing usually seem that he moved off slowly toward the wagon camp, amid the jeers of the spectators, not enough of his former spirit remaining to resent even the blows of the driver.

The services of the blacksmith were as valuable in the repairing of wagons and artillery carriages as in the shoeing of horses and mules. Most of the men were ingenious, and ready for all emergencies—"Jacks of all trades," in fact, and (contrary to the old adage) *good at all*. Circumstances often made their work difficult, but their unusual willingness and efficiency made them a worthy element in the great hosts who so bravely did service in various ways.

A Tough Customer.

AN ARMY FORGE.

XXXVII.

ADVANCE OF THE CAVALRY CORPS.

In the Van.

UCH of romance and fascinating incident came into the ordinary life of cavalry soldiers, and their dashing style and daring spirit of venture gave more opportunity for interesting study than any other branch of the service. Circumstances developed original characteristics, and brought into prominence both brigades, special bodies and individuals, where infantry could have accomplished nothing. The cavalry were always in close contact with the enemy —on scouting duty, in raids, on advance picket, or as videttes. In an advance they were the first to develop the enemy's position and the first to receive fire; and in retreat they were the last to stand against the enemy's attacks. They moved about with a rapidity scarcely imaginable, and during an active campaign seemed to be omnipresent.

I once witnessed the advance of a cavalry corps when the main army moved against the enemy. Orders had been received for the movement, and there was soon great bustle in the cavalry camp. Tents were struck. Heavy traps were placed in the wagons, blankets and ponchos were strapped on the saddles, and in quick time the regiments were drawn up in line ready for motion. Even the horses seemed to "snuff the battle afar off" as they stood in the ranks impatiently champing their bits. At the sound of the bugle the lines wheeled into column of fours, and with fluttering flags and guidons moved towards the rendezvous. The cavalry corps numbered twelve thousand men, with ten light batteries, and they marched forward and took position in the open country in front.

I sat on my horse in rear of the lines, and as far as the eye could see watched the masses of horsemen come into position from either flank. Light batteries were aligned in the open spaces between the brigades; and back of all, near the center of the position, was the commander, Sheridan, surrounded by his brilliant staff. Officers and orderlies were rushing about, and all was soon ready for the order "Forward!" The bugles sounded the advance, and a host of skirmishers, with carbines in hand, moved to the front. The main body followed slowly; but the country was rolling and broken up with frequent woods and streams, and as the great mass of horsemen advanced they broke into various formations at the sound of the bugle. The brilliant moves and changes could be likened only to a kaleidoscope.

Men in the advance removed fences and other obstructions to facilitate the movements of the main body, and in an hour's time the enemy's videttes appeared to view. They retired slowly toward their main line of skirmishers, who showed their position by open carbine fire. The Union lines were steady under the fire, and, moving cautiously forward, returned shots at every opportunity with tact and coolness. Up hill and down, through woods and swamps, over fences and ditches the line steadily advanced, rallying to each other's support when resistance in front became too great, and taking advantage of cover, however slight, as protection from the hot fire. Now and then a horse and rider would fall; and here and there could be seen a rider leaning forward on his horse's neck coming slowly to the rear, with the ashen gray face that suggested a mortal wound. Officers did not escape the bullets, and were frequently seen wounded and tenderly supported in the saddle by their men. As soon as they were assisted safely to the rear a surgeon would be sought for—in a neighboring farm-house, perhaps, where a hospital had been established. Many times a man would be mortally shot and fall from his horse; then the frightened animal, with streaming mane and tail, would rush terror-stricken across the field.

With a sudden dash by quite a force of the enemy the Union line of skirmishers was driven back, but in the movement took all possible cover to harrass the foe. Many of our men dismounted behind stone and rail fences and groups of trees, and, leaving a limited number to attend to the horses, poured a rapid carbine fire upon the advancing line. This was now broken, and the Rebs, in turn, took to cover to re-form. Reinforcements were soon sent from our rear, as "Jeb" Stuart's entire cavalry confronted us. Fighting along the whole line soon became furious. Batteries on both sides were heard from, and bursting shells and whizzing round shot increased the clamor. The enemy gave way reluctantly, under pressure of the Union advance; their main line soon took position, and the masses of cavalry were drawn up on the further slopes. In rear of them horsemen were moving rapidly, and large clouds of dust rose in the still, warm air.

General Sheridan, to test the enemy's strength, pushed the Union line forward, and, keeping as much as possible under cover, moved on until our whole force was within a mile of the enemy's position. Then about six thousand horsemen started on a trot toward the enemy, and hot shell fire from all the guns in range opened upon the Union men. The light Federal batteries had meanwhile crept toward the front, and took position on a rise of ground. The Union cavalry, harrassed by opposing artillery and skirmish fire, steadily advanced until near the Confederate line, when the bugle sounded the charge. Now, amid clouds of dust, thousands of horsemen dashed in solid masses up the slope, and cheers and yells of the struggling host rose up amid the rattling carbine fire. The enemy held fast, fighting bravely, and concentrating upon our men forced them back with heavy loss. Hundreds of wounded men came from the front, and great numbers of horses, some of which were badly wounded, were running about the field. The main body of our men retreated to their original position, accompanied by quite a number of prisoners, who seemed to enjoy their bondage. Our lines were soon re-formed, and a spirited attack made by the exultant enemy was easily repulsed, our batteries in the advance obtaining hot cross fire on their masses.

The Confederate position was evidently too strong for our cavalry, so the commanding general awaited an infantry reinforcement. When it appeared, however, the enemy vanished. The Union forces advancing occupied the enemy's evacuated position, and, riding forward, I was able to inspect the scene of the charge. Many dead and wounded men and horses were scattered about the crest of the ridge where the hottest contest took place, and around an abandoned gun a mass of men and horses were lying.

Several regiments were sent after the enemy to accelerate retreat, but the main body of our forces went into camp, and were soon cooking supper with as much expectant interest as though a battle had never taken place. I sought out some friends and, while partaking of their coffee and hardtack, listened to stories of those who were fortunate enough to escape.

Coming out of the fight.

THE CAVALRY SKIRMISHER.

XXXVIIII.

OFFICERS' COOKS AND SERVANTS.

Smoking Hot.

HE mantle of daily industry—"domestic work," as we may call it—fell upon the shoulders of the colored men or boys, for the drudgery of camp-life came to them alone, and the most laborious duties were performed by them with a never-failing cheerfulness that is seldom found in positions of servitude. I sometimes heard it stated that their good will came from a feeling of emancipation from arbitrary masters, and also because of the chance to earn a few independent dollars; but I often watched them closely under the most toilsome and exasperating circumstances, and was convinced that in most cases the willingness came of conscientious scruples to do the best they knew how for those engaged in what they regarded as the fight for their freedom.

The officers' cooks and servants were varied in appearance, but at all times picturesque in costume and figure With peculiar characteristics, they sometimes caused anxiety to their employers, but the amusement which their droll ways and odd sayings occasioned more than made amends. Some of the colored men were the experienced servants of good families, and were adept in the administering of ease and comfort. Others were field hands; yet, if not trained like the house servants, they were eager to be satisfactory, and the rough elements of cooking gleaned from plantation kitchens served a fair purpose. In winter camp the cooks' duties were easily performed; for, as the commissary was near by with necessary stores, sold at about cost price, the officers' tables were readily supplied.

The cook's kitchen was placed behind the quarters of the officers, and was usually a canvas-covered log house with a great stone chimney at the rear end. Around the sides of the kitchen hung cooking utensils, and in the corner stood the mess-chest, from whose capacious interior necessary condiments were supplied. And here, on a bright fire of pine logs, most appetizing dishes were cooked. Chickens were roasted to a turn, and when good fortune directed a rabbit to the hand of a colored cook a stew was furnished whose savor was long talked of by the partakers. Ham and eggs, griddle cakes, and all concoctions which the surroundings could produce or willing hands prepare were placed before the officers.

During a summer campaign the commissary supplies were generally with the main wagon train; and the necessity of supplying the mess, in a great measure, by what could be found from day to day made the duties of the cooks quite arduous. Temporary supplies were generally carried on pack-mules or in a mess-cart, the latter being found during a march at the rear of the column. A good cook was apt to be a good forager, and secured many delicacies along the roadside farm-houses that a less persistent and appreciative person would miss. When camp was pitched the best the mess-chest afforded would be quickly converted into something palatable for the table, and the inevitable coffee, which served the double purpose of quenching thirst and supplying nutriment, was never forgotten.

The officers' body servants were as a rule colored boys, and like all youth, were sometimes careless and forgetful. In a general way, however, they served good purpose, and their natural grotesqueness and sense of humor afforded much amusement for the men.

Instances of bravery among the colored servants were not rare. At the battle of Cedar (or Slaughter's) Mountain, Knapp's battery, which was posted near the left of the line, had a colored man and boy in service as cooks. When action commenced they were ordered to the rear, but the man said: "No, Cap'n; I'll stay with you and fight." He worked

faithfully at a gun during the greater part of the engagement, and when danger seemed almost passed the poor fellow's head was taken off by a solid shot. The boy had thus far steadily and efficiently carried water for the gunners from Cedar Creek, in the rear of the battery, but when he saw the mutilated body of his comrade he became terror-stricken, and fled to the rear.

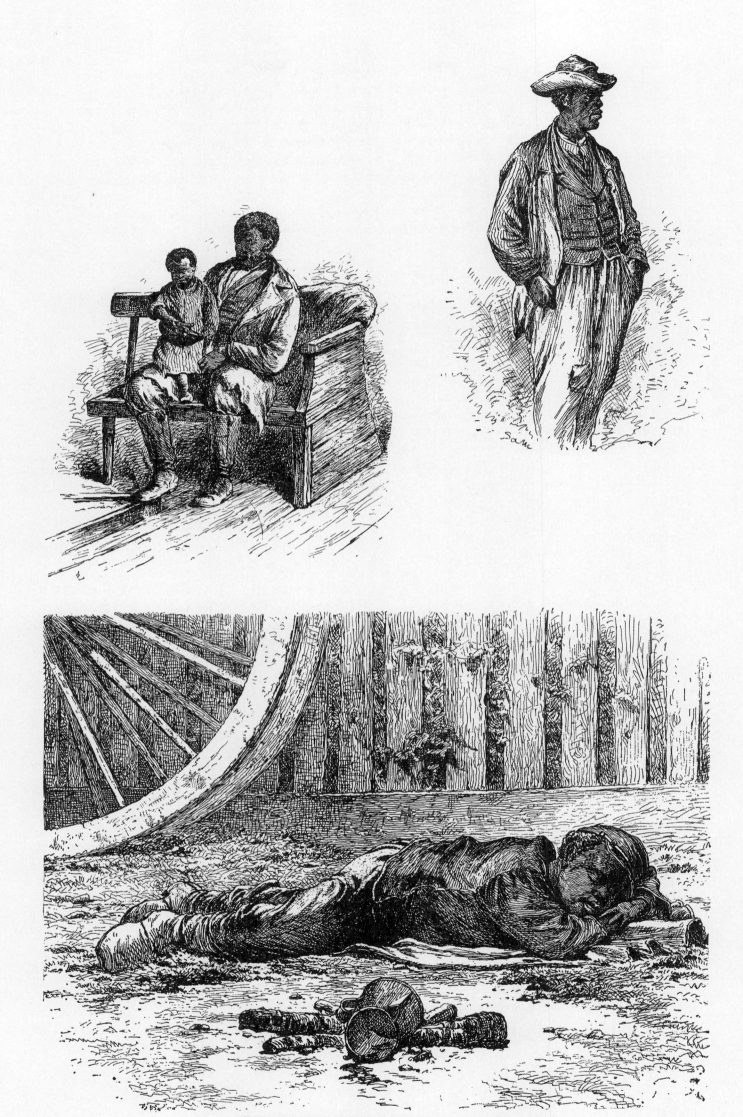

THE BURNISHED LIVERY OF THE SUN.

XXXIX.

THE CRIME OF DESERTION.

Under Guard

HEN the great wave of patriotism first swept over the country, after the attack upon Fort Sumter, men of better calibre sought the ranks than during the last years of the war. Men of all professions, graduates of institutions, and representatives of all kinds of business rushed enthusiastically to the country's defence. There was a surplus of volunteers. Men were often refused because regiments were more than full; and many young fellows were sent in disappointment homeward because of some slight physical defect.

Yet, while there seemed an overabundance of good men, many were blindly accepted who were weak in character, and some even proved false to the colors, though rarely. Later, when the armies were supplied by drafting and by the payment of bounties, recruits felt less the pressure of "patriotism" and more their own selfish interests. Many, especially of those paid bounties, would desert at the first opportunity; and then, perhaps, enlist again for a second payment. "Bounty jumping" became a regular industry. During the entire war between two and three hundred thousand deserted.

In the year 1863 I had once the opportunity of looking over a company roll-book, and was much surprised to find the word "Deserter" affixed to about one-third of the names. I asked the Captain why desertion was so common, and he replied that there was lack of proper punishment. The authorities at Washington feeling disinclined to enforce the extreme penalty, the armies were much weakened, and great injustice was thus done to the faithful. But before the expiration of that year authorities became so alarmed at the rapidly diminishing forces that tremendous efforts were made to put an end to this great crime, and orders were given for the execution of all deserters. From this time until the close of the war the penalty was enforced. Many and elaborate were the excuses made by those who were captured and returned to the command for trial. Some did not seem to realize the enormity of the offence, and felt a freedom to stay or go because having sought the service voluntarily; some disliked their officers; and a host acknowledged that the *terrible home-sickness* alone actuated them.

The professional bounty-jumpers were of course numerous. Vigilant officials sought to prevent this traffic, and guards were placed in rear of all the armies of the field. They were also placed in larger numbers along the railroads running north, and were instructed to patrol the country on each side and capture all suspicious characters. Many innocent-looking parties, dressed in clothing which they had purchased or picked up, were brought into camp, and, when subjected to the examination of the provost marshal, often proved to be Northern bounty-jumpers in search of fresh pastures. They were then passed to their regiments, where courts martial quickly attended to their cases.

I once saw a party of five men who were convicted of desertion and sentenced to be shot. Until the day of execution they were imprisoned in an old barn in camp, and placed under a strong guard.

On the day appointed the whole corps to which they belonged were ordered to parade. The troops were assembled in long lines on the side of a shallow valley. The condemned men, with their guards, marched out of the barn, and took an allotted position in the column. This was headed by a brass band, followed by the division provost guard, who, under command of a captain, were to act as the firing party. Behind the provost guard marched eight soldiers bearing two coffins, and after them, accompanied by a Catholic priest, marched two condemned men dressed in white shirts and blue trousers; then two more coffins carried by soldiers, and two condemned men accompanied by a Methodist minister; after them a single coffin was borne along, and behind it walked the fifth deserter (who was a Jew) attended by a rabbi. The burial party followed, carrying spades. When all was in readiness the band played the "Dead March in Saul," and to its solemn strains all marched in front of the military lines on the hillside, halting at the place of execution, in front of the center of the corps. Thousands of spectators from neighboring camps covered the hill, and those whom I could see seemed to realize the solemnity of the occasion. Graves had been previously dug, and in front of them the coffins were placed, and the men ordered to sit down upon them with faces toward the firing party. Minister, priest and rabbi stepped forward and, after holding a whispered conversation with those of their faith, retired a short distance. The officer of the guard then stepped behind the men, and quickly blindfolded them with handkerchiefs which he took from the breast of his coat. Then, stepping to one side and in front of the firing party, he gave the deadly order: "Ready! Aim! Fire!" At the volley the five white-shirted figures fell back without a struggle, except one, who rolled convulsively off the coffin. Surgeons in attendance stepped forward, and after a brief examination pronounced the men dead.

The troops soon returned to their various camps, and before they were out of sight the coffins were lowered into the graves and covered. Scant trace of the tragedy remained, and the valley resumed its quiet. Dramatic effect was intentionally sought in this execution, to put an end to desertion; and time proved it to have been a wise proceeding. But while it produced good results in a general way, it did not deter two men of the same company to which the deserters belonged from slipping away on the very night of the execution; and they were never captured.

Dishonoured Graves.

THE PENALTY OF A GREAT CRIME.

XL.

THE REAR OF THE COLUMN.

"Pomp" and Circumstance of War.

ONLY the hard work of the march in the opening of a campaign brought to notice the most characteristic oddities and peculiar varieties of men and things. But, however much of interest there might have been in the changing scenes of the great panorama, no part of it comes back to me as vividly as the picturesque confusion of the mass toward the rear. Rapidity of movement was of the first importance, and foot soldiers who could not keep pace fell out and drifted back; when cavalry horses and artillery gave out riders would dismount and lead them; ambulances, with the sick and slightly wounded, were found in the rear; also the officers' servants and cooks, and pack mules with their drivers swelled the variety.

The chronic malingerer was found here in full force, and his constant groans and disconsolate face were calculated to oppress the spirits of his comrades. Bare-footed soldiers, whose shoes had worn off in the march, limped painfully along. Drummers and fifers found place here, except when they were ordered forward for march duty; also officers' servants and the whole number classed as "not in action" during a battle. Families of negro refugees often joined the column, looked back at the old home with momentary regret, but soon joined in the general laugh and chatter, with no apprehensions of the future.

It was impossible to fall out entirely on the march, for that meant capture, and visions of Andersonville and Libby prisons urged many a footsore soldier forward when he otherwise would have lost sight of the main column.

Good nature generally prevailed among this promiscuous company, misfortunes often being made a source of jest. Others in the column were much amused at the odd collection, and laughed heartily at both their enjoyments and mishaps.

Discipline was lax at the rear, however, and men took advantage of all opportunities to lighten their burdens; horses and mules were "confiscated," loaded with soldiers' traps, and marched along. Farmers on the line of march no doubt bear these rear characters in regretful remembrance, as, like the Bummers in the advance, they were most accomplished foragers, and it was but seldom that any physical ailment would prevent a pursuer from capturing a turkey, chicken or fat hog. Milk and honey were most thoroughly appreciated, and many a gentle cow received rough milking from the Union soldiers. Two men would hold a cow's head, each seizing a horn, a third would secure a firm hold of the tail, while a fourth with tin cup in hand would approach and, speaking gentle words, would commence milking. Sometimes the milk was obtained with difficulty, for the cow would become terror-stricken and, struggling and kicking, would often spill the precious draught, and send the milker sprawling upon the ground.

I once sketched an odd group at the rear of a column. A tall colored boy, in an old gray uniform, was leading a forlorn mule, laden with the most varied assortment of war material I ever saw gathered together. Hanging over the back was a canvas tent rather the worse for wear; around the neck three belts and cartridge boxes were hung, and on the sides were fastened a miscellaneous collection of muskets, cartridge boxes, bayonets, tin cups, kettles and canteens. He made a ludicrous appearance as he tramped along, for nothing could be seen of the mule but legs and ears.

I made another picture of an elderly colored man leading an old white horse, to which was fastened a collection of household effects. While I was making my sketch the man seemed frightened, and nervously fumbled a piece of white paper. He protested that he "warn't no spy," and said that the paper in his hand was a "parse" from Colonel Somebody. I asked him why he thought I took him for a spy, and he answered sheepishly, "'Cause, boss, you're a writin' too much about me."

I was soon able to show him the finished sketch, and knew by the hearty laugh that he recognized his own portrait and realized that he was in no danger.

Army Milkers.

THE FAG END.

SHERIDAN ON THE WINCHESTER ROAD.

XLI

TRAFFIC BETWEEN THE LINES.

A Friendly Overture.

URING the early part of the war men on both sides entertained the mistaken idea that because those on the opposing side were enemies they ought to be shot at and killed, no matter what the conditions might be; but as time advanced they learned to realize the cowardice there was in firing upon individual men, and by tacit, mutual consent all shooting of pickets and outposts was abandoned. This rule made much better feeling, and many who read in the papers of the terrible rancor that existed in the hearts of the men of the contending armies could not conceive of the really pleasant intercourse that existed at times between the hostile troops.

During the winter of '62 and '63, while the Confederate Army of Northern Virginia confronted the Union Army of the Potomac, which was posted on the opposite side of the Rappahannock River at Fredricksburg, friendly communication between the pickets along the banks was of almost daily occurrence. Confederate soldiers would cut a shingle into boat-like shape, and rig it with a mast and paper sail. They would then freight it with a hank of leaf tobacco, and would address a note to "The Yanks," in which would be a request for the return of a ration of sugar or "real coffee." The little craft was usually returned re-laden. The Virginia to-bacco was of good quality and most acceptable to "the boys." Sometimes the gray-coats would attach the name "Virginia" to the little boat before launching her, this being the Southern name for the ironclad "Merrimac," but the "boys in blue" were not to be outdone, and would, good-humoredly, return the miniature vessel marked "Monitor."

The Monitor.

This and other pleasantries were indulged in during the winter, and served to brighten the dull monotony of camp.

During the long siege of Petersburg a truce on the picket line was of quite frequent occurrence. The main line of forts and breastworks were but a few hundred yards apart in places, and the advance pickets were thus brought within speaking distance.

During active hostilities the men were under cover in pits, in front of which were slight rail or log breastworks to protect their heads, and during the long, hot days of the summer of '64 interchange of shots was kept up across the sunburned fields.

Several times when news of a truce was passed along the lines the soldiers were more than glad to creep out of their cramped positions. On one occasion a gray picket (evidently belonging to the class known as "poor whites") called out: "Yanks, hev you 'uns got any newspapers? 'Cause, if yer have, I will give terbaccer for 'em; and if you 'uns has got coffee we 'uns would like to git some." "All right, Johnnie," came the reply; and, leaving their guns behind, several pickets from each side advanced and, seating themselves on the ground and stumps of trees, soon made a satisfactory trade.

The Southerners were especially cut off from news owing to the scarcity of paper in the Confederacy, many publishers being reduced to the extremity of printing their sheets on the backs of wall-paper rolls; so that a few newspapers from the Northern soldiers were a treasure indeed when they could be had, and were eagerly received and read. Many a joke would be passed at such times, and brief discussions were often held on the possibilities of

News from the Yanks

the war; but when word was received that the time was ended the Rebs would shout, as they hurried toward their own ranks, "Git back to your holes, Yanks," and the good-natured reply would be, "All right, Johnnie; don't fire till we're under cover."

Such incidents as these served to mitigate the cruel and savage elements of war; and, when the conflict was over and those who had been spared returned home, the feeling of antagonism that was so intense in the beginning was no doubt alleviated in recollection of the many pleasant exchanges. To this day, if you hear a man breathing out particulary hot talk about the South or "Confederate Brigadiers," two to one you will find that during the war he was snugly at home making money or earning promotion in politics. Such self-seekers cannot conceive the fraternalism that grew up even between opposing armies after hearty fighting, followed by the fellowship of traffic between the lines.

COFFEE AND TOBACCO TRADING—A TRUCE.

XLII

THE HALT OF THE COLUMN.

Dropped Asleep.

HE sight of the army upon the march, with the columns of troops stretched along the road, would probably lead one who had not been there to think that a certain number of miles should be regularly covered in a given time. The average speed of infantry in heavy marching order on fair roads was about three miles an hour, but there were many causes to impede progress and prevent an even movement. Perhaps the heavily-laden wagons would become mired in soft ground, or the ascent of a long, steep hill would cause the drivers to "double-up" teams, and thus compel troops in the rear to halt until the difficulty was over.

It was impossible in a long column to have a uniformity of movement. Perhaps at one point men would be pushing along rapidly to close a gap in front, and at another point a halt had been ordered because men were exhausted, and they could be seen scattered in shady places on both sides of the road. Often when the march had not been severe but a halt for some other reason had been needed, the men would gather in groups and amuse themselves story-telling, card-playing or in lunching from the haversack till the order to "fall in" was given. Then there would be a scrambling back to the ranks, and the long blue line would soon resume life and motion.

During a severe campaign, when marching and fighting were continuous, the fatigued men would welcome a rest of but a few moments. At the word "Halt!" column would be quickly broken, traps unslung, and, dropping upon the ground, the men would fall asleep in an instant. Many times I have ridden along the road where ten thousand men who had been briefly halted were lying as if dead. Dust-covered and powder-stained, and with the hot sun beating upon their faces, they lay stretched upon the ground oblivious of surroundings or conditions.

Sometimes, when time would permit, an hour's halt was made at midday; then fires would be built, coffee made and cooking done. The pipes would be afterward lit and card-playing be indulged in by many. Some would take the time to fill their canteens with water, while others would stroll off in search of fruit or vegetables. No apple orchard was ever ignored, for although the quality of this fruit was poor at the South it was much more acceptable than the meagre ration; cherry trees were stormed and stripped; in fact, every eatable thing was devoured that came within grasp.

The saddle-horses appreciated the long halts, for they were allowed to graze by the roadside after oats had been eaten from the nosebags. The rest was none the less welcome to the mule-teams, and they "he-hawed" and "he-hawed" until the midday meal was forthcoming. When the order was given to "fall in" it seemed, in the confusion of slinging knapsacks, blankets and canteens, as if to get into column and on the march would be a work of hours; but in a few moments of time the men would be in order in the middle of the road, and at the command "Forward!" would tramp along in the best of cheer.

A halt was oftentimes obligatory, and instead of being an interval of rest would be a period of severe labor.   A swampy spot in a road was sometimes reached that could not be crossed until corduroyed.   Then axes were distributed, and the men, under the direction of officers, would cut down trees and, dragging them forward and placing them side by side across the road, would make it passable for the wagon trains.   Or perhaps the Rebs had been indulging in their well-known accomplishment of burning a bridge; then both the labor and skill of the Union troops would be called into requisition.   In a limited time their willing hands would get together a bridge which, if not in architecture "a thing of beauty," was a structure over which they could march with safety.

A Roadside Argument.

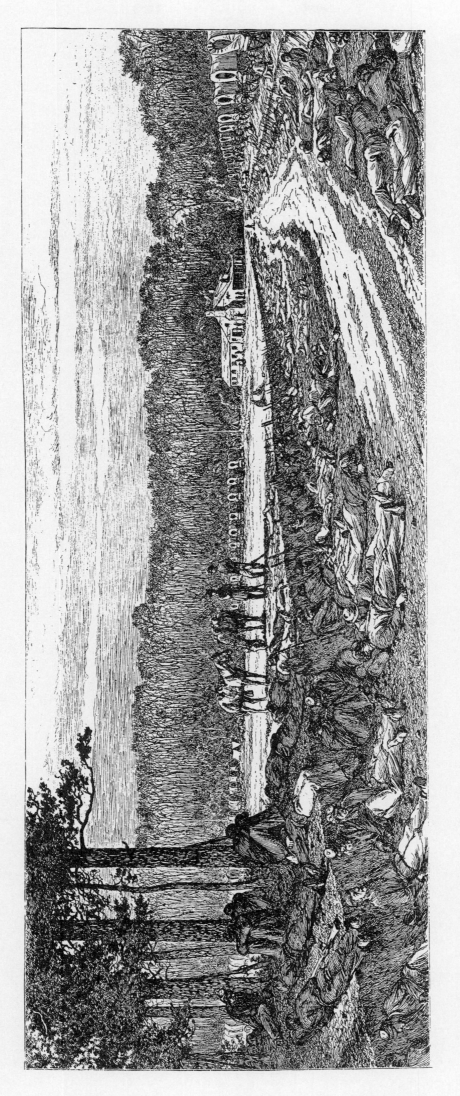

A TWENTY MINUTES' HALT.

XLIII.

WASHING DAY.

A Tale of a Tub.

OLDIERS' clothing became much soiled and worn, especially during an active campaign; yet they were expected at all times to keep their uniforms in reasonable repair and all of their clothing as clean as circumstances would admit of. The facilities of winter camp made their duties of easy performance, but when on the march the task became a much more difficult one.

A soldier's cabin was considered incomplete in its appointments unless furnished with a home-made washtub. These were made from barrels, cut down half way, with the exception of one stave at each side, which were left longer than the rest, to have holes cut through and serve as handles. The tubs when complete were much lighter and more convenient to move about than those made for household purposes.

No special time was set aside for washing, except that fair weather was taken advantage of. It was quite an amusing sight to see the stalwart fellows scattered about in the camp streets, bending over the washtubs. In most instances the gray shirt sleeves would be rolled to the elbow, and the clothes washed and rinsed with the skill of a laundress. After being deftly wrung out, coats, trousers and underclothing would be laid over logs to drain, and afterward hung upon lines stretched from hut to hut. The great numbers of garments as they fluttered in the wind and dried into brightness made an odd and pretty scene.

At the Brookside.

Ironing was a luxury that had to be dispensed with; all the soldiers could do after the clothing was washed was to stretch and smooth it into as respectable an appearance as possible.

As might be expected, there was much mending to be done, and most of the soldiers carried a supply of needles and thread. They were able to mend, darn and sew on buttons, and many, by constant practice, were able in time to do quite expert work.

During the summer march, sun, rain and dust and the contact with twigs and briers soon ruined the uniforms, and the men often presented a forlorn and battered appearance, as opportunities for cleaning and repairing were few. Washing was done hastily during the short halts, the clothes getting only (as the soldiers put it) "a lick and a promise." Time for drying was not to be thought of, and shirts and socks and bandanna handkerchiefs were often attached to the muskets, and fluttered and dried in the breeze as the soldiers marched along. The ever-rising clouds of dust did not improve the color of the washed garments, but the brave fellows learned early to live without the luxuries of private life, and accepted gratefully any comforts that came to them, however slight they might be.

Many times when moving along behind the Union breastworks I have seen a great variety of clothes hanging out to dry. Some would be hung across the top of the pup tents, some on the ends of the ridge-poles, and others scattered about on low limbs of trees. Advantageous as these opportunities seemed, however, the clothes were often perforated by bullets.

Clothing of the officers was washed by the colored servants; and as there were no "boiled shirts" and no ironing the duty was easily performed.

Washing Day in Camp.

CLOTHES-DRYING ON THE MARCH.

XLIV.

CONFEDERATE CHARGES.

Over the Breastworks.

HATEVER else may be said of the Southern soldiers, their soldierly qualities were very remarkable. One of their finest characteristics was the dashing bravery with which they would attack the most formidable positions or forces, so that their charges—while often withstood, effectively met, or successfully countered by our own men—were always regarded with a wholesome respect, even a reasonable fear.

The magnificent charge of the Rebel army under Albert Sydney Johnston at Shiloh, or Pittsburg Landing, almost destroyed the Union army on the first day, and gave to our Western soldiers the first significance of the desperate bravery of their antagonists. The attack by Van Dorn on the fortifications of Corinth, held by Gen. Rosecrans, was also a brilliant charge. The Southerners fought with reckless spirit, and retired after terrible slaughter with naught but honor left. The charge and turning movement of Bragg's army upon ours at Stone River will always deserve mention in military history as one of the most effective efforts of the war.

The advance of the Confederates under Bragg at Chickamauga was perhaps the greatest of all charges made in the West, and would have been fatal to the Union army had it not been for the heroic defense of that great soldier, Geo. H. Thomas, appropriately named the "Rock of Chickamauga." The charge by Gen. Hood on our works at Franklin, though an ill-judged and reckless movement, will hold prominent place in the annals of our war, for defeat could not sully the record of men who had made such noble sacrifices.

The Army of the Potomac also experienced the prowess in attack of the Confederate armies. The first of the great series was the charge made at Fair Oaks, when our army was made to realize that to capture the Rebel capital would be no child's play. The charge at Beaver Dam, and the terrific attacks made at Gaines' Mill, Glendale, Charles City Cross Roads, White Oak Swamp, and on other fields during our change of base from the Chickahominy to the James gave further evidence of fearless fury; while the culminating charge on the Union position at Malvern Hill, even though disastrous to the Confederates, proved that defeat did not lessen their valor. The charge of Longstreet's veterans at the battle of the Second Bull Run, when he turned and drove back the left wing of General Pope's army, was perhaps as bloody an attack as any made by the enemy, but victory, as in other instances, compensated for the terrible loss.

The great charge made by Stonewall Jackson at Chancellorsville was second only to Pickett's famous charge at Gettysburg, and was a success because the over-confidence and carelessness of General Hooker and some of our corps commanders made a surprise possible. This advance and attack were made with bold valor, and promised for a time to destroy the Union army. Troops were brought later, however, from other portions of the field, and our position was at last maintained.

The battle of Gettysburg is famous for more desperate and gallant charges than any single battle of the great war. Here came the culmination of the efforts of Lee's army when it for the last time threw itself so recklessly against the Union line. Subsequent battles occurred in other localities, but never again was life so prodigally spent.

The charge of the first day on the position held by our First and Eleventh Corps at Seminary Ridge, although finally disastrous to us, gave time for General Meade in retiring to secure the much more advantageous position of Cemetery Ridge. Although our force was inferior, the losses of Lee's advance corps were enormous, for our men made one of the most gallant defenses of the war. The charge of General Longstreet on the left of the Union army on the second day was just as valorous as that of the first, but not so brilliant in results; circumstances were against the Confederates, as the most of our army had then concentrated on the field. The charges made upon the position at Cemetery Gate and Culp's Hill at nightfall were bloody and stubbornly prolonged, but fate was against the attacking forces; for, although success first promised, the tenacious courage of the Union troops turned the tide.

The charge of Pickett's force on the third day will go down in history as the most resolute and daring attack ever made against the Union armies. Lee has often been criticized as lacking judgment in allowing this attack to be made, but there was another side to the question before the event settled it, and Lee, although a bold commander, was not a reckless one. Even when the splendid army of brave men under Pickett were ready to advance, both Lee and Longstreet hesitated to give the word, fearing that the desperate venture would prove a forlorn hope. But after two hours of cannonading our center from a hundred guns the word was reluctantly given, and a gallant body moved to death, never wavering till our converging batteries and the showers of bullets from behind the Union breastworks cut them down in ranks.

The after-sight, at the point where they turned, was simply terrible. The Confederate dead lay in long lines, as if a giant reaper had been driven over the ground to reap a human harvest. Nothing but admiration ought ever to be felt for the discipline, the splendid courage, of these brave men; while posterity will wonder at the misdirected zeal which brought forth such valor in so unworthy a cause. We shall gain another view of this grand charge in the next chapter, on Field Artillery.

Pickett's Charge.

Ricketts-Charge—July 3." 1863,
"Scene at the Grove of Trees."

A GALLANT DEED OF ARMS.

BUELL AT PITTSBURG LANDING.

XLV

AMING THE BATTERIES.

Watching the Shot.

HETHER in camp, on the march, or on the field of battle, there was a strength, an evident power in the artillery service that left an impression on the mind of the spectator not liable to be effaced, and no scenes in war are more terribly suggestive than an array of batteries in position, ready to open fire at the word of command. The preparatory movements are full of excitement and anxiety as the guns are wheeled into battery and unlimbered. Each man and horse knows his allotted position, and performs his duties with the exactness of an automaton, but with an elastic intelligence.

Perhaps the battle of Gettysburg afforded the best opportunity for study of this branch of the service, for owing to the splendid defensive position and the open ground in front our artillery was able to show more fully the effect of its power than at any other engagement during the war. On the first day, July 1st, the Confederates had the advantage, driving back our advance from the village of Gettysburg and securing the best position, on Seminary Hill; on the second day there was much hard fighting, but the enemy made no serious gain, while our line was concentrated along Cemetery Ridge.

I remember most vividly the third—the last—day of the great battle. Just at daylight, with the morning's red glow in the east, and the country covered as yet far as the eye could reach with a veil of smoke from the camp-fires, we were sitting about, eating breakfast and discussing a continuation of the fight by the enemy. Suddenly a faint sound of cannon was heard from beyond Culp's Hill, and the crash of a shell above the guns posted between the hill and the cemetery instantaneously followed. It seemed like a morning greeting from the Rebs—an inquiry, "*Are you at home?*" No return was fired for several minutes, and the enemy continued a persistent dropping of shells on the crest of the Cemetery Ridge, as if insisting upon a response to their summons. But the Union line soon awoke, and sent a few shots forward; then, as if by common consent, both sides settled down to steady fire, and the ground trembled with the continuous concussion.

To the right of our line of guns, in the woods of Culp's Hill, deadly work was doing, for the noise of musketry was incessant now, rising to a grand roar, then dying down to an intermittent rattle. It was a fierce, wild music, with crash of cannon and shell for the tremendous bass. I watched the line of guns through my glass, and wondered at the discipline and coolness displayed in that iron hail. I could see the stricken ones go down— men and horses attached to the limbers and caissons; and could distinguish the efforts of the survivors as they dragged the dead and wounded to one side.

Behind the batteries were long lines of infantry in support, hugging the ground for protection, as no breastworks sheltered them. Further to the left could be seen a nest of batteries posted around the Cemetery Gate—the center of our position—which presented the appearance of an active volcano as the clouds of smoke rolled away in masses. The white tombstones, among which guns were scattered, could be seen quite distinctly, and one could but wonder at the strange commingling of the living and the dead. From four o'clock in the morning until ten I watched this giant double cannonade, and then saw it gradually lessen and die down as if the enemy had become disheartened. The terrific musketry fire along Culp's Hill soon receded too, and by midday the sun looked down on a comparatively peaceful scene. Upon Seminary Hill, the ridge beyond the town of Gettysburg from which we had been driven on the first day, could be seen with the glass the enemy's line of guns, mere dots in cultivated fields. They stretched for miles to the left in a great circle, quiet for the time but ominous of disaster. Facing them, on Cemetery Ridge, toward Little Round Top Hill, stood our continuous line of guns, silent and grim; and down the slope in front were our blue lines of infantry, with tattered flags softly fluttering.

The varied fighting of the morning having made no essential change in relative positions, General Lee determined to disable our artillery, and then carry the Cemetery Ridge by assault. He placed 115 guns on Seminary Hill in front of Longstreet's and Hill's corps; these fronted our 80 guns in line and 120 more held in reserve. Quiet prevailed until about half-past one o'clock, when a sudden roar broke out along the center of the enemy's line; and in an instant of time our whole front, from Culp's Hill to Round Top, was belching fire and smoke. Great columns of flame shot up from bursting caissons, and for more than a mile on the crest of the hill innumerable shells from the enemy's guns sought out the weak places in the Union lines. The terrible cannonading failed to shake our lines or cripple our artillery, and when it died down a new feeling of security came to the infantry. Although it had been of but two hours' duration it had seemed like an age.

A pause ensued. I could not see what was going on below the front of our ridge, but soon, from the rapid recurrent fire of the Union artillery along the crest, it was reasonable to conclude that the enemy were attacking the front of our position—as indeed they were. It was the magnificent charge of Pickett's division. The awful roar of our musketry in front of the guns now crashed in with the bellowing batteries. Pickett's division of 4,000 Virginians, with 9,000 supporting troops, came straight at our artillery center on Cemetery Ridge and into the focus of our converging fire from right and left wings. It was a gallant deed of arms—the crisis of the great battle; but doomed to be a splendid failure. Even such a column could not withstand the terrific Union fire of artillery and infantry—front, right and left. It melted away—killed, wounded, captured, retreating. And the battle was ended.

I could not visit this portion of the line until the next morning, but even then the sight was ghastly. A great convulsion of nature could not have made more universal destruction; everything bore the mark of death and ruin. The whole slope was massed with dead horses—sixty-two lying in one battery. Most of the human dead had been buried, but even yet in front of a line of slight breastworks, where infantry had been posted, the ground was so covered with Confederate dead that it was difficult to step without treading on them. The earth was ploughed and torn by the terrible artillery fire, and under fences and in corners, and anywhere that slight shelter offered, the dead lay in dozens, showing the spots fought for. The destructive effect of artillery fire, both on animate and inanimate opposing force, could never have a more effective and frightful illustration.

Going into Battery Under Fire

PULLING INTO POSITION.

XLVI

RETURNING FROM OUTPOST DUTY.

Packing Up

INSTEAD of thinking it a hardship, soldiers looked forward with pleasure to detail for picket duty. There was a fascination about the life on the line that came of the relief from routine duties of winter camp; and orders for return to camp—even though they meant more comfort—would be sorrowfully received. The men were often soaked with rain and half-frozen with sleet and snow, even when not in danger from the foe; and the reserve pickets were perhaps roused up in the night to prepare for anticipated attack: but the newness and novelty of this life seemed to compensate for the hardships, and the knapsacks were always sadly packed for the return.

The new detail (usually a regiment) would be sent to take possession of the rough shelters; and squads would be sent out to relieve the pickets, who would march back with knapsacks, blankets, and other traps slung over the shoulders. With a regretful look at the old shelters where so many pleasant hours had been spent, they would start on their way back in column formation, and, arms at will, they would tramp over snowy roads and fields till camp was reached.

At last the old camp home was sighted, and a former line of associations began to arise. Footsteps quickened in the approach of the last half-mile. Then they came to the general camp. As they marched through the camp streets, past the huts, many a jest was heard on their soiled and bedraggled appearance, for soldiers never miss a chance for a joke. How familiar it looked as they halted at the end of their

Making Preparations for a Frost

own company street, although no smoke was seen issuing from the mud chimneys and the old log shelters had an air of desertion!   But on dismissal "the boys" quickly proceeded to set their houses in order.   The cheerless heaps of cold gray ashes were removed from the hearth, and soon a roaring fire glowed in their place, and the cheap newspaper pictures on the walls, in the light of the blazing pine wood, appeared like old friends.

Knapsacks and traps were soon unpacked, the pine needles in the bunks shaken up, and blankets spread.   The canteen was hung on the proper peg; the musket found its old place on the wall; and, last of all, the old frying pan and tin cup were hung near the fire, ready for use.   By this time the men became possessed of the usual soldier's appetite, and made their way through mud and slush to the sutler's tent, at the lower end of the camp. Others were there before them, and, as the whole throng stood clamoring over the pine counter, quite an interesting picture was made.   Canned goods and other luxuries were quickly bought at perhaps a cost of half the monthly pay; and then, eager for a feast, all hurried back to the huts.   Supper was hastily prepared, and the soldiers revelled in the enjoyment of a hot and substantial meal.

Officers' houses had meanwhile been put in order by the servants, and were soon in readiness to receive any friends who might call to partake of the hospitalities of the mess. Crackling fires and savory odors spoke of the cook's endeavor toward hospitality, and the announcement of a ready dinner came none too soon.   Old comrades dropped in,; stories of picket-life were rife, and the atmosphere of camp was not long in resuming its former attractions.

Old camp-work was now renewed.   Drills, guard-mount, and dress parade at first seemed irksome: but force of habit quickly made ancient duty the natural thing; the recreations and pleasures of the camp brightened the routine; and before many days the tour on the picket line became a memory.

Home Again

BACK TO WINTER CAMP

XLVII.

ARMY UNIFORMS.

A Specimen Pair.

TYLES and varieties of uniform, in both the Union and Confederate armies, were numberless during the war.

In the long interval of peace that preceded the secession of the Southern States, the military force of the country consisted of a small regular army, scattered about on the frontier among the Indian tribes and at the ports on the seacoast. The uniforms then were quite plain and substantial. The infantry wore dark blue coats trimmed with light blue cord and brass buttons, light blue trousers with full spring over the instep, and dark felt hats ornamented with black ostrich plume and badge in form of a brass bugle. The cavalry uniform was a dark blue jacket with brass buttons and yellow trimmings, light blue trousers with yellow trimmings, and dark blue cap with badge of crossed brass sabres on the top. The artillery uniform was similar to that of the cavalry, except that the trimmings were red and the badge on hats and caps was composed of two small brass cannons in crossed position.

The militia of the different States were uniformed in various ways, but gray was the prevailing color. When the war note sounded out, the volunteers from loyal States moved toward the front in an infinite variety of uniforms. Most of them were based on the stylish and natty chasseur costume of the French army. A few regiments adopted the Zouave costume, or modifications of it. Southern uniforms were generally of gray color, with but little variety of shape. Blue, yellow or red trimmings were used, however, to indicate the different arms of the service.

In the early part of the war young men were much taken with bright uniforms and glittering trappings, and when recruiting at the North the ranks of a command were soon filled when a showy uniform had been adopted. Of course in the early pride that filled the young men's breasts neither officers nor men dreamed of change; and when the authorities at Washington, for economy's sake, issued the plain blouse and trousers, loud lamentations were heard at relinquishing the fine uniforms.

Regiments from large Eastern cities indulged more in showy uniforms than those from the West, and when they started for the front made a striking appearance. Among the handsomest were the Fifth New York (Duryea's Zouaves), the Hawkins Zouaves, the Fire Zouaves, the Brooklyn Fourteenth, the Collis Zouaves, and many who wore the French chasseur costume of dark blue coat, flowing blue trousers and "kepi," or small blue cap with straight visor. Time proved these showy uniforms to be less serviceable than the plainer ones, as a few months of field service dulled their brightness, and marching and fighting in woods and underbrush tore and destroyed them. Bright costumes were also a mark for the enemy, and many of the gaily caparisoned regiments that went early to the front suffered the penalty of heavy loss. The Western regiments wore the regular army uniform and black felt hat.

One of the most conspicuous badges was worn by the Pennsylvania Bucktails. Attached to the side of hat or cap was a buck's tail, with the white side turned outward, which served for so positive a mark that many of the troops fell, shot through the head.

Many soldiers indulged individual taste in the ornamentation of uniforms; among other conceits several well-polished buckles were fastened on the strap of the cap in front. Many regiments wore leather leggins over the lower part of trousers and shoe; but those not possessed of such luxuries thrust the trousers into their heavy gray stockings, and thus escaped the mud which, when caked on the inside of the trousers leg, was a great impediment to marching—to say nothing of cleanliness.

A long light blue overcoat was given to the troops in winter. It was made with a cape, which was generally thrown over the head in stormy weather. An India rubber poncho was also issued, and lent great protection when the men were obliged to sleep on wet ground. In a driving storm it served good purpose also when buttoned around the neck and allowed to fall over the shoulders.

The general officers of the Union army in most instances wore a dark blue frock coat, with brass buttons and shoulder straps denoting their rank; dark blue trousers and riding boots; and a black felt hat, with black and gold mixed cord and tassel, and brass laurel leaf encircling the letters "U. S." on the front. Members of staffs suited individual taste as to headgear, but as a general thing wore the regular army uniform.

The general officers of the Southern army wore a dark gray uniform, with sleeves heavily trimmed with gold braid, and the designation of rank on the collar instead of the shoulder; a gray felt hat with gold cord and tassel was worn also, or a gray cap with visor. Top boots were desirable when obtainable, but money often failed with which to make the purchase; the Rebs, however, never disdained to confiscate any that came in their way. The color of the Confederate uniforms oftentimes lent protection from Union fire, as it was impossible to distinguish them from rocks, fences and trees, especially when the battle smoke was dense; but in the bright uniforms of the Union army the contrasts in color only brought them out in greater relief. As the war advanced the Southerners found it difficult to obtain clothing, and would often exchange their rags for the good clothing of the Union prisoners. Even the dead and wounded were stripped, and it was not an unusual sight to see dead figures lying perfectly nude. In all cases shoes were taken. This was, no doubt, a fair and often necessary spoil of war. In both armies, however, there were too often those who hesitated not to search the pockets of the dead merely for the chance of gain; but when there was opportunity the dead were decently buried, and the parties in charge of this duty protected their helpless bodies from desecration.

However varied and gay the uniforms started out for service, it did not take many months of weather and war to reduce all to "pretty much of a muchness," so far as color was concerned. As the days of "shoddy" advanced in the shops of the North the veterans of the field, whether "boys in blue" or "boys in gray," became gradually softened and harmonized to a soft butternut brown.

An Old Campaigner.

ONE OF THE BUCKTAILS.

Officers & Non. Com.
Penn' Zouaves. Camp Pardee Va April 17th 1862. E Forbes

A GROUP OF PORTRAITS.

187

XLVIII

CROSSING THE PONTOONS.

Sharp Work

T a casual glance a pontoon bridge seemed a slight affair, but the greater part of them used during the war were carefully and substantially constructed. In the early days, however, a style was adopted which a few trials proved to be insecure. Its supports, instead of being made of wooden scows, were formed of inflated India rubber bags. A scene comes back to me where one was laid across a river, and the general in command came down with his staff to the bank to witness the crossing, as did many stragglers, wagon men and others not doing military duty. A cavalry band of music first made its appearance, followed by a brigade of mounted troops, who were glorious with fluttering guidons and bright colors and noisy with jingling accoutrements. The band struck up "The Mocking Bird" as it marched on to the bridge, and the column followed in order. They had gone but a short distance when the motion and weight of the horses caused the bridge to sway from side to side. Great consternation prevailed. The music suddenly ceased; the musicians carefully dismounted and stood for a few moments, that the bridge might settle into place; then they cautiously moved on, followed by the cavalrymen slowly leading their horses, and all reached the opposite bank in safety. All this was fun for the spectators, from whom came peal after peal of laughter until the journey across the river was accomplished. I believe this was the last time that style of bridge was made use of.

A most interesting movement in my army experience was the crossing of the James River during the advance of the Army of the Potomac on Petersburg. The longest pontoon bridge that was built during the war was here made use of, and was crossed by the left wing of the army, while the right wing made use of steamboats further up the river near City Point.

Crossing the James River.

I took position near the head of the bridge, and watched the column in its course. Regiments of infantry came surging along at route step, ragged and footsore, their faces much discolored with powder-stain and dust. Officers were scarcely discernible from privates. The latter were laden with all kinds of traps and plunder, and the pack mules and horses had more than the usual burden. Everything bore the terrible imprint of a month's hard fighting, and made sad contrast to the hopeful men who in new uniforms had so recently started out from the winter camp near Culpepper, under the great commander, Grant. The forces had been terribly reduced in numbers, but with the same determined spirit that always pervaded the troops, even in defeat, the column marched promptly and cheerfully forward. Out from the shore was a fleet of war vessels to protect the bridge, and upon one of them was a group of newly and jauntily dressed sailors, who had evidently experienced no hard service. With open-eyed wonder they watched the progress of the column, and laughed loudly at the grotesqueness that misfortune had given to many groups of soldiers. There was indeed great contrast in the two arms of the service, but my heart went out in sympathy to the poor fellows with tattered clothing and blackened faces. All day the throng poured over the bridge, and with each moment came changing scenes. This was heightened by the many steamboats and sailing crafts anchored in the river, and on the steep bluff of the farther bank arose Fort Powhatan, an abandoned earthwork, which had been thrown up by the Rebs to dispute the ascent of the stream. Low muttering like distant thunder was after a time heard from the southwest; the advance had arrived at Petersburg.

But before long the sun sank to rest, and evening brought a beautiful picture. Hundreds of bright camp fires on the river bank lit up the bridge, which, with the colored lights flung out from the vessels, looked like fairyland. The trains clattered noisily along, and the many sounds of a moving army rose in the still night air, and were accompanied by the boom of distant cannon—that solemn suggestion of deadly conflict. Long into the night I watched this moving panorama, until from sheer exhaustion I sought repose.

Sometimes the crossing of a river was a matter of grave difficulty, and accomplished only with heavy loss. The building of the bridge and crossing of the Rappahannock at Fredricksburg, under General Burnside, preliminary to the great battle, brought about serious encounter, and was the bloodiest event of like character during the war.

The enemy's position was a strong one, being under cover of houses and commanding both banks of the river; so that, from the time the first pontoon boat was pushed into the water, our men were compelled to work in a shower of bullets, which came without warning through the dense fog. As fast as the poor fellows fell others promptly took their places, and the structure gradually crept out on the still water until progress was no longer possible, it having become absolutely fatal to approach the line of completion.

Then a terrific bombardment was ordered, and for more than an hour an awful shower of shot and shell was poured into the ill-fated town. But most of the missiles passed over the heads of the Confederates, as they crouched behind outhouses and fences. When the fire was slackened, the following plan was adopted: A number of boats were filled with troops who, on command, pushed for the opposite shore and, with a yell, bounded out on the slippery bank and, with quick formation, charged up the steep ascent. They soon cleared the ground of Rebs, who retreated to a plain in rear of the town, where they awaited the advance of the Union columns. It was a successful but costly crossing.

There were other dangers menacing pontoon bridges, which were difficult to guard against. Most of the Southern rivers were narrow, and rapid in times of flood, and the eyes of the workers were always cast up stream in apprehension of tree trunks and other dangerous drift of a torrent. Anchor ropes would strain and lift with the tremendous pressure, and sometimes the bridge would break and a section be swept down stream. Willing workers were in readiness and, dashing into the water—often waist deep— would quickly repair the damage.

I have often heard veterans refer to these scenes and say they never could forget the exciting pontoon crossings, with the tramping troops and the rumbling of the guns on the plank floor of the frail, sway- ing structures.

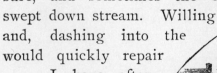

Making A Landing.

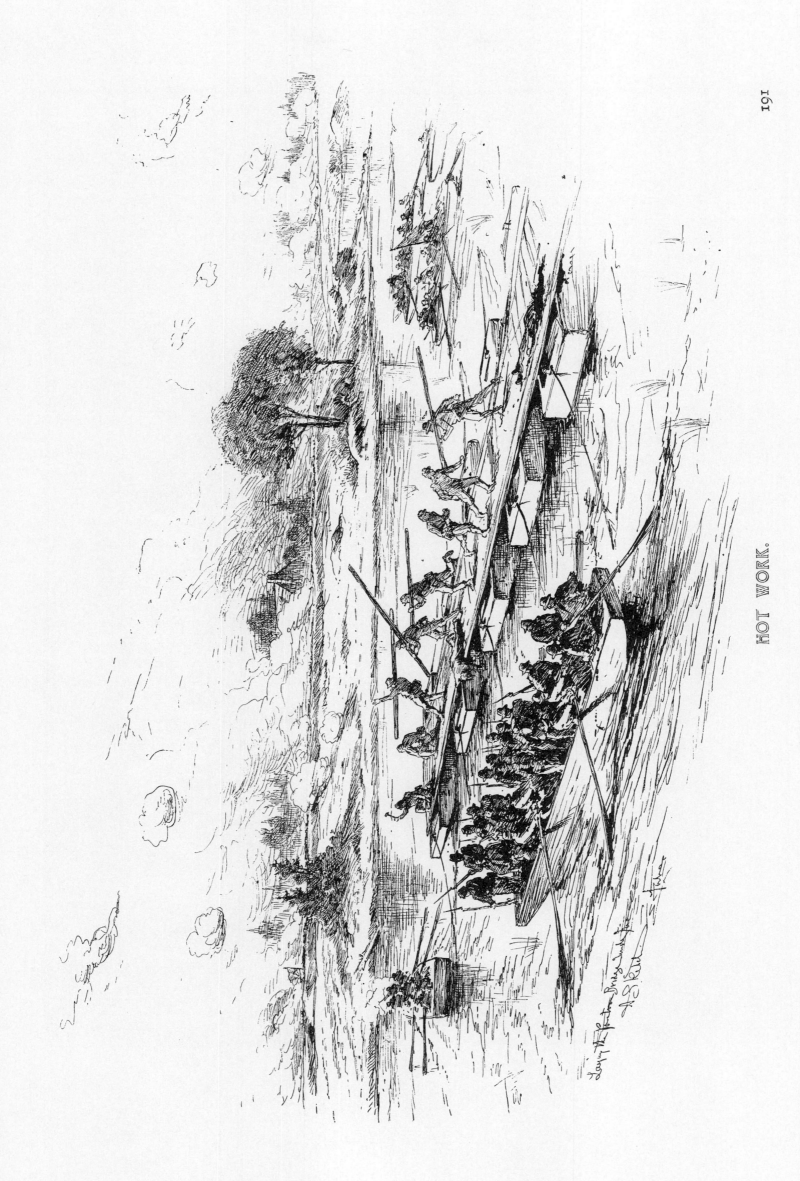

HOT WORK.

ROSECRANS AT STONE RIVER.

XLIX.

THE SIGNAL SERVICE.

On the Mountain-Top.

TO those unfamiliar with the method of transmitting news by flags, which was made use of in our late war, it had much that was interesting, for, when railroads had been destroyed and telegraphic communication cut off, it was often the only means of sending information; and in many instances it enabled a commander to frustrate the plans of the enemy.

The signal corps of our army was composed of soldiers who had received special training for the service. They moved mounted, with the advance of the army, squads locating themselves on the way in elevated positions, at intervals of about seven or eight miles. They were thus enabled to signal back from one station to another until intelligence reached headquarters. They were provided with the usual soldiers' supplies, also flags, telescopes and torches.

The sign-language is made by three movements of a flag or torch—one to the right, one to the left and one downward to the front. This seems almost too simple to be intelligible, but the repeated and combined movements are so complicated as to make a complete alphabet, and full messages can be sent and comprehended.

The upper left-hand sketch (1) of the group on page 195 represents a signal station on the summit of Pony Mountain, near Culpepper, Va., during the spring of 1864, just before the advance of the Army of the Potomac into the Wilderness. The signal station was made of pine logs, with a rough flooring on top, and was surrounded with a hedge of pine branches, which broke the wind and served the purpose of a partial screen from the enemy. It was made quite substantial and picturesque, from the fact that the soldiers were in winter quarters and had ample time to construct it; but when the army was on the march the roughest kind of stations were improvised.

The signal officer in charge invited me to spend a day with him, and on ascending the station I could see the picket lines of the Union army in the foreground and camps stretched to the right and left for miles. Beyond the Rapidan River, at the foot of the distant mountain, a distance of eight miles, General Lee's army was encamped. Through the telescope I could plainly discern the figures of the Confederate soldiers as they moved about camp, performing their duties. I could see men cooking their meals over fires, others feeding their horses; and at one point close to the river a body of men was throwing up breastworks, evidently preparing for a possible advance of our army. On the summit of this mountain was a signal station (indicated by black dot in sketch), and the men could plainly be seen waving their flags. Our flagman, whose flag appears at the bottom of this sketch, was more cautious, flagging all intelligence behind the station, out of sight of the enemy.

The sketch (2) immediately below the foregoing is a scene in the attic of a farmhouse near Williamsport, Md., during the pursuit of Lee's army by General Meade. This position was on the advance lines of the Union army, and through the glass could be plainly seen the Confederate columns three miles distant, beating a hasty retreat toward the Potomac River. Their wagon teams moved slowly and heavily, as if laden with spoils captured from the Dutch farmers of Pennsylvania. The flagman who waved the news from this to the next station sat in the scuttle-hole above the observing officer, with legs and feet only in view. While making my sketch I noted the old spinning-wheel and bits of quaint furniture that the attic contained, and thought the turmoil of the moment a heartrending contrast to the peaceful days of patient spinning in the past.

The lower right-hand sketch (3) illustrates a signal officer and men whom I met just after the commencement of the battle of Gettysburg. They were hastening to the top of a high hill known as Little Round Top, to locate a station.

The signal station in the tree (4) I sketched at the battle of Chancellorsville, Va. Very little of either army could be seen at this point, as the battle was fought in dense woods surrounding the hamlet. Yet it was a wonderful sight. Woods that had been set on fire by the cartridges were burning for miles, and as the light smoke ascended to the clouds it looked as if a great city was being consumed. High up in the air were round puffs of white smoke, made from the bursting of shells, and the continuous roar of cannon and musketry made the earth tremble.

The station shown in the upper right-hand sketch (5) on the roof of a house, was established at the battle of Cedar Mountain, Va., and was directly on the line of battle. While shells exploded and bullets rained about the brave men on the roof, the family of the house fled in terror to the cellar, and I, after making a hasty sketch, retreated into safety.

The manner of signalling with a torch is also illustrated (6) in the group of sketches. The lights could often be seen all night throughout the mountains, and except for the regular movements which an observer in time takes note of, one might think them mysterious balls of fire moving about from some unknown cause.

The signal corps did important service during General Hood's raid in the rear of Sherman's army, then occupying Atlanta, just before the "March to the Sea." The enemy, upon positive orders from Jefferson Davis, sought to disable Sherman by destroying railroads and seizing supplies in his rear, the most of which were at Altoona. Sherman signalled at Vining Station over the heads of the Southern army for General Corse, who was at Rome, to hasten back to the assistance of the garrison at Altoona; but when Sherman reached Kenesaw Mountain he learned at the signal station that there had been no response to his call. This gave him at first great anxiety, but he soon caught a glimpse of the tell-tale flag, which signalled "Corse is here." Some hours after news came that the enemy had been repulsed, but Corse wounded. It was not known how severely, but the next day, amid apprehension of his danger, the following characteristic note was received from Corse: "I am short a cheek bone and an ear, but can whip all hell yet."

During the battle of Kenesaw Mountain, General Sherman noticed a group of the enemy observing him and his surrounding men with glasses. Anticipating a fire from them, he ordered a battery close by to fire upon the group, and rode down the line. He heard the volleys fired; but had no knowledge that the shots had taken effect until he returned at night to a signal station near his headquarters. The signal officer then told him that by study he had learned the ene- my's "key," and had about noon read a signal of theirs, "Send an am- bulance for General Polk's body." From this they knew that General Polk had been killed, and learned afterward that he had been struck at the time of General Sher- man's order. General Sherman, however, could not even tell in the dis- tance that the men were officers — much less who any of them were. The order was simply a matter of course, and Sherman rode away be- fore his orders to fire were executed.

GROUP OF SIGNAL STATIONS

L.

ABANDONED PICKET HUTS.

Buzzards' Roost.

THE sudden coming upon an old picket hut bereft of its inmates gives rise to many tender thoughts and memories. Where are they who had so carefully fashioned the shelter and sat in comradeship about the door? Groaning in hospitals perhaps, or scattered in lonely graves by the wayside. Silence pervades the little structure, and naught remains to mark the interior save the dead gray ashes from their last bright fire. Crows and turkey buzzards haunt it now, making a perch of the roof and passing in and out without fear. A regret, too, comes over one that the result of so much hard labor should serve so temporary a purpose.

In many instances the characteristics of the former occupants of deserted huts could be determined by the way the structures were built and finished, some being carefully made to shed rain and effectively protect the inmates from snow, while others were carelessly thrown up with only the roughest consideration of comfort.

Strolling out in the woods one day I found an abandoned hut which was built near a road where a small stream crossed. It was quite a substantial structure, and had been made by first driving into the ground twelve feet apart two posts with upper ends forked; a stout pole with ends resting in the forks had been placed across, and from this slender poles rested and slanted to the ground. Over these, pine boughs had been scattered, which gave to it an air of completeness; but desolate it looked now under the red sunset sky. The pine beds inside were just as the occupants had left them, and among some large round stones were ashes and débris of the camp fire, with the improvised support for the kettle still in place. A rabbit startled by my steps darted off through the bushes and across the stream, and a flock of crows rose disturbed in the twilight and sailed away, slowly uttering their dismal cry.

Forsaken

Thus it was wherever the army had camped for a length of time, these deserted shelters stood as remembrancers, and their lonely and forsaken aspect had a living significance that pen could not indite or language portray.

LI.

EXHAUSTION.

Played Out.

CAME upon a most pathetic picture of an exhausted soldier as I was riding along a road to Petersburg during its siege, whose attitude suggested utter abandon, and whose pallid face caused me to think him dead. I dismounted and found him motionless upon his back, with bare feet and legs hanging over the bank. His old grey blanket was around his body, a gun was slung over the left shoulder, and his haversack, containing untouched rations, rested on his hip. I began to sketch so interesting a subject, and at first supposed him to be a white man; but as I carefully drew his lineaments I noticed the unmistakable fulness of feature and wavy black hair which showed him to be a mulatto, and probably a member of a negro regiment in the Eighteenth Corps.

As I continued my work I was suddenly startled at a trembling of the eyelids and the languid opening of his eyes. He looked at me in a dreamy fashion, then drowsily closed his eyes again as if too exhaused to interest himself in anything, and remained motionless. I finished my sketch and left him in the care of those who would look after him.

With no reference to the many who died in the service, of deprivation and exposure, this was but one of thousands whose strength was taxed to the utmost and health no doubt permanently impaired. With slight rations to sustain strength for arduous campaign work, on the move from daylight till nightfall, over rough roads, through storm and swamps and underbrush, skirmishing and fighting at intervals, was it a marvel that thousands dropped by the wayside? Pitiful indeed they often looked as they lay stretched upon the ground with haggard, upturned faces, utterly indifferent to surroundings. When nearly overcome with sleep, they would often refuse to fall out, but resolutely stagger on with eyes half-closed, and after a time regain self-control until camp was reached at night. And perhaps even that halt would bring no respite, for orders to fortify the lines were often given. Picks and shovels were then distributed, and without an interval of rest the brave fellows would work at that. There were times when this work of marching and entrenching had to be continued for weeks, and under the strain I have seen officers and privates reduced to shadows of their former selves.

The life of cavalry and artillerymen was just as full of suffering, and I have seen the men asleep, swaying from side to side on their horses, and trusting to the instinct of their animals to keep them in column. Typhoid fever claimed numberless victims. It was in most cases the result of over-exertion, and many poor fellows were taken to the hospital, there to meet a linger- ing death.

201

PARADES AND DRILLS.

Cavalry Drill.

D ISCIPLINE in the army was never wholly relaxed, and to keep the troops up to the mark, routine of military work was necessary and continual. The infantry batallion-drill generally took place in a level pasture near camp. The troops would be first drawn up in line and then put through the manual of arms by the Colonel. Then they would break into columns of companies and go through a most interesting practice, though of complicated appearance to any but the professional soldier.

The cavalry drill was very fascinating and exciting, and the arrival of a brilliant regiment at the parade-ground always called forth the enthusiasm of spectators. The breaking into column, the advance at a trot with the accompaniment of the bugles, was a brilliant sight; even the horses seemed susceptible and dashed about with dilating nostrils and glittering eyes. But the charge was the grand culmination of the movements. Moving slowly across the ground at a walk, the regiment would wheel into line at the further end, then at the sound of the bugle would first advance at a walk—break into a trot—and finally, at the sound of "charge," the whole line would dash across the field at a gallop, sending up a cloud of dust and shaking the solid earth. The artillery-drill, although equally interesting, was not as rapid as that of the cavalry, because of the weight of the guns, but there was a grandeur in the movement of so many spirited, well-trained teams and heavy pieces, not seen in the other branches of the service. Target-firing was also practiced to a high degree of excellence.

Dress parade at close of day had also many attractive features both to troops and spectators. Regimental inspection brought forth erect figures, bright horses and clean guns; and when the inspecting officers dropped the ramrods in the soldiers' guns the sharp metallic sound, which proved them to be clean, fell cheerfully on their ears. Both inspection and guard-mount, however, showed the peculiarities of the different regiments. Some were poorly disciplined and slovenly, while others would appear in white gloves and orderly condition generally, and perform their duties with military dignity.

Still, lack of discipline and shiftless attire was not always a criterion of effectiveness on the field, for I call to mind a regiment whose appearance on parade-ground resembled that of a mob of tramps, but whose bravery shortly afterward against Stonewall Jackson at the battle of Port Republic was unequalled. Not always do "Fine feathers make fine birds." There is another saying, about the "deceitfulness of appearances,"—and sometimes, even under the yoke of laziness and thriftlessness, "a man's a man, for a' that!"

Inspection.

Double Quick March

Played Out.

LIGHTS AND SHADOWS.

LII.

THE FODDER QUESTION.

The Nose-Bag.

MOST difficult problem in our war was how to feed the animals attached to the different branches of the service. Facilities were better in the winter season, as most of the forces were connected with the base of supplies by railroads. There were exceptions to the rule, however, when all stores had to be hauled long distances over poor roads. This was often a terrible strain to the animals, and the dead horses and mules lying along the road attested the severity of the task.

When Chattanooga was besieged by Bragg, it was almost impossible to obtain supplies for man or beast, and hay and grain became so scarce that draught-animals died by hundreds. Those that survived were so weak that had a retreat been ordered all trains and batteries would necessarily have been abandoned, and it was not until communication had been established by the "Cracker Line" on the Tennessee River that the army was rescued from its perilous predicament.

The difficulty of hauling supplies over the mountains of East Tennessee was one of the greatest obstacles in holding Knoxville. But little could be obtained in the surrounding country because of its broken and wild character, and also because of the persistency with which bushwhackers attacked foraging parties.

During summer marches, animals were fed on standing grain, in fields by the roadside which in a few hours looked as if there had been a flight of locusts; and fields of standing corn would disappear like morning dew. Grain would sometimes be found cut and shocked. This was a most acceptable sight to the army, and would soon be swept away; but the poor farmers were pictures of consternation when they stood helpless and saw a whole summer's harvest disappear in an hour. In many instances grain had been gathered and stored, but the soldiers had no respect for the wayside barns and corncribs, and captured their contents when necessity urged and opportunity offered.

The passage of a great army was a severe lesson to the farmers of secession proclivities, and had many of them realized what war would bring them, I think they would have been less hot-headed in the political movement that brought it on. Although Sherman's march was a comparatively bloodless one, it brought more significance to the planters of the interior South than all the fighting that had previously taken place along the Border States, for, with the wide swath of destruction cut through nearly a thousand miles, came a realization and terror that distant descriptions could not have effected. It was long years before the damage of the marching columns was repaired, and solitary chimneys to this day still mark portions of its course.

One could form no conception of the quantity of forage necessary for an army until visiting a depot of supplies. Then could be seen thousands of bags of oats, stored under long sheds, and bales of hay piled almost "mountain high." And what scenes of noise and confusion the depots were! Long lines of trains of empty wagons would come from all directions, and amid shouts of drivers and braying of mules would be loaded and despatched to camp. Immense trains of cars packed to the doors would arrive continually and their stores soon melt away like snow in the warm south wind.

One unfamiliar with the labor of handling supplies would readily conclude that, after delivery at a camp depot, distribution would be easily accomplished; but in reality this was the most difficult part of the work, for the army corps were scattered over a great extent of country, and the mud in the roads was often so deep that wagon wheels sank hub-deep. I have watched them labor along at snail's pace in the yellow mire, through valleys and over barren hills, halting when a team was stalled, and then plunging and tugging slowly onward until camp was reached.

During an active summer campaign, although the roads were in better condition, the task of feeding the animals was an arduous one, and a never-ending source of anxiety to the officers and men of the quartermaster's department. When the armies were engaged in a rapid forward movement it was not always possible to bring up supplies of forage by rail. Then the country was scoured in all directions and all grain and forage was requisitioned. It was a perilous work, and many a lively fight ensued before the loaded trains could be driven back to camp. Sometimes when hay and grain were not attainable, animals were grazed in the pastures or in fields of rye and oats; but such fodder was a poor substitute for creatures so hard worked as the army draught-animals.

Often during a hard march the cavalry columns would leave the road and file into the fields. At the sound of the bugle each man would dismount, and holding the horses by the bridles would allow them to feed until hunger was satisfied. Then, at the order, they would mount, fall into line and take the road again, refreshed and ready for emergency.

Cavalrymen become much attached to their horses, and I have been much interested in watching their anxiety to get a nibble for the faithful beasts; and the real comfort they seemed to feel in their horses' enjoyment often made them careless of the enemy's horsemen within gunshot.

A HALT BY THE ROADSIDE.

BURNSIDE AT FREDERICKSBURG.

LIII.

A MUD MARCH.

Mired.

O CLAMOR of press and people during the great war became so exasperating to commanding generals and the authorities at Washington as "Why don't the army move?" The cry was incessant, and all except those in the service seemed to think that the great hosts could move in any direction, at any time, irrespective of local conditions or existing circumstances.

Thus matters stood in December, 1863, when the Army of the Potomac under General Burnside lay camped on the Heights of Falmouth, confronting General Lee, who was camped at Fredericksburg, on the opposite side of the Rappahannock River.

Our army at this time was in snug winter quarters, and cries for an advance came urgently from all directions. Roads were yet in good condition, for winter frosts with intervening rains had not rendered them impassable. Army officers realized that a few hours of changing weather might greatly transform conditions; and, when a command to advance came from Washington, orders to break camp were given with great reluctance. But the die was cast. "On to Richmond!" was the cry. So, huts were dismantled, tents struck, impedimenta packed, and the different corps marched on the roads towards the upper fords of the river. The warm December sun shone through the winter haze, and the air was as calm and peaceful as a June morning; yet the silvery cirrus clouds that stole across the sky looked inauspicious.

The troops were in fine spirits, and as I watched the columns of brave men hurry by I thought I had never seen them more vigorous and cheerful. The artillery and cavalry were in grand form, the animals especially so, having become much improved by the weeks of rest, no suggestions of the gaunt look—which came from previous strain—remaining. The mules looked well,—as in fact they always did—and were invaluable to the service, for they seemed scarcely susceptible to ill-fortune and were always a reliance. Altogether the Army of the Potomac was a magnificent column as it moved along the road toward Kelly's and the United States Ford. By afternoon the sun was dimmed by dense clouds, but the columns pushed on till nightfall. Then a halt was made for camp, and soon the fires lit up the country for miles around, and noises of the great throng resounded through the woods. But late in the evening pattering rain drops foreshadowed the morrow's march, and the blanket-wrapped troops lay down to sleep with doubts of what was to come.

They rose with early promptness, however, and, with steps somewhat less quick than the day before, filed into the roads which had not yet become difficult to travel. But the strong east wind soon brought the rain in torrents, and the roads that had been passable became quagmires. The infantry picked their way as they could, but were soon covered with yellow mud and soaked to the skin by the blinding rain. The artillery horses plunged onward, dashing up showers of yellow paste, which stuck to everything upon which it fell. Drivers and horses assumed the same color, and the guns almost lost distinctness of form. Witnessed through the clouds of vapor which rose from the overworked teams, the scene was a weird one, and sympathy went out to the poor animals who plunged along with such willing effort in the emergency. The cavalrymen were a sorry sight, dripping with mud and water, all trace of the jaunty appearance of the day before having disappeared. But the wagon trains met with terrible difficulty, for the heavy loads were more than the animals could draw through the churned mass of mud and water.   In spite of the frantic efforts of the negro drivers, a line of teams would be stalled at intervals of two or three hundred yards; mules would sink in the mire to die, and by midday everything was at a standstill; nearly one hundred thousand men with guns and transportation mired; and the long-sought-for opportunity of a battle postponed perhaps for months. Never was there a more disheartened body of men.

But the problem of how to get out of this dilemma now presented itself. The distance back to the old camp was not great, but difficulties increased each moment, and it was doubtful if the teams would be equal to the task of extricating the trains from their predicament. Word soon came from headquarters that the movement was abandoned, and the troops were ordered to return to the old camp. Simple enough instructions, but how difficult of performance!

The brave infantry, however, bedraggled and demoralized, soon took up the backward march; the artillery turned about and toiled through the swamp-like roads, losing horses by the dozen in the mire.   Order was not thought of; the only consideration being to get out of the sad predicament.   Pontoon-trains were come upon in some places securely anchored, and in others whole regiments of infantry tugged at long ropes in the vain effort to move the unwieldy boats on their trucks.   Slowly the great army retraced its steps, and the men revived in spirits when the old camp-ground appeared to view. But what a motley body they were as they drew up on the parade-ground facing the dismantled huts!   How unlike the splendid array of a few days before! Even the flags looked dispirited as they hung limp and dripping from the staffs.

But soldiers are proverbially light-hearted, and order soon began to manifest itself. Tents were pitched, old huts re-roofed with canvas, and the blue smoke ere long ascended from the mud chimneys as of old. Slowly the trains returned, and for days dejected "coffee coolers" appeared with their original pleas for delinquency.   In a week, perhaps, matters were again set to rights, and except the relating of incidents of the "mud march" the men resumed the "even tenor of their way."

The Mud March.

A TOUGH PULL.

LIV

ON THE RIVER BANK.

WHETHER among the mountain ranges or on the flatlands near the sea, rivers of the South possessed a dreamy and poetic character that would not be easily forgotton by one who appreciated scenic beauty or had sought adventure upon their banks. From mountain to seashore, down rocky slopes and through swampy flats, they moved leisurely along, and their peaceful murmurings were often a deep contrast to the sounds of struggles near their banks.

A River Picket.

During the summer of 1863, while the Army of the Potomac was lying in peaceful camp upon the north side of the Rappahannock, I thought one day I would ride along its beautiful shore. Starting on horseback just after dinner I moved toward the stream, riding along through shady roads and pleasant lanes. I arrived at a hill overlooking a lovely valley, through which the stream wound in and out on its way to the sea. Pausing awhile to take in the beautiful landscape, I saw two blue-coats coming up the hill, whom I accosted, to gather what news I could of things along the line. I was assured that a visit to the pickets would be perfectly safe, as no firing was allowed on either side. I followed a winding road down the hill and soon came in sight of a post near the river. Men were lying about lazily under improvised bough-shelters, and were so indolent and happy that one might suppose a menacing enemy the most remote thing in the world.

Noticing the rising blue smoke of a camp-fire in an orchard beyond the stream, I inquired what it was, and was surprised to learn that it belonged to the enemy's pickets, with whom our own men were on the most friendly terms. This was soon proven, for looking across I saw a party of gray-coats on the bank, one of whom was fishing, with the hope, I suppose, of hooking a stray perch to add to the mess. I could see their faces plainly, and was surprised at their youthful appearance. They were quiet in manner, but a laugh now and then suggested enjoyment; and the sun glistening on their muskets was the only thing that spoke of war. Seated around the camp-fire mentioned were a party of men and boys who decided that I was a stranger, for they rose from the ground and sauntered toward the bank with a look of interest. I retired back among the trees, not feeling quite secure in such close proximity to a foe, and took a seat by the camp-fire among the Union pickets. They assured me that Lee's army was most certainly moving toward our right, evidently intending to take advantage of our reduced numbers, as nearly forty thousand men had been discharged since the battle of Chancellorsville. A negro from Culpeper had crossed the river that morning and he reported that large bodies of cavalry, infantry and artillery were marching toward Chester Gap in the Blue Ridge. This was important news, and I watched with renewed interest the men on the opposite bank, who had evidently been placed along the stream to prevent news of their movement coming to our side.

I accepted an invitation of the officer commanding the picket to accompany him on his tour, and strolling up stream passed on the other side groups of Southern soldiers every few yards, who were quiet but watchful. At one point we saw a number of men and boys bathing, who were full of pranks and appeared more like schoolboys than soldiers. The officer had cautioned his men to keep a bright lookout till we reached the end of his command, then, seeing that everything was placid, we turned about and were soon back to camp where the boys were cooking supper.

I was invited to partake of their meal, which I did, sitting on a fence rail, and passed a delightful hour listening to the jokes and witticisms of the young soldiers. Across the river the faint blue smoke still drifted off among the trees, and the Confederate pickets were evidently enjoying such comforts as were obtainable. Now and then a gray-clad figure would come from the well of an old farm-house in sight, or an equestrian figure would ride slowly down the road on a tour of inspection. But the "shades of night were falling fast," so I bade the men a cordial good-bye and left best wishes that their stay by the river might continue to be peaceful. I mounted my mare and glancing back at the strangely placid scene cantered up the hill. At this point I halted and turned to look at the valley at my feet as it lay bathed in the light of the setting sun. I caught a glimpse of the narrow river winding among the lovely groves of trees, and at intervals along its banks columns of smoke ascended into the still air, which mingled together, then drifted away.

It was scarcely possible to realize that within so short a distance were men who at a moment's notice might engage in deadly conflict; but war is a series of singular contradictions, and it is strange to reflect that the men who do such deadly work are free from actual malice.

I now turned from the scene of beauty toward camp and rode musing under the overhanging trees in the gathering darkness. Reaching camp, report of the enemy's movement was confirmed, and orders had been given to pack up and be in readiness to start at daylight. Far into the night I listened to sounds of the army in preparation, and just before the sun appeared the troops, with loaded backs, came pouring into the roads. Soon through the dust-laden air myriads of men and animals were moving towards the mountains, and naught was left to me but to follow the column.

"All Quiet on the Picket Line."

On The River Bank.

On Picket.

WATCH AND WARD.

LV

WAITING FOR SOMETHING TO TURN UP.

The Warrior's Rest.

HERE would be intervals of calm during a great battle, when both commanders had come to a standstill, or some new scheme was in contemplation, and the great hosts confronting each other, while wary and watchful, were grateful of a rest for weary limbs even though the hot sun poured down upon them.

At such times, along the lines on the extreme front, an occasional skirmish-shot might be heard, but so infrequent as to appear more like accident than design; or an unexpected solid shot or shell would occasionally whizz through the air, cutting off limbs of trees and sending up a cloud of dust from where it struck the ground. And it was strange what slight agitation these deadly messengers aroused, so accustomed did the men become to them.

Even for temporary rest and protection from the sun, the soldiers would make shelters of boards, fence-rails and brush, and with knapsacks for pillows would doze away, oblivious of dangerous surroundings. Here and there parties of men could be seen putting final touches to breastworks,—critically placing a headlog or deepening a ditch in front. If a party of men among whom were gray uniforms, were discovered approaching from the direction of the skirmish-line in front, some interest would be aroused, and the men would collect along the works to get sight of the prisoners coming in.

Among the batteries a similar spirit of indolence and indifference was manifested; even the horses appreciated the quiet interval and stood half asleep, munching their food. Some-times a man would be sent to climb a high tree with a hope that some news of the enemy's movements might be gleaned, for the dullness would at times become oppressive.

But off to the right, perhaps, the skirmish fire would begin to increase in a defiant way, and soon settle into a steady roar. A new interest would now be aroused in the men. Some of them would climb on to the breastworks, and looking along the face of the works through a scattered growth

EXPECTANCY.

of trees determine the locality of the fighting by the ascent of the light blue smoke. When agitation had reached this point, a few deliberate shells would be thrown from both sides, which, when bursting in the air, had a sharp, metallic ring, while those in the woods sent out a low, muffled roar. A movement along our lines might next be seen, and large bodies of infantry would march toward the threatened point, gun-barrels glistening in the sun, and even the men who carried them being distinguishable from the distant place of quiet. But oftentimes such a demonstration would be only a local affair, perhaps a small reconnaissance or a contest for a farm-house and outbuildings, prizes always coveted by both armies as a shelter for sharpshooters. But at such times the firing soon died down, and the movement of troops ceased.

And so days might pass, with only a whizzing bullet as an occasional reminder that the enemy was still in front. In these quiet intervals, many could be seen reading the well-worn papers and passing them from hand to hand to wile the tedious time away. The arrival of the mail was a great pleasure, and one and another from the expectant groups gathered about the carrier would grasp a welcome letter and hasten away to devour the contents. What touching significance a letter had in those days! "News from home" spoke volumes. Truly, "Home is where the heart is," and the soldier went back to the old scenes as he read the pages, and at night placed the missive in his knapsack, only to be re-read when the reveillé sounded.

But however dull the days, sunset brought brighter aspects; horses had to be fed, and camp-fires had to be re-kindled in the ravines in rear of the ranks, where smoke could ascend out of sight of the enemy. If fresh beef was issued, it had to be cooked in any utensil available; but it was always acceptable to the hungry men, however primitive the arrangements might be. After dark an air of apprehension pervaded everything, for the stillness along the line seemed like a "calm before the storm." Additional pickets were sent forward by the officers, with many cautions; but thousands of men settled down to sleep, careless of when or where the awakening might be.

THEY ALSO SERVE WHO ONLY STAND AND WAIT.

219

LVI

BREASTWORKS, ABATIS, TANGLES, Etc.

A Hard Road to Travel.

DESPITE the fact that the Union army at first ignored picks and shovels, and thought all defences except those naturally available beneath a soldier's dignity, experience proved fortified lines to be a necessity, and for the many perfected accessories of defence our war stands pre-eminent.

The early battles both East and West were fought on open ground, and it was not until McClellan's campaign in the Peninsula that artificial defences were made use of. The character of the country would not admit of engagement with unfortified lines, the dense woods enabling the enemy to concentrate its great masses unseen. Their surprises therefore made the holding of a Union position of great difficulty, and compelled some plan of resort to check their first rush.

The Rebs were the first to avail themselves of this cover, and as early as the date of their occupation of Manassas Junction and vicinity, had constructed splendid lines of defence. On the evacuation in March, 1862, I visited the ground and was amazed at the extent and completeness of their work. Around the Junction they had built a large number of detached forts, with embrasures and platforms for guns. Each fort was surrounded by a deep ditch, and the whole by abatis and chevaux-de-frise. At the town of Centreville, six miles nearer Washington, a line of forts had been constructed six miles in extent. They were connected by a substantial breastwork, and in front were heavy chevaux-de-frise and slashings, which made the line almost impregnable. No artificial defences were used during the battles of that summer, those of Cedar Mountain, Second Bull Run, South Mountain and Antietam being fought on open ground, except when the combatants took cover of fences or buildings, and at the "Sunken Lane," in which fight our loss was terrible.

At Chancellorsville, the Union commander engaged in digging and slashing (felling trees with the tops towards the enemy). The whole front was covered with earthworks, and beyond them the woods were slashed so that when the enemy charged, the lines were thrown into inextricable confusion, which, with the heavy Union fire, completed their distress. Stonewall Jackson's charge on the right of the Eleventh Corps was, no doubt, disastrous to us; and, if it had not been for the breastworks and slashings, his course could not have been checked before reaching Chancellorsville house; in which event, the Army of the Potomac would have been cut in two, and the greater portion captured.

It was a wonderful sight to see what men could do with axes, even during the battle, for the trees of a vast wood would fall as if by magic touch, men working like beavers to make all possible obstruction for the enemy. Although the battle was a virtual defeat for us, the experience was of great value to the Union army.

At the battle of Gettysburg, which occurred a few months later, full use was made of breastworks; although with the exception of the line of works on Culp's Hill, fighting was done on open ground during the first two days. But when Lee advanced to his final attack on the third day, our men were under cover of rough breastworks, rocks, and other shelter.

The science of artificial defence was not reduced to practical completeness until the campaign of General Grant during the next year. The ground from the Rapidan River to

the James was dug over, and scarcely a mile was traversed that did not have breastworks
and tangle.   In many places the Confederate and Federal lines were close enough to admit
of conversation, and no movement could be carried on except over abatis and breastworks.
The sound of pickax and spade was incessant, and the line of clay breastworks extending for
miles in every direction along our front became monotonous.

At Spottsylvania Court House and Cold Harbor the two armies could have been likened to columns of huge ground squirrels buried in the earth, from whence it was dangerous
to emerge.   Great yellow earthworks and forts covered both armies, and over the intervening
ground were scattered thousands of daring skirmishers, insecurely protected by shallow holes
in the ground.

At the sieges of Petersburg and Richmond, the use of earthwork fortifications reached
a culminating point in the East, and the number of miles built by both armies could scarcely
be estimated.   The grass-covered lines can to-day be traced in any direction where the two
great armies sought to fight out their strife.

The Union armies in the West were at first prejudiced against fortifications, while the
enemy, being on the defensive, took advantage of every possible means to strengthen a position.   The battles of Fort Donaldson, Shiloh and Stone River were fought on open ground,
and heavy losses consequently incurred; but after the successful defence of Corinth by General Rosecrans, a well-fortified front was appreciated, and earthworks were thenceforward built
at every available opportunity.   The following campaigns in fact became digging-matches,
when opposing forces vied with each other in the building of breastworks, forts, tangles, and
other impediments.

The sieges of Vicksburg and Port Hudson were good examples of the value of fortifications, and the works built by both armies served admirable purpose.

During Sherman's series of battles from Chattanooga to Atlanta, the whole country
was covered with a net-work of forts and rifle-pits, so that it would have been fatal for either
side to make a front attack.   An advance by the Union forces was possible only by flanking
the enemy's position and forcing them to fall back.

The capture of Atlanta and defeat of Hood by General Thomas at Nashville ended
the building of fortified lines in the West, and when Sherman's army left Atlanta on its
glorious march to the sea, and Grant moved toward Five Forks to turn Lee out of Petersburg, the men laid aside pick and spade and brought hard labor to a triumphant end.

BUILDING OBSTRUCTIONS.

SEDGWICK AT RAPIDAN RIVER.

LVII.

THE OUTER PICKET LINE.

A Cautious Scrutiny.

HE great Union armies during the winter months might have been compared to hives of bees who had garnered the sweets of the summer and settled down to drowsy hibernation. Of course there were duties and occurrences that aroused them into activity, such as drills, camp-work, amusements and a jolly ball now and then, but they apparently droned in indolence a great deal of time away.

Yet, camped in a hostile country, enough of apprehension pervaded these great hosts to guard against the attacks of an ever-persistent enemy. Supplies for men and animals were received from a depot sometimes hundreds of miles in the rear, and to protect the approach to camp was no easy task or slight responsibility. A farmer whose son was an officer in the Army of the Potomac visited him in 1863 and said "Sakes alive! I expected to find yer hull army on a farm of a hundred and fifty acres; but, law me! I've rode ten mile on the cars from Acquia Creek, and as fur as I could see on both sides was camps! camps! camps! and I guess I know now what an army is." From this primitive description, a reader may conclude over what miles of country our picket line had to extend, and imagine the dangers they were exposed to, so hostilely surrounded. Neighboring people would locate a post carefully, note details of numbers and defences and communicate with the enemy. With such authentic information a dash of theirs was apt to be disastrous to us, for we never received warning except from an occasional faithful negro.

The picket line was strongly fascinating to me, for the men were always apprehensive and cautious, making constant preparation for difficulty. In the early spring of '64, when camp-life was to be seen at its best, I made a visit to the line that extended along a ridge of hills on the Rappahannock River above Beverly Ford. It commanded an extensive view of the country toward Washington and Little Washington, which for beauty could not be surpassed in Virginia.

In the foreground was a line of rude picket huts, tenanted by groups of soldiers, while within short distance men on duty were passing up and down with guns at a shoulder. Across the Rapidan, about fifteen miles to the south, was a range of hills on which Gen. Lee's army was camped, and from which with the aid of a glass faint columns of ascending smoke could be discerned. Nearer to my position were the blue crests of Thoroughfare Gap and Cedar Mountains, where Banks' division made so gallant a fight against Stonewall Jackson's superior force. Further to the left, Pony Mountain could be seen, with a log signal-station on its rocky crest. At its foot lay the sleepy old town of Culpeper Court House, and from the woods and fields around, the blue smoke drifted from Union camps there located. Less remote, near Brandy Station, could be seen the headquarters camp of General Grant, snugly ensconced in a pine grove. The Rappahannock meandered through the brown fields of the valley beneath, lost to sight here and there among groups of leafless trees on its banks. The snow-capped Blue Ridge Mountains rose in the western horizon, their azure tint suggesting the origin of their name. Scanning their summits from the south to where they faded towards Harper's Ferry, I recognized Chester Gap, through which I passed with Banks' Division in the summer of '62, on the way to Cedar Mountain. Ashby's Gap, the scene of many desperate cavalry fights, was visible; also Manassas Gap, through which the railroad passes into the valley. Snicker's Gap could be discerned, and far to the north could be seen indistinctly the dip at Harper's Ferry, that wonderfully beautiful rocky gateway, through which the Potomac passes on its way past the national capital to the sea. What thrilling stories that historic range and its surroundings might echo! "Dark and bloody ground" it all is; scarce a hill but has been a scene of struggle, and along its roads and paths and in deep recesses of woods terrible tragedies have been enacted. Thousands of shallow graves were scattered through this country, and thousands of human bones have lain bleaching in the sun.

And yet this beautiful landscape suggested peace, as the shadows of the morning clouds passed slowly along.

But in any calm, if a column of smoke rose, coming perhaps from a farmer's burning brush, all eyes were attracted toward it with the idea that it might be a signal of danger; and a bright gleam in the trees on a distant river bank suggested the glimmer of the sun on a gun-barrel. The slightest movement of any object for miles around, or the faintest rustle near by, had a significance of danger to those faithful watchers, the picket guard. All day long the ground was scanned, and at night the vigilance increased, for surprises were frequent, and Union deserters or Rebel spies made their way about under cover of darkness. And when there was good reason to suspect hostile movements in earnest, word was sent back and mounted parties would be despatched to go further and faster that the infantry pickets could penetrate, to search out and if possible ascertain the facts. The deep scrutiny of the pickets might have been likened to the eyes of some insects who see with numberless lenses.

In many ways experience on the picket line was a good school for the soldiers, and would often restore ambition lost in the aimless life of winter camp.

Danger Ahead

THE ARGUS EYES OF THE ARMY.

227

LVIII.

SCOUTING.

Off, and Away!

ETAIL for scouting—not by the regular scouts, but from the general force—was always gladly welcomed, as it was such a pronounced change from the dull routine of camp-life. A party of this kind was generally composed of men noted for their courage and good horsemanship, and commanded by a young and energetic officer of tried experience. On most occasions duty was specific,—such as locating the enemy, capturing an isolated body, or destroying bridges or depots of supplies; each task calling for a brave and determined party. After the detail, ammunition and supplies were given to each party, and under the guidance of some one familiar with the roads they would start out of camp.

The journey was necessarily one of caution. Making their way toward the enemy with advance guards thrown out to prevent surprise or ambuscade, they would scour the country on all sides. Sometimes a small body of the enemy would be met, and a lively encounter ensue, the weaker judiciously giving way. If the enemy retreated, the party would continue the advance cautiously, until the expedition was accomplished—or not, as circumstances would have it. A party would often divide into small squads and scatter on different roads in search of information. Suspicious characters were generally picked up, and many an innocent-looking farmer was captured, who, when brought to camp, proved to be a bushwhacker.

A scouting party was sometimes sent to destroy a railroad in possession of the enemy. This was always a dangerous proceeding, as all bridges of importance were protected by breastworks or a block-house. A lively contest usually took place, and even if the bridge-burners were victorious, the killed and wounded were often left, as the attacking party had to leave hastily to escape the enemy's reinforcements, which generally arrived in very quick time. A running fight back to camp would then follow, and the man who was not knocked out of the saddle and ridden over by the pursuing Johnnies had cause for congratulation.

Often the expedition would be a pleasant and peaceful ride. The men would stop at farm-houses and feast on goodly viands, such as fruits, honey, and milk from the spring-house. Under the apple-trees the repasts would take place, and the soldiers often declared there were some bright spots in the service.

An adventure full of excitement was when a depot of supplies was to be destroyed, for the guard fought savagely to protect stores so much needed, and often many men were killed before the black clouds of smoke ascended which told of success.

But sometimes jolly, hopeful parties, who left camp in great glee, met with disaster or capture. For days no news would be received from them, and after long waiting one or two would straggle back to camp, forlorn, or wounded, or both, with a mournful story of misfortunes. Despite their dejected appearance after a failure, men were just as ready to venture again, and no visions of death or Andersonville prison seemed to discourage them. When soldiers first entered the service fear of death was felt, but danger became so constant that realization of the great risk they ran seemed to lessen, and they were intent only on the fun of adventure, the excitement of danger, or the grim determination to do what they had undertaken.

OLD CAMPAIGNERS.

A Good Provider.

ECOMING a veteran was not so much a matter of time as of events, and many youthful recruits, who, with tear-filled eyes received their mothers' blessing, in a few short months became inured to the hardships and dangers of an active campaign. From the recruiting office to the field of action elapsed but a brief interval of time, and in the desperate need of troops, young men would be forced into action who scarcely knew the use of a gun.

A company of New York City recruits joined a regiment at the battle of South Mountain, Maryland, on their third day of service and took part in the fight. Inexperience made them fearless, and veterans watched their wild excitement in surprise. They were ordered to charge a stone wall, from which was coming a steady fire. As they advanced and attacked, one of our boys seized a graycoat by the collar, dragged him over the wall and made him prisoner. When the action ceased he was exhibited with pardonable pride. Another—a playmate of my own—scarcely more than a boy, left for the front on Thursday and on the following Tuesday advanced on the skirmish line with Burnside's charge at Antietam. Surely an early "baptism of fire"!

Recruits were easily distinguishable from old campaigners, who had become wise in service, and realized when danger was most imminent and how to avoid it. Time-acquired instinct told the soldier when to fight and when to shun it; how to march, eat and sleep; when and where to forage; and in fact how to make the most of all opportunities. The veterans were to be recognized by their easy, swinging gait and caps thrown jauntily to one side. Their baggage was always light, for old soldiers learned that roads would be strewn with discarded surplus articles of the inexperienced, when a battle was contemplated. With these they were able to refit at short notice. In camp, the old campaigner had an easy manner of meeting difficulties and shirking responsibilities that new-comers were not accomplished in. In winter camp, his hut had an air of comfort, inside and out, that told of experience, and his summer tent was always pitched in the most desirable locality.

Through battle he often seemed possessed of a charmed existence, so wonderful was his escape from bullets, and appeared at roll-call in good order. Much preservation of life came from facility of cover; and the perfectly the value and tree, and even ground, during an of the enemy. Dana zest to existence, played through long-fatigues was simply

Well Fixed.

in taking advantage old soldiers knew of every stone wall inequalities of the advance in the face ger seemed to give and the spirit discontinued trials and marvelous.

A VETERAN.

A scouting party.

A PEACEFUL START.

231

LIX.

THE RELIABLE CONTRABAND.

Finding the Army.

HILE this name was given in derision to the unfortunate race who were so unconsciously the cause of the great rebellion, there was to those who saw and knew them a touch of pathetic realism in its appropriateness. I do not know of a single instance when one of them proved false to a trust. Their assistance to the sick and wounded was invaluable, and their lives were often imperilled in efforts of appreciation and gratitude to the Union army. Their dark faces were often beacon-lights to escaped prisoners, who, hungry and footsore and oftentimes wounded, were piloted with patient courage and passed from hand to hand with an admonition that those who received the charge should be faithful to the trust.

The knowledge of the intricate wood-paths and river-fords which the colored people had gained in stolen night visits about the country, aided greatly in simplifying the movements of the Union army. When an important movement was contemplated, the commanding officer would send for some negro in the neighborhood, and if, after close questioning the man was evidently familiar with the surrounding country, his services would be secured. When the column moved he would take position beside the commanding officer at the head, and guide the column through swamps and woods that were apparently impassable, with the intelligence of an Indian hunter.

The name "contraband" was a popular taking up of the ingenious declaration of General Benjamin F. Butler, who, in the early days of the war, asserted that escaped slaves, being capable of rendering aid and comfort to the enemy if returned to the Rebel lines, were "contraband of war," and therefore to be received and made use of by the Union forces. The name "reliable contraband" was at first used frequently by the army correspondents, who reported startling probabilities or important movements of the enemy on the authority of some frightened refugee, and the epithet was continued ironically because of the *unreliable* intelligence they sometimes brought into the Union lines. Any discrepancy in statement, however, came from a lack of knowledge and not a desire to mislead. The secessionists were always cautious about making statements in the presence of the slaves relative to the number or movements of their armies, and the slaves in their bondage were of course ignorant of local geography; so it is not to be wondered at that they failed to estimate the numbers of an army or give an accurate account of its movements.

The colored fugitives who made their way to our lines were always welcomed and their grotesqueness was a source of amusement to the cavalry outposts. They often came with valuable information, yet many times with exaggerated and indefinite reports. For instance, if asked about the enemy's numbers, they would reply "Oh! dar was a right smart lot of 'em, massa, mo' dan I eber see befo',"—a statement which though literally true, meant but very little.

The negroes were of invaluable assistance in the East in the construction of works of defence — rifle-pits, earthworks, forts, camps, etc., and they were gradually taken into the forces and utilized as non-combatants in many ways—as body servants, cooks, drivers, grooms, laborers, and wherever they could save work or time for the soldiers.

Later on, when it was decided after much discussion to enlist and arm them, and give them a chance to fight as well as work for their liberty, they gave a splendid account of themselves. As soldiers, the colored troops exhibited their *reliable* qualities, chiefly on the bloody battle fields of the West, notably at Fort Pillow and the battle of Nashville under General Thomas. They displayed splendid courage and discipline, and proved that the country had not erred in arming them. Their position was particularly trying, as the enemy at first refused to give them quarter, and capture at that period meant death.

Through the trials of the great struggle their fidelity never wavered and their dearly bought emancipation was but just recompense for their long years of servitude.

Lookin' for the Yankees,

CONTRABAND OF WAR.

LX.

RALLYING THE LINE.

Break, and Rally.

HEN a line of battle was making successful advance against the enemy, it was generally regular and under control. Universal discipline seemed to prevail throughout the whole body; and, although sometimes men fell at every step, the ranks would close up at command. Yet, while surmounting most serious obstacles, the enemy's fire would sometimes become so severe, that the men would lose nerve, waver, and, while not in the notion of retreating, grow unsteady, so that the lines became much confused. A flank movement of the enemy also often made a position untenable. At such times but one command could be given, and that, to "Fall back!"

This was always a difficult thing to accomplish, it seeming a much easier matter to get into danger than to get out of it. With faces to the foe, men seemed to possess a courage that deserted them in retreat. They would fall slowly back in an irregular line, loading and turning about to fire at intervals, presenting quite a regular front as they stood at bay, but making a broken and demoralized line as the enemy's fire became too hot for them. Under this pressure they would sometimes break like a flock of sheep, and run panic-stricken towards the rear.

Then the officers would make strenuous efforts to restore order and bring out some semblance of discipline. Part of the line would halt, perhaps, and seek the shelter of a fence or building, as a ship might take refuge from a storm. In the midst of excitement, a regimental flag would be thrown to the breeze, and men to right and left would rally quickly into line at the inspiration.

When the line of battle fell back because of severe fire or a lack of ammunition, reinforcements would be sent forward and the exhausted fighters rally to the rear, where they would soon recover their *esprit de corps*, and from being shaky individuals become again a disciplined body.

I have seen a line of battle in a defensive position driven back by an overwhelming force who, dashing forward yelling like demons and frantically waving their little battle flags, would deliver a rattling fire. Such an attack was difficult to resist, and I have often watched our retreating forces making vain efforts to stem the overwhelming tide that swept them along in confusion. Bravely they held every piece of advantageous ground, clinging to rocks and hiding behind walls and trees, between times sending showers of bullets back at the on-coming foe. Now perhaps the enemy were compelled to halt; then our men with renewed spirit would take the offensive, and drive them back in defeat over the ground on which they had made such triumphant advance. So forward and back the battle would rage, and both sides would become so exhausted that the men would drop down among the bushes and glare at each other like tigers.

A cavalry line under defeat was much more difficult to rally than the infantry. The horses were unmanageable under the excitement, and their great size made them fine marks for the enemy's fire. When the cavalry line was broken the horses would dash wildly about in every direction, but when the bugle sounded forth, officers' commands could be heard, and circumstances were favorable, they would gradually take regular form and again present a solid front to the enemy. It was especially difficult to re-form cavalry under a heavy shell-fire, until a hill or a wood offered shelter; but horses as well as men had felt the organizing power of discipline and could generally be rallied.

There was much perplexity in handling the artillery batteries when the line of battle was being driven back. Horses were killed and wounded, and upon the battery thus disabled the exultant enemy would press with redoubled vigor, with the desperate intention of seizing the pieces. At such times artillerymen exhibited a stubborn pride of possession, and contested every inch of ground by firing cannister into the face of the enemy, and defending their guns even with pistols and hand spikes. At the same time the pieces would be slowly moved to a safe position by hand or dragged by *prolong*, as the long rope coiled on the trail of the gun is called. All guns were not of course always rescued, but the enemy paid dearly for all captures. When the line of guns was rallied it was not always symmetrical; but, despite the missing horses from the teams and men from the guns, the old spirit remained, and as they growled forth new defiance, our forces took on fresh courage—for the artillery was really the back-bone of the line of battle.

Many a rally, following upon what seemed like a disgraceful break and even rout, exhibited the genuine courage and steadfastness of the soldiery far more notably than a battle in which the same men had been favored with victory from start to finish.

CAVALRY RALLY.

A RALLY ROUND THE FLAG.

Thomas at Chickamauga.

LXI

THE SUPPLY TRAINS.

No food, no fight.

HE enormous trains of wagons on which the army relied for regular food and ammunition were more a source of wonder to observers than any other portion of the army. They seemed to compose the greater part of the great force, and could be seen (so to speak) *everywhere*. They filled the roads on the march and covered miles of fields in every direction, when the main body halted. Their management was a constant and difficult problem to the commander-in-chief, as the success or failure of a campaign depended on their safety.

At the beginning of the war the trains were unnecessarily large, troops being furnished with quantities of material that was afterward deemed unnecessary. Sibley and wall-tents were used by both officers and privates, requiring for their transportation quite a large train. Camp-equipage was used unsparingly by everybody at this period, the movement of a single regiment using more wagons than a brigade required during the last year of the war. Those used by the Union army were heavy four-wheeled vehicles, with a canvas cover stretched over a light frame. On the cover was marked the name of the Corps, Division and Brigade to which the wagon belonged; also the nature of supplies, whether quartermaster, commissary, or ammunition,—kind and caliber of the latter being indicated.

The wagons at first were drawn by six-horse teams, but later, when the superiority of mules became appreciated they were substituted. They were harnessed in most substantial fashion, as the wear and tear upon the gear was terrible, and guided by negro drivers, who bestrode the saddle of the near wheel-mule, and managed the team with a single line fastened to the near leader's bit. None but the colored drivers were really successful with the mule teams, there seeming to be an occult understanding between them.

All camp-equipments, stores and ammunition were moved in these trains, and when an army of one hundred thousand men were on the march, the wagons, if stretched in a line, would reach a distance of fifty miles. To move thus would not have been practicable, as the troops could not have been served with dispatch. The trains were therefore broken up into manageable divisions, and under the care of officers and guards would take different roads in the rear and on the flanks of the moving columns where they could be protected from the vigilant enemy. Cautiously they would creep along over mountains and through valleys, looking, as some writer has said, "like a string of white beads," sending up clouds of dust in the dry weather and showers of mud in the wet. Guards of infantry or cavalry were detailed with the trains when in proximity to the enemy's forces, and walked or rode alongside the wagons.

If a surprise was feared, they would take position off on the flanks, keeping a vigilant eye, and paying attention to all crossroads, at which points a dash from the enemy's cavalry often occurred.

While the Army of the Potomac was on the way to Mine Run in the early winter of 1863, I remember an instance which illustrated the daring of an attacking force and the skill of successfully carrying out a design. The troops had crossed the Rapidan and were moving slowly towards the enemy's position, followed by their trains, the Fifth Corps train taking the road from the Germania Ford to Wilderness Tavern, then turning sharply at a right angle into the Orange Court House road, which led to Mine Run. At this sharp angle the enemy's cavalry made a dash at the train. Riding up to the wagons they ordered the first driver to turn about towards Chancellorsville and all the wagons to follow, and at the same time sent a squadron of cavalry on the road toward Germania Ford to prevent a rescue by the guards. As soon as a sufficient number of wagons had been turned off the road, the enemy fell back toward Chancellorsville until safe from pursuit, when they unhitched the teams and plundered the wagons of all valuable stores easily carried, and then set fire to them, leaving nothing but ashes and old iron. Quite a number of train-guards were captured, and a handsome young artillery officer in charge of the ammunition wagons disappeared headlong in the melée with drawn sabre. He was a gallant young fellow, whose name I have forgotten, but I have often wondered what his fate might have been.

Mosby's men were the particular scourge of the wagon-trains, and exhausted the life-blood of the quartermaster and commissary trains in Virginia. Many desperate struggles took place among the wagons on the lonely Virginia roads, and the men in charge of the teams never felt safe from the reckless bushwhackers.

At camping time the trains left the road and parked, in long lines, in adjacent fields. These scenes were full of life and variety and seeming confusion to a looker-on; but there was method in every movement, and after the wants of men and animals had been supplied the busy hive settled down to comparative order and quiet.

Confederate wagon-trains were not as well appointed and equipped as those of the Union armies. The wagons were generally taken from the farmers, and were on the style of the old "prairie schooners." They were high at both ends, their name probably having originated from this peculiarity. They were always fair game for the Union cavalry and scouts, and many thousands were captured, plundered and destroyed. They were driven by negro slaves, who, when captured, gladly exchanged the tattered gray clothes for the blue, and thankless service for "Uncle Sam's" pay.

Attacked by Bushwhackers.

THE ARMY MULE TEAM.

LXII

THE SUTLER.

Necessary Luxuries

LTHOUGH the men who catered to the needs of the soldiers, selling goods at enormous profit, were not looked upon as public benefactors, yet in furnishing a variety of supplies otherwise unobtainable they served the purpose of enabling the men to endure hardships through which the meagre rations would scarcely have sustained them.

The position was much sought after, especially in the early part of the war. It fell to those, however, who could command the greatest influence and pay the largest fees. Profits were whatever they chose to make them, and many retired at the close of the war with comfortable fortunes. In the French army the sutler is a soldier detailed to that service; in ours, he was a civilian who got appointed to the post. All were under military law, and were severely dealt with if found guilty of frauds or irregularities towards the soldiers.

There was generally one of these money-makers attached to each regiment, who in summer carried his goods in two-horse wagons. He was always supplied with a large tent, which could be pitched on short notice, and when a halt was made it was the center of attraction. The sutler and his clerks were busily employed from morning till night in dealing out supplies. Soldiers never seemed so happy as when buying something to eat, and anyone who did not dispose of his limited monthly pay in three weeks was thought to have a failing appetite.

Sutlers usually received their goods from parties at the army's base of supplies, who had secured the right to furnish them. When the Army of the Potomac was in the vicinity of Fredericksburg, supplies were sent down the Potomac River on schooners and retailed to sutlers who came to Acquia Creek and Belle Plain. Hundreds of thousands of dollars' worth of goods would be disposed of in one day, yielding enormous profits to the syndicate who controlled the business between Washington and the camps. When a fresh supply arrived there would be great activity about the sutler's tent: soldiers would swarm from all directions, and crowding about the front would devour with longing eyes the contents of the shelves. When their turn came they would "fish" deeply in their pockets for money with no complaints of price, or request the sutler to charge purchases to their accounts. This was always a safe proceeding, as the paymaster paid all sutlers' bills and gave the soldiers the balance. When supplies were brought to the army in summer time by wagons, they were often captured by the "Johnnies." Every such accident was a god-send to them. They always made a clean sweep of all luxuries and retired to their lines, where they were received with loud cheers by their hungry comrades.

When such a catastrophe happened to one of these camp-traders, general sympathy was not extended to him; on the contrary, there was a feeling of exultation and cries of "Served him right!" "Glad somebody's got the better of him," etc., were heard.

It was suspected, and not without ground, that some sutlers carried on a large traffic in contraband goods and reaped a rich harvest, for facilities enabled them to furnish medicines and other articles of small bulk to the enemy, who in their great need paid dearly for supplies.

Many Hebrews secured permits as sutlers and were said to be noted for their great shrewdness. Observation led me to conclude, however, that Americans were equally keen, and that the sutler's profit was a matter of opportunity and not nationality. The chance of making extravagant and unjust gains out of other people's needs, is a temptation that appeals to selfishness, and finds response in all times and in all countries. "Human nature is pretty much of a muchness," and there never was a war—however patriotically undertaken and carried on by the bulk of a nation—in which some men did not come out of it enormously richer than they went in. This was notably so during our Civil War; and the fortunes made in selling the Government poor arms, shackly wagons, shoddy blankets, overcoats and uniforms, wretched shoes, and all manner of fraudulent supplies, should make us chary of severely criticising the sutlers. They took their humbler chances, and did indeed make undue profits, but as a rule they furnished honest goods and were, if a "necessary evil," a very welcome one to the soldier.

After Canned Goods

The Sutlers Tent.

QUICK RETURNS AND LARGE PROFITS.

LXIII.

ON THE ROAD TO CAMP.

A Day Off.

CENES on the way from camp to the base of supplies in the rear were always full of variety and interest. In summer long wagon-trains lumbered along through the clouds of dust to and fro, those going to the front being laden with hard-tack, salt pork, beef, and other commissary supplies, also corn, oats, and hay—all destined for the quartermaster's department. Here and there in the train a sutler's wagon could usually be seen, the sutlers as a rule having smiling faces, no doubt in anticipation of their great profits in the near future.

Groups of jolly officers would often pass along toward camp, returning from commissary headquarters at the general depot, where good cheer always prevailed. Stray cavalrymen appeared at intervals, and infantry also, who picked their way on the edge of the throng, keeping in the fields beside the road as much as possible to escape the great clouds of dust.

Sometimes a regiment of recruits would be met, looking bright and smart in new uniforms. Their white skins were in great contrast to those of the sunburned and weather-beaten fellows, and the eager, curious observance they made of all surroundings was unlike the careless, indifferent manner of the men in long service. Droves of handsome, fresh horses, remounts for the cavalry, could be seen moving along in the throng toward camp. Their full sides and glossy skins were in strong contrast to the faithful, broken-down animals whose burdens they were sent to take up.

Amid this variety, groups of convalescents under guard would wander slowly along toward camp, their steps faltering more each mile. Their knapsacks were restlessly shifted from side to side as if to lighten the load, and permission asked to halt when a shaded place was reached.

Great droves of cattle ("Beef on the Hoof") would often appear wandering from side to side in search of a green nibble, wholly unconscious of the slaughter that awaited them at the near-by camp. The herdsmen were a characteristic set of fellows, mounted on mules or horses, and could be seen urging the bellowing herd along, sometimes dashing into the field to head off a straying ox or hurrying to the front lest the animals should turn into a cross-road. Wagons of the Sanitary Commission laden with delicacies for the sick were among the variety, and passing soldiers glanced with covetous eyes at the stores furnished by that noble organization. Our troops would often smile at the civilian's dress of the members, which was so out of keeping with their own, but they had a kind word for the charity and appreciated throughout the war the grand effort to relieve the sick and wounded.

Dashing along at hunter's speed with rolls of newspapers thrown over the saddles would come the newsboys, each horse galloping under stimulus of the whip, every rider being desperately determined to keep the lead and secure the first sales.

In moving from camp to the rear, empty wagons formed a good portion of the panorama. They rumbled along with quick and hurried motion, their object always being to reload and return to camp before dark. Ambulances loaded with sick and wounded intermingled with the trains and passed slowly along toward the general hospital.

Groups of cavalry horses no longer fit for service were sent to the convalescent camp. Some of them were very lame; others perfect skeletons, oftentimes being past restoration.

Government veterinary surgeons took charge of them, however, sorting out and selling the worthless ones and turning the remainder out to grass.

Occasionally, a woman seated in an ambulance under officer's escort would give rise to much conjecture. She might have been an officer's wife, or nurse in the Sanitary Commission. In any event, a woman was a novelty, and was always earnestly stared at.

Groups of escaped slaves could now and then be seen on their way to the supply depot; the men and boys sought work in the commissary or quartermaster's department, and the women and girls in the hospitals, as cooks and washerwomen. During one of these scenes I noticed a commotion far down the road toward camp, and out of the cloud of dust appeared General Grant (then commander-in-chief), surrounded by his staff and accompanied by several members of Lincoln's cabinet, in civilian's dress. They had evidently been to headquarters to consult about army matters, for as they swept by their faces had an anxious expression and they leaned forward on their saddles listening attentively to the words of the great commander.

These varied sights were always intensely interesting to me, and I often compared the road from the depot of supplies to the main artery in the human body, along which pulses the life-blood, and without whose continuous action life would cease to exist.

The Road to Camp

A RACE FOR CAMP

LXIV.

SUPPORTING A BATTERY.

Weary Work.

RONE upon the ground in the rear of the guns, the soldier in line had ample opportunity to realize the danger of his position, without having occasion to join actively in the fight and thus end the strain on his nerves. Nothing in a soldier's experience was more dreaded by the men than the unpleasant duty of supporting a battery. How anxiously they watched the fragments of bursting shells which often carried destruction to their prostrate ranks! They envied the men at the guns in front, who, in the intense excitement of battle, lost sight of danger. Hour after hour the supporting line would lie upon the ground, a prey to the enemy's sharpshooters, who were located in distant trees, and at whom they could not return fire. The position of those unhurt would from mental strain become unbearable; and when word was received that the enemy's infantry was preparing to charge the battery, a feeling of relief would prevail along the line. At the Colonel's command to "Fall in!" the whole line would spring to their feet with a shout, and really delight in the thought of a fight where the privilege of a return fire could be enjoyed.

Excitable movements of the men in the battery would follow, which would suggest that "business" with them was about to commence; and the men who served ammunition would rush back asking for cannister, and dash forward to the guns again. When the enemy would advance on their charge, the yells could be heard plainly enough to indicate the extent of their line. The men at our guns would then work like demons, loading and firing the pieces with incredible rapidity. When the yells and fire in front told of the enemy nearing the guns, a portion of the regiment would be moved toward each flank of the battery where their fire could be most effective, and soon after a steady roll of musketry would tell that our men were intensely at work. Perhaps then a part of the enemy's line would get to the guns and drive our gunners, even though they might make stout resistance, to the rear. At such times the enemy would make a desperate attempt to turn the guns on our men; but when the gunners had had quickness enough to carry off the ramrods, the Rebs were baffled. Then the force in the rear of the guns would show their mettle, and gallantly respond to the call of the officers, firing a volley into the faces of the scattered men among the guns, and pressing forward with bayonets, sweep the ground clear. This enabled the artillery to rush forward again and train the pieces on the demoralized lines of the enemy, hurrying back toward their own forces. We were not always so fortunate, of course, for many an attack could not be repulsed, and the battery with all its horses and equipments would fall into the hands of the enemy, who would lose no time in turning our guns against us.

When evident that the enemy's onset could not be stayed, guns would be hastily "limbered up," and amid frantic lashing of horses hurried to the rear with the hope of obtaining a good position.

These retreats were scenes of terror and confusion; the heavy guns and caissons bounding on the rocky fields, and the firing and fierce yells of the exultant foe, seemed to increase the speed of the excited and frightened horses. Infantry that had supported the battery would then fall sullenly back and reform on the next hill behind the position secured by the guns.

At times the cavalrymen were compelled to support the batteries during an engagement, and being unable to take cover were exposed to great danger. Shells would plough through their ranks, mutilating men and horses, and bullets would cut them down. But there was no retreat; they stood as targets for the enemy's fire. When an order came to resist a charge it was gladly received. There were times at rare intervals when a stone wall provided cover, and an advancing enemy then met with a hot reception.

But no soldier ever liked to be posted in defence of a battery; it was always a dangerous and thankless responsibility, and, unless there was an actual attack, none had the feeling of individual compensation that comes in the exciting success of actual battle.

Defending a Battery.

Defending A Battery

CHARGE AND CHECK.

GILMORE: SIEGE OF CHARLESTON.

LXV.

WATCHING A BATTLE.

Of Local Interest.

O THOSE inexperienced in active service a great battle is thought to resemble a grand review, without any greater risk to a spectator, and in a rehearsal of exciting events the ridiculous questions with which one is continually interrupted make an old soldier smile.

I fully expected, when I started for the front, to accompany the troops into battle and seat myself complacently on a convenient hillside and sketch exciting incidents at my leisure; but how greatly reality differed from imagination I will tell you.

On my first approach to a battle-field (that of Cross Keys, Va.), I found the troops moving through a partly wooded country, and a mile further on in advance I could see the smoke of our guns, which were posted on a wooded ridge commanding ground in front. I could hear musketry fire and, being anxious to witness a charge which was then evidently in progress, I sought a desirable position from which to see it. But my efforts were vain; for the ridge where our guns were posted was swept by the enemy's batteries and the ground in its rear was raked by shot and shell for at least half a mile. The sight of the desperately wounded who were being carried to the rear did not re-assure me, and my ideas of witnessing a battle underwent great change. I concluded to wait for a more convenient opportunity.

I was more fortunate on my second attempt, at Slaughter or Cedar Mountain, for I had been on the line of battle the night before, and was quite interested the following morning watching evidences of an enemy in our front. The Rebs kept well under cover, but showed several battle-flags along the edge of a distant wood, and at intervals with my glass I could see a horseman ride across the field along the line. Nothing to alarm a spectator took place until early in the afternoon. I was then watching some soldiers who were boiling green corn in a large iron boiler that they had obtained from a farmer, when I was suddenly startled by a rattle of musketry in front. I ran towards my horse, which was tied to a fence near by, and hastily mounting rode forward to the crest of the ridge on which Knapp's battery was posted, and halted near it. I soon realized that a battle had begun. The Confederates were posted on a ridge parallel to the one occupied by our forces, their position being rapidly developed by the opening fire of their guns.

Off on our right their infantry advanced, preceded by a cloud of skirmishers, who kept up an incessant fire on our men, but the compliment was returned two-fold. In their center I could see, with the aid of a glass, several batteries advancing and firing, and I knew their practice was good, as their shells burst over our heads and in rear of our position too often for comfort. The sight was magnificent, but trying to one who had no active duty to perform, so I rode over to the right, where the infantry were engaged, and saw Gen. Banks and his staff on the main road directing operations. This place soon became too hot for me, and I galloped back along the line to my original position. On my way I saw a body of Union cavalry making a charge towards the foot of Cedar Mountain, the enemy's center. It was a foolish movement, for the enemy's shells raked them badly, and this, with the ground being cut up by numberless fences, soon caused them to fall back. I watched the battle until the fire became unbearable, then, putting spurs to my horse, retreated in remarkably good order to a safe position about a mile in the rear. I here listened to the ebb and flow of the battle until, under pressure of largely superior numbers, the Union forces were compelled to fall back. I had several narrow escapes during this battle, and realized that to be a spectator was nearly as dangerous as being a participant.

It was often impossible to catch the faintest gleam of a battle because of the density of woods. Two hundred thousand men were engaged on both sides in the battle of the Wilderness, but all the satisfaction that could be gleaned by a spectator was to watch the dense clouds of smoke that rolled up from the woods and listen to the roar of the guns.

The second battle of Bull Run, or Groveton, was quite different, and afforded a favorable chance for sketching. The most of the Union army was on open ground; so that, looking from Bald Hill, on the south of the Warrenton turnpike, the engagement reminded one of a great review. When the Union army was driven back on the afternoon of the last day I lost a chance to witness the final act of the drama, the concluding and most desperate fighting taking place on the very spot where I had stood as a spectator early in the afternoon.

The battle of Antietam was probably the most picturesque battle of the war, as it took place on open ground and could be fully viewed from any point north of Antietam Creek, where our reserve batteries were posted. The battle was a dramatic and most magnificent series of pictures. At daylight Gen. Hooker advanced with the right of the Union army, then followed Sumner's attack on the enemy's center later in the forenoon, and, until the concluding attack and repulse of Burnside's corps on the enemy's right, the engagement was a spectacle which was not surpassed during the whole war. Thousands of people took advantage of the occasion, as the hills were black with spectators. Soldiers of the reserve, officers and men of the commissary and quartermasters' departments, camp-followers, and hundreds of farmers and their families, watched the desperate struggle. No battle of the war, I think, was witnessed by so many people.

Gettysburg was also fought in very open country, but it was impossible to see much of the actual fighting on the Union side except from Cemetery Ridge, with the line of battle, and this place was so storm-swept with bullets and shell that it would have been folly for a looker-on to venture.

It may be believed, therefore, how difficult it is at times to witness a battle, and how, even when one is favorably placed—but without responsibility—excitement and confusion put to flight a realizing sense of events. Soldiers engaged in the thickest of a fight do not know what is taking place within a few hundred feet of them, and learn of results in a general way only after the fury has subsided.

A PRIVATE BOX.

THE DISTANT COMBAT.

LXVI.

ABANDONED CAMPS.

War Relics.

IT WAS my good fortune to visit the camps that had been occupied by the Rebel army at Manassas and Centerville shortly after the evacuation in the spring of 1862. I started from near Union Mills, on the historic Bull Run, and first bent my steps toward Manassas Junction. There I found great villages of solidly-built log huts. They were chinked with clay, had strong chimneys and split pine doors. Each collection of huts seemed capable of housing five thousand men. They were arranged in rows with streets intervening, officers' quarters being located at the ends. From the substantial appearance of things, the Confederate commander had evidently expected to occupy the position for an indefinite length of time. The officers' houses were built with great care, of the best material, and the roofs were carefully shingled.

I inspected the interior of many, and was amazed at the quantity of material left by the occupants. Broken trunks, valises and boxes were scattered about in all directions; clothing of all kinds, camp-utensils and furniture, and every imaginable thing that green troops could secure, were littered in all directions. In many of the huts were articles of convenience made by the men, that exhibited much ingenuity, some of the chairs were really attractive and the rough beds and lounges were comfortable and well put together. Thousands of playing-cards were scattered on the floors; also paper-covered novels, letters and other home souvenirs innumerable. They were evidently too bulky to be taken in the hurried exodus. Near the camps were great numbers of old-fashioned "schooner" wagons, the abandonment of which proved that there had been a scarcity of horses.

Continuing my stroll toward Centerville, I found at short intervals in the sheltered valleys log camps of the same character as at Manassas. The villages were more frequent; stretched on both sides of the Warrenton turnpike, behind the line of fortifications, they dotted the landscape as far as the eye could see. The whole number of huts built by Joe Johnston's army in this vicinity would have comfortably housed fifty thousand men. During the later part of the war the Rebs began to appreciate labor and material, and made structures less substantial; but in 1862 and '63 such great quantities of wood were used that when a camp was abandoned, forces of negroes were sent to tear the huts down and haul the logs to the Orange and Alexandria Railroad, where they were used as fuel for the engines.

The Union camps would not bear comparison with these, for previous making of log huts, which were the universal dwellings of the poor whites at the South, was an experience that our soldiers had not had. Ours had but four layers of logs, and were canvas-covered; not very substantial, perhaps, but picturesque and varied as the taste of occupant suggested; mud, logs, cracker-boxes and barrel-staves were all made available.

No scenes in the army were more pathetic than those deserted and silent ruins that had so often echoed to the tread of brave men. The substantial bunks spoke of skillful handiwork, conveniences for holding arms and accouterments suggested ingenuity and order, while the pictures culled from the newspapers and pasted on the walls gave evidence of some refinement. No signs of life appeared about these deserted places except the ever-present crows and turkey-buzzards, on the lookout for stray bits of food.

Summer shelters consisted only of light canvas stretched upon poles ; and when abandoned, a forest of sticks, barrels, cracker-boxes, and other trash appeared. A dead horse or mule was often seen in the rubbish, and many times lonely graves, with head-boards from cracker-boxes, lettered with name and date of death of the poor fellows who had died of their wounds or succumbed to typhoid fever, resting

> "Where no sound of tender weeping will be heard,
>   Where goes no loving step of kindred."

MONUMENTS TO DEPARTED LIFE.

The Abandoned Camps
and Defences of Centreville Va.
Forbes
April 18th 1862.

THE QUAKER-GUN FORT.

LXVII.

"HOME, SWEET HOME."

"Home Again."

I WAS attracted one afternoon by strains of this sweet old melody, and as they touched the chord of memory so easily aroused in the desolation of army life, I strolled in direction of the plaintive sounds and came upon the scene my large picture portrays. I stood at a respectful distance till the air was finished, for it seemed like intrusion to come suddenly upon the two men whose thoughts I knew floated off to lonely Northern homes; but the notes soon ceased, and the violinist smiled a welcome as he laid down his instrument.

Stepping forward, I asked permission to examine the unique *Cremona*. The body was improvised from a cigar box, with the name "Figaro" burned in the wood. The neck was of soft pine, whittled into shape, and containing holes for the crude pine keys. The bridge and tail-piece were made of cedar, and the strings, which were of good quality, were obtained in Washington. The bow was skillfully made of pine wood and reddish-brown horse-hair.

Noticing the color, I said, "Where did you get this horse-hair?" The fellow remarked sheepishly, "From your mare's tail, when she was tied near here. I took it because it was so long." I assured him that no harm had been done and talked a bit with his companion, a drummer-boy. I found him to be a loquacious youth, like most of his craft, and also that he considered himself an authority on the beauties of music. I said I should like to hear the violin again, and the drummer suggested various tunes—some pathetic, some lively, and a number of military airs popular in camp, the performance of which he criticised quite professionally. "Home, Sweet Home" was repeated with amusing effect at pathos, but I had to admit that the tones were wonderfully good from so rude a little instrument.

Most of the soldiers' feelings found expression in music Its influence both saddened and brightened their lives as they went from "grave to gay." Their life seemed to make them simple-hearted, and merriment gave a zest to existence while the shedding of pent-up tears many times alleviated sorrow—especially the soldier's greatest grief, home-sickness.

The soldiers' love of home was an ever-present memory. They universally kept up a regular correspondence with their families, and the mail at headquarters was equal to that of a fair-sized city. There was a regular system, each regiment, brigade and corps having a mail department, where letters were collected daily and promptly sent North. Those received from home were delivered without delay, troops often receiving letters while lying under fire.

It was always a difficult matter to obtain a furlough; but when an application was granted, the soldier's spirits became most jubilant. Young as most of them were, right from the home fire-side, with not the remotest idea of the hardships to which they would be exposed, it is not to be wondered at that a visit to the old home was a great pleasure. I can see them now, with bright faces and spruce new uniforms, donned for the occasion, bidding good-bye to comrades and hastening to the railroad depot. These visits were of great benefit, often restoring to health and spirits ill and dejected men. Received at home with jubilation and sent off again with honor on their return they would step briskly into the ranks and march forward to battle or to long and weary marches with cheerful courage.

None but a soldier knows what the terrible army home-sickness was; how the men drooped and grew listless in the longing for home, and how many really died from the malady.

Thoughts of home came to the sick and wounded who were at time placed under trees or exposed to sun and rain, and their despondency often aggravated their condition. If a soldier was fortunate enough to get to a large general hospital in the rear, how his heart would beat with joy at the sight of some relative, who had come on to wait upon him or if possible to take him home!

Ah yes, whether in the camp-fire's blaze, on the long march or in the crash of battle, the song of our soldiers most often heard was

"Home, Sweet Home!"

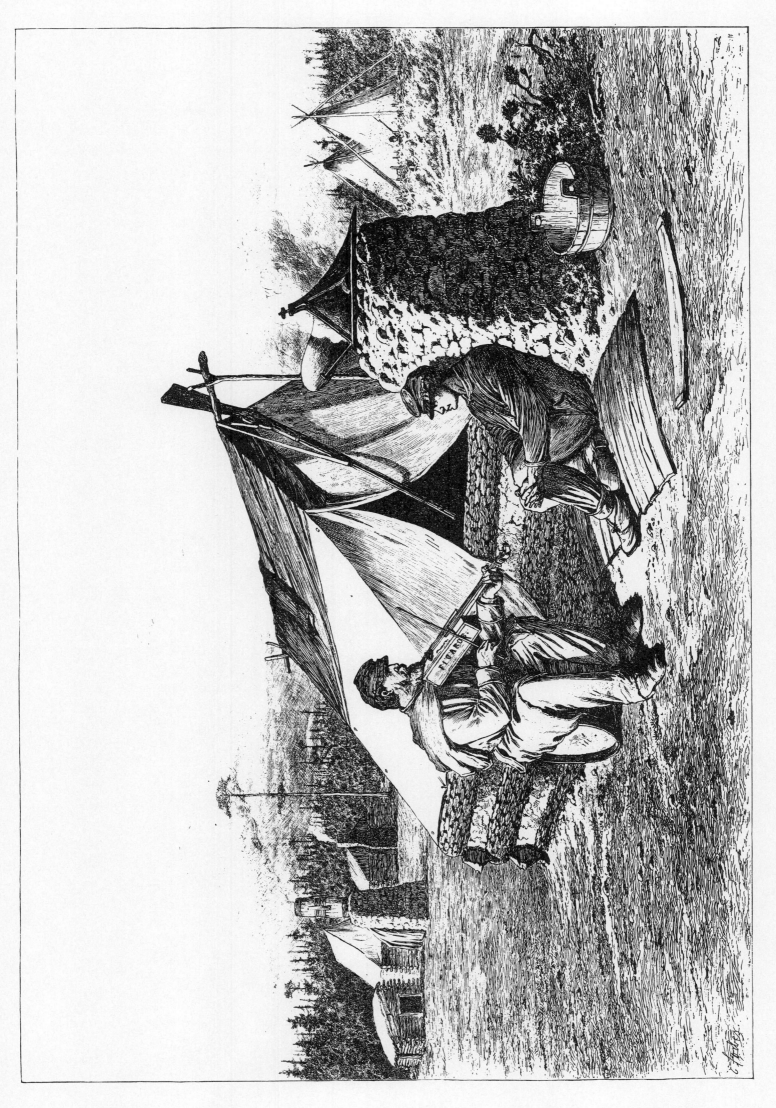

MUSIC HATH CHARMS.

LXVIII.

MILITARY RAILROADS

"*A daddy-long-legs.*"

ONE of the most serious problems presented to the commanders of the Union armies was the transportation of supplies to troops scattered over thousands of miles of territory. It was easy of solution at the beginning of the war, but as the armies advanced they found railroads rendered useless by the destruction of tracks, bridges, and all rolling-stock that could not be moved.

This universal destruction made the formation of a special railway corps imperative, and a bureau was formed for the building, repairing and operating of all railroads within the enemy's lines, until the close of the war. The responsibility was no sinecure, for the forward and backward movements of opposing armies made arduous work, as a retreat of either side left a wake of destruction. A pursuing force often found it necessary to rebuild bridges, relay tracks, and perform other work which had been well done but a few months before. This necessitated an enormous quantity of material to be kept on hand, and depots were established at many points, where hundreds of men were kept busy, making duplicate bridges, collecting ties, rails, rolling-stock, and other necessary material. This military bureau made early examination of the lines of roads likely to be used by our troops, and as far as possible, duplicated the bridges in advance of disaster. Then, when one would be destroyed, its counterpart would be loaded on platform cars and immediately hurried forward, so that in many instances the bridge would not have ceased burning when the repair train would appear, with workmen and train-guards sitting in groups upon piles of lumber which was to compose the new bridge. Quick work would begin, and in a few hours the structure would be complete and render futile the plans of the enemy, who had counted on many days' delay.

The railroad construction corps were very much taxed in the Western departments; the campaigns under Grant, Sherman, Rosecrans, Buell, Curtis and others extending over a greater extent of country than those of the Eastern armies, which were mostly confined to Virginia. The roads running south through Nashville to Chattanooga were particularly subject to destruction by the enemy—Morgan's, Wheeler's and Forest's cavalry spending much of their energy to thwart the railroad builders. The work of the enemy's military forces was ably seconded by the rebellious civilian element, who under the names of Bushwhackers and Guerrillas, swarmed on all sides of the Union armies. The railway corps were so energetic and dispatchful, that they were literally on the heels of the advancing columns, and brought forth the humorous remark from a rebel soldier, " It's no use to break up tunnels, for old Sherman carries duplicate tunnels with him."

In the early part of the war the troops in the field built extensive and substantial bridges of very rough material. This was illustrated during the early summer of 1862, while the army commanded by General McDowell was camped on the north bank of the Rappahannock River opposite Fredericksburg. It became necessary to reconstruct a bridge over the river for the passage of trains of supplies for a contemplated advance to join General McClellan in front of Richmond. The river at this point was several hundred feet wide, and both deep and rapid, while the grade of the railroad was about sixty feet above its surface. No building materials were on hand, and the special corps had not yet been formed. So, skilled mechanics were detailed from various regiments and at once set to work.   Parties were sent into adjacent pine woods, felled and trimmed the largest trees, then hauled them by ox and mule-teams to the bank of the river.   Rough timber was cut at various saw mills in the surrounding country and work was soon under way.

In a short time quite a sightly structure appeared to view.   Many, however, considered it insecure for the passage of a train, or even a locomotive, and when the day for trial arrived great throngs from all the surrounding camps gathered in expectation of difficulty. I heard one soldier ridicule its appearance by calling it " A daddy-long-legs bridge."   The locomotive crossed at a snail's pace, in safety ; the bridge creaked, however, in an ominous way, and settled perceptibly under the weight.   Experimental trips, fortunately, were all that it was called upon to endure, as the defeat of our army in front of Richmond and the shifting of the struggle to the line of the upper Rappahannock compelled the abandonment of Fredericksburg, and the bridge soon went up in smoke.

Another bridge of the same character was thrown over the river some distance above, at Rappahannock Station, where the Orange and Alexandria Railroad crossed.   It was used by troops who fought the battle of Cedar Mountain, and held by General Pope later as he fell back toward Bull Run before the combined armies under command of Lee.   The scene at this point during the retreat was intensely interesting, with the enemy holding the approach to the southern end of the bridge in strong force and the Union troops in secure possession of the hill at the north end.   One of the most savage artillery duels of the war took place for the possession of this bridge.   Batteries on each side, in almost point-blank range, sent destructive fire and killed and drove men from their guns on the other side.   Trains arrived and departed with great regularity during the contest, some pushing to the extreme front, where steam of locomotive mingled with smoke of batteries, and shriek of whistles with sound of bursting shells.   This combination was not unusual when a train bearing troops or supplies had to run the gauntlet of well-placed batteries.   The engineers and train men required rare pluck and coolness to perform their duties in such cases.

The bridge at this point was destroyed and rebuilt several times during the war, and in the summer of 1863 the whole road from Culpeper Court House to Bull Run was laid waste by the army under General Lee, every bridge was destroyed, every tie burned, and every rail heated and bent, so that when the Union army under General Meade again advanced in the fall to occupy the line of the Rapidan River the entire road had to be rebuilt.

Thousands of freight cars were required for military purposes, and one of the most singular sights was to see cars bearing the names of familiar railroads in such remote places   The first car in a train might read " New Jersey Central," the second " Pennsylvania Railroad," the third a western railroad, and so on.

Victory could have boasted of but slight achievement without the help of military railroads, and although the men were not as greatly exposed as in the fighting forces, they could yet show a large list of killed and wounded, from accident and the enemy's weapons. Those who watched their movements pronounced what they accomplished marvelous, and those who write history for future generations should pay full tribute to the arduous work.

Running the Gauntlet

"ALL ABOARD."

REYNOLDS: FIRST DAY AT GETTYSBURG.

LXIX.

TAKEN PRISONER.

"I Surrender!"

SOLDIERS in both armies generally shrank from the thought of being taken captive; but this, like all rules, had exceptions, and some were willing to take a risk of which they knew nothing rather than defy the fate of wounds and death. No army is made up of brave men entirely. Even Cæsar, we presume, had specimens of the genus "Coffee Cooler." Capture was at first a more serious matter to the Confederates than to the Union soldiers; for, having arrayed themselves against the Government, they had staked all upon the success of their cause, and to be taken prisoner might be the end for every one. The greater portion of the Southern army was made up from the class of "poor whites," and their politicians and newspapers had so impressed them with the idea that they would receive cruel treatment in Northern hands that they were most apprehensive of danger, and would fight desperately to avoid capture. Later, this was somewhat changed.

Great numbers of prisoners were taken on both sides during the war, a constant stream being brought into the lines in the interim between battles. The armies of the South were most successful in securing prisoners, as all fighting occurred in their own country. Scouts and bushwackers were familiar with its features, while the people assisted them, acting as spies on every possible occasion. The Union army controlled no territory in the theater of war, except that within its picket lines, and all outside was full of every imaginable danger.

Perhaps the largest number of men captured at any one time by the Union army was at the battle of Vicksburg, where thirty thousand laid down their arms at the feet of the victor, General Grant. At the final surrender at Appomattox, twenty-eight thousand gave up, and if consideration had been made of all who had been brought in during the campaign the number would have been doubled. Union soldiers captured by the enemy numbered hundreds of thousands. Not over five thousand were taken at any one time, but the aggregate was more than our capture of their men.

People at home had strange ideas of how prisoners were captured, and invariably asked the ridiculous question, "How did they know when to give up?" This was no mystery to the soldier, who fought unto death while chances were favorable, but who dropped his gun and threw up his hands like a man when all hope was gone. Prisoners were well-treated by their immediate captors, on both sides, for true soldiers respect brave enemies; but when sent to the rear and placed in charge of home-guards, trials began. Captives from the Southern army were sent to prison depots at various points in the North, and were comfortably rationed and housed, which—without wishing to revive painful memories—I cannot refrain from asserting was a consideration that our men when captured did not receive from their keepers. I witnessed the capture of large bodies of the enemy at Gettysburg, Rappahannock Station and Spottsylvania Court House. I noticed especially their kind treatment by the Union guards, who did everything to alleviate the condition of the prisoners. Many times I have seen prisoners, right out of the heat of battle, chatting pleasantly with their guards as they were brought to the rear, while Union soldiers emptied their haversacks of the scanty store of hard-tack and held up their canteens of coffee to refresh the men who in the roar and crash of battle had so recently sought their destruction.

A most interesting incident in the battle of Gettysburg was the bringing to the rear of nearly five thousand prisoners taken in Pickett's charge. It was about four o'clock on the 3d of July that I was sitting on my horse on the pike near Powers' Hill, watching the travel along the road and seeking information relative to the situation at the extreme front. Every one was in a hopeful state of mind, for the terrible attack on our center had been repulsed with great loss of life to the enemy, and all felt that victory was ours. Scanning the ridge where the Union line was posted, I could see a large body of men clad in gray drawn up as if in preparation to move toward our rear. Soon the column started, and I took a favorable position to see them. They soon appeared at hand, led by several officers whose rank was determined by an ornament on the collar and bullion on the sleeve. So many were they, and so solidly did they advance, that General Meade, who had just come upon that part of the field, at first thought them a force that had successfully penetrated our lines. Most of them were finely-formed fellows, with resolute faces, and evidently good soldiers. They seemed to be in cheerful mood, and chatted pleasantly as they marched along, guarded on each side by Union infantry and cavalry. They were poorly clothed, in a variety of uniforms, a dingy gray color prevailing; some wore jackets, others gray-skirted coats trimmed on collars and sleeves. There were many ragged slouch hats, and caps of various kinds with visors. Some wore boots, others shoes, and many were bare-footed.

The column was marched some distance to the rear, across Rock Creek, and turned into a field, where the men were made as comfortable as possible, and guards were placed about them to prevent escape.

After the retreat of Lee those men were sent to prisons in the North, and never again took up arms against the Union army.

Prisoners from the front

PUT OUT OF HARM'S WAY.

LXX.

SOUTHERN HOMES—SLAVE CABINS.

Puttin' de chimley out.

THE dwelling-houses which added much beauty and picturesqueness to Southern landscapes were varied in their style of architecture. The large, roomy plantation houses of upper Virginia, with colonnaded fronts and old brick walls covered with moss and vines; the low, cool mansions of the Gulf States, with a luxuriant growth of vines over the broad verandas, were all beautiful to look upon; but the latch-strings, as a rule, were not hung out to the boys in blue; on the contrary, scant hospitality was extended to all who sought food and shelter within their walls.

Grouped in rear of the mansions of the wealthy, peeping out from the shadows of vines and trees, were the modest cabins of the house-servants and farm-hands. Their shabby exterior was scarcely in keeping with the warm welcome always offered to the "Linkum sogers" by their inmates, whose utmost sympathy could always be depended upon; and thousands of soldiers can recall with pleasure kindnesses received from these dusky people. Delicious pies and cookies made by the old "aunties" were freely handed out to the hungry groups who stood about the door; the sick and wounded soldiers were never turned away, and escaped prisoners received food and guidance, and were assisted to places of safety by the slaves, irrespective of their own danger. It was often a difficult task, but they would take great risks and pass the fugitives from one refuge to another until the Union lines were reached. It was wonderful, in their irresponsible positions of simplicity and servitude, that they understood as well as they did the final meaning of the presence of our soldiers, and waited with such hopeful, quiet patience the great accomplishment of their emancipation.

The cabins were invariably built of logs, generally squared and jointed at the corners; the peaked roof was roughly shingled, and the chimney was built outside of the house, at the end. It was sometimes built of stone, but oftener of sticks, crossed at right angles and heavily plastered with clay. Still another variety was sometimes seen, which was made of but two walls of logs. The inner ends were fastened to the house, and the others met at a point, thus giving a triangular form and affording opportunity for a very wide fire-place.

Sometimes a cabin would be seen with two and three chimneys. This at first mystified me, but on inquiry I found that when one chimney "burned out" another was built, the first serving no other purpose than to add variety to the cabin. In many instances I noticed a rough ladder which led from the ground to the peak of the roof near the chimney; and occasionally there were two, one on each side. No amount of conjecture satisfied me as to their use, and I one day questioned an old negro about it. "Laws, massa," he answered, "dem ladders is to put de chimley out." "Out?" I said, "why, it *is* out — outside." "Laws! I mean dey is to put de chimley out when it cotches fire — 'n' dat's bery off'n. Yer see we takes up a pail o' water and po's [pours] it down to stop de blaze. We couldn't git 'long 'out dem ladders, no how."

Many of the cabins were overgrown with honeysuckle, the beautiful trumpet creeper and other vines indigenous to Southern climates, and often an arbor was built in front of the door, under which the pickaninnies could romp or take shelter on rude benches. Water-buckets stood outside the wall, and hanging from a nail over them were gourd dippers with which to drink. A rude square table was usually seen in front, on which "aunty" ironed and performed other household work.   Near the outside corner of the cabin generally stood a wooden vessel, of bowl-like structure, though with tapering top, used for the making of lye for the manufacture of soap.   Old iron pots lay carelessly about, and numberless ducks and chickens gave animation to the picture.

The interior of these cabins, however, seldom ever bore out the promise of the outside view.   Many of them were divided into two rooms, while others had but one, which served the purposes of sleeping, cooking and eating.   The furniture was rude and scanty, consisting only of one or two benches, an old arm-chair and a bed.   A spinning-wheel and loom often found places in the corner, and when "homespun" was being woven, the scene was always an interesting one.   The large fire-place was at the end of the house, furnished with andirons and a crane with chain attachment, on which a cooking-pot was usually hung. Logs were used for fuel, and the great back-log usually emitted a thin curl of pale blue smoke, which lazily made its way up the ample chimney.   The thought of ornamenting the walls evidently did not occur to the simple negroes; but, had they desired it, the smoked surface would not have admitted of embellishment.   Overhead was an attic, where sweet corn, pumpkins and other supplies were stored for winter use.

Gone forever these days may be to the slaves unfettered and the soldier boy long since mustered out, but thoughts of the past will awaken grateful memories in both, and they will drift back in imagination to the time when they first clasped hands in mutual helpfulness—

"Away down in de ole cabin home."

Waiting for Dinner

Gone off with the Yanks

A slave cabin

RELICS OF THE PAST.

LXXI.

FIELD HOSPITALS.

Hard Times

THE medical field-service of the Union army was of great magnitude. Those who lived through those trying times and saw the long rows of wooden buildings about Washington and other northern cities will never forget the scenes where the sick and wounded were cared for after having been sent back from the front. Everything possible was done to alleviate suffering. There were comfortable beds, unlimited surgical and medical attendance, medicine without stint, and capable nurses whose conscientious care of their charges has never been thoroughly appreciated.

In the field, however, the wounded could not receive the same careful attention. When a battle was imminent, the officers of the hospital department would secure all barns and available farm-houses for use, and fling to the breeze the yellow flag—the badge of the Medical Department. If buildings were insufficient, large hospital tents would be erected in shaded localities, and by the time the engagement opened everything would be in readiness.

The boom of cannon and rolling of musketry would scarce have commenced when long lines of ambulances would appear, coming from the front laden with wounded men. Groups of soldiers could be seen carrying wounded officers or comrades on stretchers; many less severely wounded were helping themselves along as best they could, and the tented village would soon be peopled. No estimate could ever be made of the number of wounded that would need care during and after a battle, and the accommodations provided were often inadequate. When great numbers were rapidly brought in, many improvised shelters were resorted to: tent flies were stretched, boards were laid across the fence-corners and inclined from the fences to the ground, or laid with one end resting on stakes, and even blankets and ponchos were made use of as tent-shelters in the great need. Every room in the farm-houses would be full of the wounded, and on the barn floors—often among corn-stalks and hay—men were thickly laid in rows. Circumstances like these required close attention from the surgeons, and the rapid but calm way in which they worked was marvelous. When a wounded man was placed upon an operating table a surgeon would quickly probe the wound with his finger to see if a bone was fractured. If such was the case, a word would be whispered to assistants, chloroform administered, and an operation performed. Attendants then lifted the death-like figure from the table and removed him to an adjacent shelter, while, if it had been a case hopeless of mending, some one took the severed leg or arm away and dropped it on a ghastly pile that had arisen near by.

Sometimes the wounded were without shelter of any kind, tents not being obtainable because of insufficient means of transportation. Then a shady spot was sought, a pine grove perhaps, or an old apple-orchard. Here the men would be laid in rows, while the attendants moved from place to place administering to their wants.

Even during the day there was much about the field-hospital that was death-like and sickening; but at night the light of the torches and glow of the camp-fires produced so grim and somber a picture that anyone, except those thoroughly accustomed to the effect, would shrink from the scene. In case of defeat it was sometimes necessary to abandon the field-hospital and leave the most seriously wounded to the tender mercies of the enemy, thus adding imprisonment to physical suffering.

At the battle of the Wilderness, when the commanding general resolved to push on towards Spottsylvania, orders were given to abandon the hospitals and establish new ones at Fredericksburg. Facilities for transporting eight thousand wounded men could not possibly be found on short notice, and orders were given, for all that were able, to make their way to the town. All empty wagons were positively jammed with men variously wounded. Single horses and mules bore the burden of two and three men upon their backs, and many lame soldiers limped along in pitiful fashion, offering to each other such assistance as was possible; so that between the battle-field and town a procession of misery, unequaled by any similar event of the war, passed slowly by.

Sometimes the field-hospital, placed in a presumably safe location, would become a scene of desperate encounter, the tide of battle sweeping over the spot. Those who could run would dash for a place of safety, while the desperately wounded would hug the ground and pray for a safe delivery.

After the battle all who could be removed were loaded on cars or in ambulances, and if contiguous to river, transportation was taken on steamers to hospitals of the North, where the tender care of friends or nurses of the Sanitary Commission would do much toward restoring them to convalescence.

A Field Hospital

PERFECT VENTILATION—NO PATENT!

LXXII

JACKS OF ALL TRADES.

A Railroad Builder.

N the soldier's fond dreams of army life previous to his entrance into service, he had not the slightest conception of how a variety of accomplishments would be called into use. Sleeping and waking, his mind was filled with the glory of successful battles and the brilliancy of grand reviews, without a tinge of coloring suggestive of the hard work that in time fell to his lot.

The ordinary duties of camp and field were arduous in comparison to home employment, but when soon after his arrival at the front the recruit was detailed on a wood-chopping expedition, he underwent an experience of aching limbs and stiffened joints which, though new to his life, possessed not the least particle of pleasurable novelty. The use of the axe was not acceptable to teachers, students or clerks, many of whom were in the ranks, and their attempts at first were most ludicrous; but in spite of blistered hands and aching backs they were generally persistent in the performance of duty, and brought back to camp the allotted quantity of logs. Cutting ties or logs for track-laying or bridge-building was work that they often had to do, and a crowd as busy as bees would swarm along the road.

When an abandoned locomotive was found, men would be sought for who had made machinery, and under speedy and skillful manipulation an apparent wreck would assume new usefulness, and, placed on a rebuilt track, would soon be sent puffing backward and forward, to the gratification of the men who had worked so diligently to make repairs.

Those accustomed to clerical work often found occupation in the various departments, and accounts were accurately kept and office-work was generally well done. Many who were detailed for hospital service did most conscientious work, and the careful assistance rendered to surgeons in many cases afforded an opportunity for pursuing the medical profession after their return to the North.

Occurrences on the march forced soldiers into odd capacity, and my picture over the page, of the pontoon-train stuck in the mud, represents a regiment furnishing strength expected only of mules, for with the aid of a long rope and a universal pull the unfortunate train was started on its way.

When opportunity offered, men were sent to take possession of grist-mills, where grain was quickly brought, ground and distributed to the surrounding corps. Or, may be, when boards were needed, an old saw-mill would be taken possession of, the wheel started, and in a few days a large pile of well-sawed planks would reward the workers. A great portion of the soldiers became expert diggers: to this the hundreds of miles of breastworks, forts and defenses built during the war bore witness. Necessity developed many latent domestic accomplishments, such as washing, mending, sewing on of buttons, etc., and many became expert in shoe-mending. The building of quarters, making and mending of beds, tables, chairs and household conveniences, and multitudes of ingenuities, were achieved by them. Even slaughtering and dressing cattle was practiced successfully after a little practice, the cuts served out to the troops often suggesting the work of skilled butchers — as, indeed, it sometimes was. Most of the cavalry or artillerymen could repair a harness, or, if necessary, nail on a horse-shoe, and many a village blacksmith of after years acquired his first lessons during the time that he followed the flag.

Men of all trades and professions made up our ranks, and opportunities were infinite for turning talent to account. Lawyers, doctors, professors, bank officers, merchants, clerks, farmers, students, mechanics of all kinds, and men of every conceivable calling, made up the Union host, and thus by brain or muscle most difficulties were overcome. And when these many elements of mental force and physical strength were welded by discipline into one great power, it need not be a marvel that they accomplished so many wonderful things.

The reader who has thus far followed the brief descriptions of the many scenes caught in the artist's sketch-book will appreciate the almost infinite variety of labor called for in pursuit of the work of a great army; but yet the old proverb falls to the ground, for although the boys in blue were — and had to be — "Jacks of all trades," they could not be said to be "masters of none," since they arrived at so efficient a mastery of the grand art of war.

A Present for the Colonel

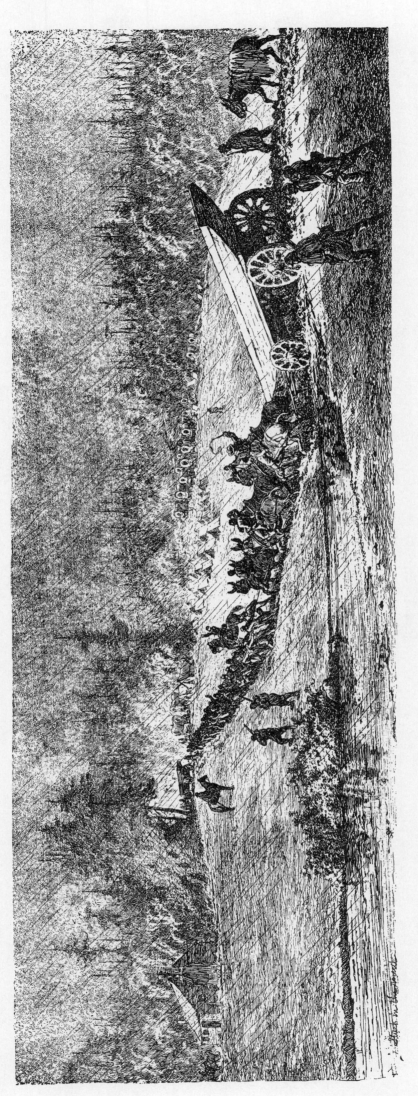

THE HUMAN MULE-TEAM.

HALLECK AT THE SIEGE OF CORINTH.

LXXIII.

NEGRO REFUGEES.

"Whoop!"

AT the beginning of the war the question of how to dispose of the colored refugees that sought our lines was a difficult one to decide. They were undoubtedly a source of strength to the seceding States as laborers, in the raising of crops, also in building breastworks and working on fortifications, while the greater portion of the white population was fighting in the extreme front. The Northern people at first were strongly opposed to any interference with the slaves, and Washington authorities were for a time obliged to defer to that strong sentiment. Generals Frémont, Hunter and Butler, without authority from headquarters, attempted to cut the Gordian knot; but these movements seemed premature, public opinion not warranting extreme measure until after the battle of Antietam.

Previous to this, the negroes coming into our lines, while generally obtaining employment about camp and the supply depots, did not always receive the warmest welcome; but after the Proclamation of Emancipation by Lincoln they were heartily received and their services made available. The men were used as teamsters, cooks and for general work about depots and camps, as well as later enlisted regularly and organized as troops, in which capacity they gave manly account of themselves. The women and children were sent to refugee camps and maintained until the close of the war. The news of emancipation spread over the South like one great wave and bore on its bosom to the dusky people its glorious intelligence.

There were never more pathetic pictures than were seen in the unceasing streams of slaves who then in their new-found freedom sought the protection of the Union lines. Wherever our armies marched, those hapless people dropped their tools, implements and small possessions, and flocked to us. At all times and places they could be seen tramping along the roads. The mature and strong carried the helpless "pickaninnies," who, with round, wondering eyes, were at a loss to understand the change; the elder children would trudge along clinging to their mothers' dresses; the old folks would sometimes be in carts or wagons, and sometimes hobbling along on foot; but all making as much speed as possible toward the goal of safety.

I saw a quaint family come into camp one summer day in '63 at Culpeper Court House. I was at a picket post southeast of the town, when I noticed a vehicle approaching that was a mystery. I knew that no single baggage-wagon would come from that direction, and on waiting for a nearer approach found it to be a party of refugees. The team was composed of an old white horse, a white ox, and a mule. The horse was led by a man, who carried an old banjo under his arm, and a boy mounted on the mule was driver.

The wagon was an old-timer, and had evidently seen long service on the plantation. It was a so-called "schooner" in style, and its shape reminded one of a sailing vessel. It was bereft of the usual canvas cover, but three of the frame-hoops made to support it still remained, arched over the body. The occupants were an old "mammy" and her better half, —his gray locks surmounted by an old white hat,—a young woman and two children. A bonnet was suspended from one of the hoops for safe keeping. This article of feminine apparal created much amusement among the soldiers, and from the scornful way in which the young woman resented their remarks I am sure it must have belonged to her. The whole turnout made a great deal of fun for the soldiers, and witticisms were launched forth all along the line. I laughed with the rest and wondered, if the odd picture could be transported to Broadway, New York, what kind of a sensation it would produce.

Sometimes those parties appeared in little two-wheeled farm carts drawn by horses or mules. In one case I saw one of these carts drawn by a bull. He showed none of their usual ugly spirit but seemed quite tame and pulled at the traces in docile fashion. Household goods and children too young to walk would be tumbled in promiscuous confusion into these wagons. An old buggy, an old family vehicle of "massa's," would often be made use of by a refugee party. I imagine the owner would have turned pale with rage at such appropriation of his chattels had he known the use made of it; but the negroes cared not as they moved hopefully forward, yet half afraid their dreams might not be realized and that stories repeated to them about the cruelty of Yankee soldiers might all be true.

Sometimes the number of slaves that sought refuge with the Union columns was more than could possibly be managed. During Sherman's march to the sea they flocked in thousands from the surrounding country. It was not possible to care for the great hosts, and many were reluctantly left behind.

And how these simple people have adapted themselves to circumstances and settled down to the struggle for existence as freemen! They have kept good their promises, and the progress they have made is a full recompense for the sacrifice made for them and the protection they received. Their industrial value, not only as agricultural laborers, as in times "befo' the wah," but in divers mechanical callings, is gradually winning for them the appreciation of their white neighbors, and they are steadily advancing towards a proper recognition of their worth.

Will Massa Sherman.

COMING INTO THE LINES.

LXXIV.

CAVALRY RAIDS.

"Quick, now!"

ONE of the peculiar and original features of the war was the use made of the cavalry arm of the service on both sides, in raiding the enemy's lines of supplies, destroying depots and rendering useless their railroad systems by burning bridges and tearing up tracks. In wars of the past, cavalry had been used chiefly as an adjunct to the infantry and artillery in actual battle to deal the culminating blow in an enemy's defeat; or, when the opposing force was victorious, to cover the retreat and prevent a disastrous rout. Duties of scouting, making reconnaissances, foraging, picketing, of course, were also given them.

During the first year of our war, the cavalry was made use of in the legitimate way, but without very favorable results until late in the war. The heavily wooded country, cut up by fences and streams, prevented rapid movement of large bodies, and it was not until after the raids of Jeb. Stuart around the Army of the Potomac in front of Richmond, and his subsequent raid around the same army near Antietam and Harper's Ferry in the fall of the year, that the Union commanders began to realize the other uses that might be made of cavalry.

The first great raid was made at the battle of Chancellorsville, when with a largely increased cavalry force General Stoneman was sent to destroy the railroad betwen Richmond and Fredericksburg. General Lee at the time, with the army of Virginia, was in a heavily fortified position on the heights in rear of the latter town. This raid was energetically and skillfully carried out, and railroads and bridges in rear of Lee were badly wrecked. Even so, it was thought at the time that the cavalry force might have served better purpose on the actual field of battle. Stonewall Jackson's march and surprise of the right flank of General Hooker's army in that fight could hardly have taken place had the front of our army been covered by proper cavalry force; and if energetic advance had been made on the rear of the enemy's position the campaign might have ended successfully.

While not losing sight of the fact that the enemy's cavalry under Stuart was drawn from the field in pursuit of our own, their lessened force did not compensate the Union commander for the great advantage he would have had if his front had been properly covered. Had the cavalry been retained with the army, not only would it have been likely to discover Jackson's movement, but the main battle would have taken place on comparatively open ground; then, with preponderent force, the Union commander would have had an immense advantage, and his army would not have been compelled to fight a defensive battle tied up in a dense jungle. When the battle ended it was found that it had been impossible to bring one-half of our men into action. Our army lay like a great stranded whale surrounded by a swarm of sword-fish and thrashers. It was indeed "a disaster rather than a defeat."

Subsequent raids were made upon the enemy's communications with better results: Grierson's raid in the Southwest, Stoneman's in the same section, and Averill's raid into Virginia, which caused great loss to the Confederate quartermaster department, were all successful, and the last great cavalry raid of the war in Alabama and Georgia under General Wilson was very destructive. Less significance, however, was attached to this late success, from the fact that Lee and Johnston, with the only great organized army left in the field, had surrendered.

While a cavalry raid carried destruction, the aggressors were subject to disaster also. Movements had to be made with the greatest rapidity, with meager supplies and scant transportation; thus men and horses were subject to great strain, and constant action impaired the strength of both. The Confederates made some effective cavalry raids; but the fate of Morgan's noted expedition into Kentucky with two thousand eight hundred men— only five hundred of whom escaped death or capture—shows the danger of that style of operations. The most successful cavalry raids by Union forces were no doubt during the winter, when operations were suspended and the absence of the cavalry did not imperil the army's safety.

The raid of General Sheridan before the final move upon the enemy's position at Petersburg by General Grant, was a brilliant success, if destruction of roads and supplies was taken in consideration, but its effects could not be compared to the events of Winchester, Fisher Hill, and Cedar Creek, when he threw his cavalry force upon the enemy's flank in the orthodox style of co-operation with infantry and artillery.

The change in appearance of a raiding force on its departure from camp and its return was simply startling. Officers and men went forth on the dangerous mission with buoyant spirits and brilliant attire. Bright flags and guidons fluttered in the breeze, and the light batteries with their handsome horses gave character to the column. Looks of admiration and words of praise were given by the lookers-on and wishes for success went after them as they disappeared into unknown country.

But on return, however successful, the men were haggard and worn, the ambulances likely to be full of wounded, and the foot-sore horses with prominent ribs were shadows in comparison to their former condition. I heard a soldier once say of a returning expeditionary force: "By golly! those fellers look as if they 'd passed through a cyclone." Raiding was, at best, tough fun and rough work.

THROUGH THE ENEMY'S COUNTRY.

LXXV

GREAT SIEGES OF THE WAR.

About ready.

NUMBER of important positions were besieged by both the Union and Confederate armies during the war. Chief among these operations were the siege of Yorktown by McClellan, in 1862, of Corinth during the same year by General Halleck, of Vicksburg, in 1863, by Grant, Port Hudson the same year by General Banks, Chattanooga during the winter of '63 and '64 by the Confederate General Bragg, Charleston and Fort Pulaski by Union forces, the siege of Atlanta by General Sherman, of Nashville by General Hood, and lastly, the siege of Petersburg and Richmond by General Grant. These events afforded opportunity for ingenious contrivances in earthworks, and the most remarkable defenses known in modern warfare were made by both the Union and Confederate armies.

The siege of Yorktown was begun and ended by General McClellan in the old-fashioned way, something like the siege of Sebastopol in the Crimean war. He was no doubt influenced by knowledge gained during that remarkable siege, as he was detailed by the United States government at that time to observe operations of the allied forces against Russia, and made an important report of it. The siege of Yorktown was commenced with great deliberation, the approach to the enemy's lines being made with great care under cover of heavy works. Large earthwork forts, connected by breastworks, were built and all armed with guns and mortars of heaviest caliber. The intention was to shell the enemy out of a strongly intrenched position by an overwhelming fire—a seemingly feasible operation at that period of the war. The enemy, however, became unnerved at the great preparations made for their annihilation and abandoned the position before a serious attack had been made. Later experience taught that the ground should have been held, for all the guns and mortars in the Union army could not have rendered the position untenable.

The siege of Corinth had a similiar result; the Rebel armies evacuating the position and retreating southward before Halleck could make a serious attack.

The sieges of Vicksburg and Port Hudson for the first time proved to the enemy that well-built earthwork defenses could not be taken by attack in front; and disparity of numbers was of but slight disadvantage if the besieged force was properly supplied with ammunition and provisions. The enemy held its lines intact, the Union forces not being able to take any portion of them during the operations of several months, except that at Vicksburg, where the mine was exploded, a few feet of the front was secured. This victory, however, was soon neutralized by the enemy, who established a new line slightly in the rear and prevented any further destruction in that quarter. Want of provisions and ammunition, however, finally caused surrender of the place; but the fact was proven that a strong position, well fortified by earthworks, could be held an indefinite time.

The siege of Port Hudson ended in much the same manner, the defense persistently holding the line and repulsing with great slaughter all attempts of the Union forces to carry the place by storm. Arms were laid down only after Vicksburg had fallen and all hope was gone.

The siege of Charleston and Fort Sumter was prolonged and costly to the Union forces. The operations were vigorously conducted, but without definite result except the burning of part of the city of Charleston, for after months of bombardment, although Sumter became a mere mass of powdered bricks, mortar and iron, the secession flag still floated placidly over it. Attempts were then made to storm the stronghold, but in every instance our forces were bloodily repulsed. The march of Sherman, however, in the rear of the city compelled the garrison to evacuate the place, defeated but not dishonored.

Our siege of Atlanta was commenced by covering the whole front of the enemy's lines with strong earthworks, arming them with field-guns, and supporting them with infantry. No attempt was made to dislodge the enemy by regular siege approaches; but General Sherman's old trick of creeping around the enemy's flank (at the same time holding his front with heavy works) was brought into play. Hood was thus compelled to retreat, fearing capture by an attack from the rear.

Nashville was besieged in strange fashion by the Confederate General Hood during the winter of '64, but the effect proved ridiculous and abortive, for when General Thomas' preparations were complete, the besieged forces became the attacking party. Hood was then swept from his lines with immense loss of men and guns, and one of the most brilliant Union victories of the war achieved.

The siege of Richmond and Petersburg was in many ways the most remarkable of the great military events of the war. Petersburg could no doubt have been taken had General Smith moved into the town following up his successful attack on the enemy's first line of works, for nothing but a small force of home-guards garrisoned the place; but the Union commander was slow and over-cautious, and the enemy held the position by making a bold front and running a noisy locomotive forwards and backwards over the Appomattox bridge into Petersburg, leading the Union commander to conclude that Lee was pouring troops into town. Thus a golden opportunity was lost.

The conclusion of the whole matter seems to be that sieges, in our day, will be ineffectual to reduce strong and well defended fortifications, unless supplemented by strategic movements of troops to isolate the defending forces or to cut off their supplies. Even a good palisade, a breastwork, or a rifle-pit has often resisted the most gallant attacks in front by far superior forces; and a properly constructed work is a most difficult nut to crack. When this is enlarged to a series of works, or a fortified place of importance, direct attack is rarely successful. In spite of the wonderful advance in destructiveness of modern mechanisms of war, the need of "mixing them with brains," still exists, and probably always will.

Drawing Their Fire.

SIEGE-WORK.

LXXVI.

ARMY PUNISHMENTS.

Bucked.

ACK of discipline in the army would render futile the best combinations of master-minds, but under good control a body of men become a unit of force and their physical and moral strength can be used to the best advantage by a commanding general.

The Union army was not a homogeneous composition except in reference to the vital cause in which it was engaged. Men rich and poor, from all professions and trade, made up its numbers, and without strict discipline could never have made the efficient force which carried out the war to its conclusion. Thus punishments for the infraction of military rules were inflicted and courts-martial were often busy meting out correction to delinquents.

Desertion was the gravest offense, for which the extreme sentence was death. During the early part of the war this penalty was withheld in many instances because of a sympathetic feeling the authorities had for the volunteers, but during later events they became less lenient; many deserters were tried, convicted and shot; others were sent to the Dry Tortugas—in many instances for life. Of this we have already treated.

Stealing was another infraction of discipline which was severely punished. The culprits were tried by court martial, and if convicted were often sentenced to long confinements in Northern prisons. Their departure was signalized by the most terrible of all military disgraces, being *drummed out of camp*.

One summer day, while lounging in camp under the shade of a tent-fly, I heard some drummers and fifers playing the Rogue's March. Struck by the singularity of such an air I rose and walked to a bit of high ground and surveyed the surrounding camps as they lay parching in the sun. About a quarter of a mile distant I saw a great crowd of soldiers scattered among the tents of a large camp, and more soldiers on horseback and on foot were hurrying from all directions toward the scene. Seeing that it was something unusual, I ran to my tent, seized my sketch book and joined the crowd.

I found that two soldiers had been convicted of stealing from comrades, and sentenced to have their heads shaved and be drummed out of camp. The parade wheeled around the end of a line of tents and took a course through the length of the company street. The condemned men were the first in the line, and in the bright light the pink skin of their close-shaven heads was a strange contrast to their brown, sun-burned faces. Their hands were fastened behind them by bright steel handcuffs. Each man was followed by a soldier with gun and fixed bayonet, which he carried pointed toward the culprit's back. In rear of these came two ranks of drummers and fifers who played viciously the suggestive air, and seemed to enjoy the opportunity.

The odd procession wound slowly in and out of the company streets, and the gaping crowd pushed and jostled to get a sight of the offenders. They jeered and laughed at the poor fellows who had fought at their sides, but who had betrayed comradeship and disgraced the name of soldier. The faces of the culprits were pictures of humiliation and mental suffering; they would no doubt have preferred death on the battle-field to this terrible ordeal. But the ceremony finally ended, the men were delivered to the guards, who quickly departed with them, the crowd scattered and all traces of the strange scene soon disappeared.

Lighter punishments were inflicted for lesser offences, such as extra duty, bucking and gagging, carrying a log on the shoulder back and forth on a specified beat, etc.   In the artillery and among the wagon trains men were bound fast to wheels, with arms and legs extended, or hung up by wrists and thumbs.

It was unpleasant to inflict or witness these punishments, and painful for the doomed men to endure.   The penalties no doubt served the purpose of making many compliant and dutiful, and secured a completer discipline and order than could otherwise have been had; but on the whole they were very few, in comparison with the vast numbers of men under command.

The Punishment Fits the Crime

Drumming Out of Camp.

A BITTER LESSON.

SCHOFIELD AT FRANKLIN.

LXXVII

FIGHTING IN THE DARK.

Hot Work.

CENES of a battle by day are striking enough in their horror to satisfy the most morbidly disposed, for the misery spread broadcast is visible in every direction; but at night horror becomes intensified in the mystery of darkness. Confidence does not desert a soldier in daylight, even in the smoke and confusion of battle, but when in action at night only one's next neighbor in the ranks is recognizable, and the only light is the momentary flash of the cannon or of musketry along the line of battle.

I have often watched the troops at nightfall preparing for an attack from the enemy or making ready to charge a fortified line in their front.

Large masses of men would move mysteriously along over rough roads and through dense woods, with a battery here and there, or with a body of cavalry,—men and horses both on the alert, each having learned from experience when to anticipate danger. At such times, the nerves of those engaged were strained to the utmost tension, and they listen breathlessly for the first rumbling of the coming storm. The first roll and crackle of musketry brought relief, for the situation then, through perilous, was definite. As the fire increased, voices of officers in command could be heard, and masses of men in the gloom of night and density of trees and undergrowth would close up ranks, and make the best possible way forward. The batteries would soon get into position, and when they opened fire, came the opportunity to witness a battle by sound only. I have often recognized the sharp report of rifled guns and heard the low muffled sounds of shell-firing a few seconds later. Then the musketry fire would grow louder near our center, and I would know that the enemy were dashing forward to capture a battery.

On one occasion my heart almost stopped beating as the "Rebel yell" went up from a rapidly advancing line of ten thousand men in so tremendous a chorus as to nearly drown the roar of the guns; but the sound died down when they received a rolling volley from the Union infantry and voices from the "boys in blue" rang out in "three cheers and a tiger." A battery of Napoleon guns also opened on them with canister, and the crash of the terrible iron hail could be heard tearing through the trees.

The enemy was soon repulsed, for there was no response to the battery save intermittent musketry, which looked like fire-flies as it crackled among the trees in front. And here brave fellows were struck down by a seeming mysterious force, for in the darkness they could not know from whence a missile came or see to examine a wound.

Some were trampled to death by cavalry or artillery horses, and others burned, for when the woods are fired in front, great columns of smoke and flame roll up, cutting the combatants apart and placing in further jeopardy the lives of the many too badly injured to move. After such a battle, parties of gallant fellows are sent forward amid smoke and flame to bring out the wounded and to return with them clinging to their rescuers with desperate tenacity.

Such a conflict leaves the country covered in all directions with a pall of smoke, lit up at intervals by the flash of guns. As the combat comes to an end, an occasional shell bursts among the men on the front line, or creates consternation in the rear by exploding among the wagon-trains or the wounded at the temporary hospital. It is harder to be crippled by such accidental and unintentional firing or explosions than in the heat of battle; it seems an unneccessary suffering, with nothing to be gained by the sacrifice. However, it was all a part of the fortune of war; and after all, whether slain in the fight, or killed at its close, or dying in hospital of sickness or wounds incurred in pursuit of duty, the soldier is "dead in the field of honor."

Fighting in the dark was always one of the most trying and difficult phases of soldierly experience, keeping the nerves wrought up to the highest point of tension; and once the fight was over, and matters quieted, officers and men exhausted by the terrible strain dropped down upon the ground oblivious to all surroundings, and slept peacefully till daybreak.

A NIGHT BATTLE.

LXXVIII.

LOCATING THE ENEMY'S LINES.

———•———

RMIES of both sides were so large, and when moving covered so great a territory, that it would seem a simple matter to learn their position with certainty. But there was much of intricate and complicated detail that made it most difficult to locate an opposing force in an active campaign, and the armies approaching each other might be compared to two great marine animals with sensitive tentacles outspread to gain the first intelligence of each other's proximity.

A far look.

First, spies were employed by both sides to gather all possible details of numbers of men, batteries, etc. The Confederates had much the advantage of us in this respect, as they were most of the time on their own soil, and their non-combatants were always on the alert to carry important information. In addition to this disadvantage the North swarmed with the genus *copperhead*, a class ever ready to injure or betray the Union cause. The Union armies, on the other hand, found great difficulty in obtaining trustworthy information. A great number of spies were sent inside the enemy's lines, and often with good results, but the system of espionage was so rigid in the South that in many instances these men were captured and executed. Sometimes a Union man of the country would stray into our lines with a budget of valuable news, but the occurrences were rare. The negroes brought a great many reports, some of which served valuable purpose ; but with their simple minds and ignorance of military matters, commanders did not always feel safe to act on their statements without corroboration. They often gave matter worth inquiring into, however, and scouts or reconnoitering parties were sent to verify their reports.

Armies in the field were generally covered by scouts, cavalry pickets and videttes, who were thrown out on all roads both in front and on the flanks. These were the sensitive points which first came in contact with the enemy, and from them the commanding general could get some knowledge as to the force which confronted him,—its numbers, the extent of ground covered, etc. Considering the significant points and making allowance for exaggeration and mistakes, the general would move his force as his judgment suggested.

Crude use was made of the ballooning system, and considerable information was thus gained in the locating of the enemy's fortified lines. During the first advance of the Army of the Potomac against Yorktown and Richmond, Professor Lowe's balloon was quite a feature of interest and utility. It was inflated and made ascent every day ; a long rope was attached to it by which its movements were controlled. Efforts were made by the enemy to destroy it with shells, but without avail, as it was impossible to elevate the guns sufficiently to get the range. At the battle of Chancellorsville the balloon was in constant service, and General Hooker's ignorance of the enemy's movements during the battle was inexcusable, as the balloon at Falmouth overlooked the country as far as Chancellorsville and noted with exactness the movement and size of each of Lee's columns. This, I believe, was the last use made of the balloon, and the hollow ball of silk resting motionless in high air over the Virginia woods ceased to be a familiar object. I have often thought it strange that the system should have been abandoned, for it certainly was invaluable in skillful hands. Sometimes detailed parties of men were sent to the tops of high mountains to make observations of the enemy's forces, and from personal experience I can testify that few ventures were more exciting. I was once able to watch the retreat of Stonewall Jackson's army down a valley-pike in Virginia, and with a good field-glass observed the minutest details of the armed host.

Often when the armies were in close contact men would be stationed in tall trees, where they could overlook the situation of the opposing force and convey information to their anxious comrades below.   I have often watched the motionless figures outlined like great birds against the sky and heard the warning words "Look out! The Rebs are coming!" At the battle of Gettysburg, General Lee posted himself in the cupola of the college, and was thus enabled to get a fine view of the Union position.   This must have been of great advantage, as he could see along the front and rear as far as Little Round Top and also note the defenses of the Cemetery Gate and Culp's Hill.   In fact, he was so near the center of the Union line that with a glass he could discern individual peculiarities of the Union men.   On the retreat of the Confederates from the battle-field, I went up into the cupola of the town hall at Williamsport, Maryland, and from an upper window looked into their works and was able to see distinctly all their preparations for defense.   The grey-clad figures with bronzed faces were digging for dear life with pick and shovel.   It comes back to me as one of the most interesting scenes of my army experience.

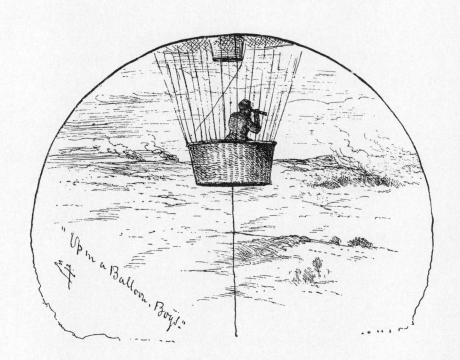

"Up in a Balloon, Boys."

Locating The Enemy's Line

Forbes

THE LOOKOUT.

LXXIX.

WINTER MARCHING.

Cold comfort.

LTERNATE rain and frost made the roads so nearly impassable that long marches were not usual in the winter months. A number of movements were made, however, in the enemy's country which were a new experience to our soldiers, for the hardships were even more severe than the summer marches, with their great heat and dust.

Several cavalry raids were made in the mountainous country of West Virginia, and the rapid streams and deep valleys made difficult of success an extended raid of a large cavalry column. While only an occasional snowstorm occurred in the low country of Eastern Virginia, the peaks of the mountains in the western part of the State were covered with snow from November until March.

General Averill with a large cavalry column carried on a winter campaign through this rough and poorly provided country, known as the "Salem Raid." The amount of difficulty encountered was unprecedented, but the point aimed for was gained, and several million dollars worth of commissary and quartermaster stores were destroyed. Large bodies of the enemy made desperate attempts to cut off Averill's retreat, but without success. His men pushed their way over snow and ice-covered mountains, and in some places where short cuts were taken they were compelled to haul their guns over the rocks by hand. Deep and rapid streams filled with floating ice were crossed, with the enemy pressing the rear guard in several places. The men were soaked to the skin night and day, and the horses were nearly reduced to skeletons by the unusual labor and exposure. At several points the march of the Union force was blocked by the enemy taking position in rocky defiles on their line of march. But General Averill commanded with great coolness and skill, circumventing all the well-laid plans of the enemy's cavalry and reaching a place of safety within the Union lines. The enemy lost heavily, while the number of Union men killed was comparatively light. The men presented a worn-out and ragged appearance on the return to camp, and the strength of the horses had been severely taxed; but a few weeks in camp soon restored both, and they were in good condition to move toward the enemy in the valley of the Shenandoah.

The mountainous sections of Eastern Kentucky and Tennessee were also the scenes of suffering during the winter, the troops being compelled to campaign without shelter or supplies. Then the men and animals of the commissary and quartermaster departments were obliged to team over hills through ice and snow, in all kinds of weather, and the trail of dead mules and scattered soldiers' graves on the line of march spoke pathetically of what they had to endure. Even in the low and warmer valleys along the foot of the Alleghany and Blue Ridge Mountains, occasional storms of snow and sleet swept over, causing great suffering and checking contemplated movements.

It was not always snow and ice, either, that made winter campaigning hard. Even as far South as Savannah, Georgia, General W. T. Sherman was badly delayed by heavy winter rains in January, making the roads impassable and swelling the Savannah River so that it overflowed a vast extent of rice fields lying along its bank. The flood swept away their pontoon-bridge and nearly drowned a division of the Fifteenth Corps with some heavy wagon trains that were trying to pass along an old causeway. Thus, drenched with rain

or immersed in flood, it may be imagined that all arms of the service would be nearly para-
lyzed by the shivering chill and consequent inability to throw off fatigue.   Horses and
mules as well as men suffered intensely at such times, and without those faithful beasts of
burden an army is soon crippled.

 Our soldiers, however, braved the winter's cold and the terrible Southern heats with but
few murmurs of complaint, until the last Rebel force surrendered.   When the survivors
turned their bronzed faces homeward, they thought of little else than exultant joy, and when
they were again surrounded by home comforts, their past suffering existed in recollection
only.   Yet true it is that while multitudes of young fellows were strengthened in vitality
and toughened in fiber by the trials to which they had become inured, other thousands were
broken in body, and went home to die or to live feebly with crippled forces, bearing about
in their bodies the marks of their devotion to Union and Liberty.

A WINTRY MARCH.

LXXX.

THE SANCTUARY.

"Dar dey be!"

EAGER possessions were packed quickly when news came to a plantation that the Yankees were holding a near-by town, and although the country was picketed with Southern cavalry close up to the Union lines, the slave family stole from the old cabin at nightfall, and avoiding highways to escape capture, tramped through wood and thicket, and came, weary and foot-sore, in sight of the Union lines at daybreak.

I saw one group that I never shall forget, it impressed me so deeply with what the Federal success meant to these dusky millions. The old mother dropped on her knees and with upraised hands cried "Bress de Lord!" while the father, too much affected to speak, stood reverently with uncovered head, and the wondering, bare-legged boy, with the faithful dog, waited patiently beside them. As the bugle notes of the reveillé echoed across the fields, and the star-spangled banner waved out from the flag-staff on the breastworks in the bright morning sun, I murmured, "A Sanctuary, truly!"

Four millions of slaves were freed during the war. At the beginning of the struggle they had an indefinite idea that their interests were vitally concerned, but so many reports reached them about the cruelty of our soldiers that some regarded us with fear. One old aunty was heard to ask if "dey had horns and tails." Gradually, as the war went on, they understood more fully that success of the Union army meant freedom to their race, and indeed, with the instinct developed by generations of slavery, the majority of them from the first knew that whatever they could do to help the Yankees was a help to their friends. I do not believe that a Union soldier ever experienced anything but kindness and eager assistance from a negro during the war.

Yet in the long interval of uncertainty they were faithful to their masters, and in household and field cheerfully performed all labor, with admirable and affectionate fidelity protecting and supporting the wives and children of the men who were fighting to rivet their chains still closer. They even obediently built forts and breastworks, from whose front issued forth flame and iron hail on the heads of their defenders. No one can realize the fears and anxieties of these people as battles ebbed and flowed, their grief when the Union lines were beaten back, and their joy when victorious. But they listened to the roar of battle and saw the flag of freedom float or fall in silence; neither did they speak when the exultant cries of the men in gray arose on the air. No joy or grief of theirs could find expression in words or song, for any open manifestation at the success of the Union army meant death to them.

One incident along the line of Sherman's "march to the sea" was typical of many similar occurrences. When news came that the "Linkum sogers" were advancing, and gray-clad couriers dashed along the dusty roads, spreading the intelligence and warning farmers to secrete their stock and make preparations for flight, much suppressed excitement was noticeable in the negro cabins. Old men would come in, and in marvelous fashion retail news picked up along the road to excited groups of negroes, in the midst of which the sudden report of a gun was heard. One black fellow exclaimed "Dat's thunder, I reckon." "Ho, no!" a second replied, "dat de Yankee guns, shore 'nuff." Then the sounds came louder and nearer, and all in a body the slaves hurried from the cabins to the mansion, where in great confusion " Massa," " Missus " and " de young folks " were packing up.   The family carriage was at the door, into which trunks and traps were thrown, when a moment after the family entered, and starting off in great haste were soon lost in a cloud of dust.   Shells now fell thick and fast, and the negroes were at their wits' ends to find a place of safety. The cellar of the mansion was soon thought of, and in its gloom, with gray faces and distended eyes, they hugged the wall for safety, and listened to the turmoil outside.   When the contest ended and the Rebel rear guard had limbered up its guns and clattered down the road to find a new position, for a time stillness prevailed.   But the triumphant cries of the pursuing force were soon heard, and the frightened negroes left their place of refuge, and creeping up the stairs found the house filled with blue-coats—new faces—the much-talked-of Yankees.

The new-comers were hungry, as soldiers always were, and on making their needs known, all available food was soon placed before them by the willing black hands.   The main army shortly after appeared in sight, and as it surged down the main street the colored folks at first stood motionless and stared at the strange sights; but when a cavalry regiment appeared with its proud-stepping horses and flashing sabers, a shout arose that would do a patriot's heart good.   And now all the negroes poured forth to join Sherman's army " marching through Georgia."   Their few traps were packed and, abandoning the old plantation, they trudged along with the column, too happy in the sense of new-found freedom to apprehend danger.

Yes, the manacles have long since fallen from the hand of the slave, and in the words of Henry Ward Beecher, " he can now organize that little kingdom in which every human being has a right to be king, in which love is crowned,—the family."   He can now choose his occupation, his rights of property are protected, the avenues of learning are open to his children, and he can keep and rear them as he pleases.   In spite of the trials and tribulations the negro must yet endure on his road to manhood and acknowledged citizenship, his year of jubilee has come. " Bress de Lord ! "

THE SANCTUARY.